GARLAND STUDIES ON

THE
ELDERLY
IN AMERICA

*A collection of monographs and dissertations
addressing specific problems facing the
elderly in a changing America*

EDITED BY
STUART BRUCHEY
Columbia University

A Garland Series

ADULT DAY CARE
The Relationship of Formal and Informal Systems of Care

Patricia M. Kirwin, Ph.D.

GARLAND PUBLISHING
New York & London
1991

Library of Congress Cataloging-in-Publication Data

Kirwin, Patricia M.
    Adult day care: the relationship of formal and informal systems of care / Patricia M. Kirwin
        p. cm. — (Garland studies on the elderly in America)
    ISBN 0-8153-0512-5
    1. Day care centers for the aged—Pennsylvania Case studies. 2. Frail elderly—
    Institutional care—Pennsylvania—Case studies.
    I. Title. II. Series.
    HV1455.2.U6K57   1991
    362.6'3—dc20

                                                                    91-2

Printed on acid-free 250-year-life paper

MANUFACTURED IN THE UNITED STATES OF AMERICA

PREFACE

With those over the age of 85 representing the most rapidly growing segment of our population, community long-term care has emerged as a national policy goal to replace the previous bias, through funding mechanisms, toward institutional long-term care.

This monograph, an analysis of area agency on aging funded adult day care programs in three southeastern Pennsylvania counties, attempts to broaden the knowledge base upon which community long-term care is conceptualized. The purpose of the study was to both describe and explain the complementary roles performed by adult day care programs and primary groups in meeting the community needs of the dependent elderly.

The study would not have been possible without the cooperation of three area agencies on aging whose deputy directors graciously provided access to the data used in the investigation. The commitment to research demonstrated by these agency administrators is much appreciated and inspiring.

I also want to express my gratitude to the Pennsylvania Department of Aging for their support of the research on which this monograph is based, to the Bryn Mawr College Graduate School of Social Work and Social Research in Bryn Mawr, Pennsylvania where the investigation was carried out, and to East Carolina University in Greenville, North Carolina for assistance in the preparation of this manuscript. The support of faculty, staff, and students nourished and sustained the process.

Special recognition goes to Lenard W. Kaye, Associate Professor in the Bryn Mawr College Graduate School of Social Work and Social Research, Co-Director of the original project on which this analysis is based and to Sherrie Schulke, research associate. Numerous others — especially Dottie Blades — were involved in gathering information from the various data sources, compiling mailings, formatting tables, typing manuscripts and, in general, assisting in all manner of means. To all thank you.

Finally, I wish to extend sincere thanks to all those older adults and their caregivers who gave of their time to respond to my numerous research questions and inquiries. Their thoughtfulness and honesty were critical to the success of this effort.

For Larry whose faith teases dreams into reality

ADULT DAY CARE: THE RELATIONSHIP OF

FORMAL AND INFORMAL SYSTEMS OF CARE

TABLE OF CONTENTS

Page

CHAPTER 3
Methodology and Definition of Terms

Page

LIST OF TABLES

Page

CHAPTER 1

INTRODUCTION

*"All would live long, but none would
be old."*
Benjamin Franklin

This is a descriptive study of the complementary roles performed by adult day care programs and primary groups in meeting the community long-term dependency needs of the frail elderly.

BACKGROUND

The number of elders in the United States is growing much more rapidly than the population as a whole. Persons aged 65 years and over increased by 28 percent in the decade of the 1970s, and the 85 and over group increased by 59 percent compared with an 11 percent increase for the entire population. The older aged are currently, in fact, the fastest growing age segment in the United States (Siegel and Taeuber, 1986).

Since those 75 and over make up the group most in need of long-term medical and/or social services, its rapid growth has lead to an increased demand for these services. Meeting the long-term care needs of these dependent elders and "treating them with justice and dignity as full-fledged members of the moral community will tax our common energies, the public purse, and our moral imagination" (Jennings, Callahan and Caplan, 1988, p. 1).

The present American long-term care system has been widely criticized for many shortcomings: it relies too heavily upon institutional services; it is too costly; it forces inappropriate levels of care upon patients by offering too few options; in too many instances it offers inferior quality care, and it places too much emphasis on caring for physical ills without concern for enhancing the quality of patients' lives (Huttman, 1985). It is thought that community alternatives, such as adult day care could ameliorate one or more of these criticisms (Weissert, Winter 1979).

A major objective of supportive services for dependent elders is "maintenance of the quality of life" (Cantor and Little, 1985, p. 745). Most often discussions concerning the quality of life emphasize the ability of the frail elderly to remain independent in the community (Sussman, 1976). The generation born between 1910 and 1926, a population that prefers to remain at home or in the community, has highlighted the critical gaps in the provision of supportive long-term care services (Torres-Gil, 1988, p. 8).

For this and other reasons, community long-term care has emerged as a national policy goal to replace the previous bias, through funding mechanisms, toward institutional long-term care (Crystal, 1982). While Hudson (1988) has indicated that 69 percent of all elderly hospital care is paid with Medicare dollars (p. 24), nursing home care accounts for 42 percent of total Medicaid expenditures (Crystal, 1982, p. 69). And, half the $25 billion annual nursing home bill is paid by elders themselves or by their families (Jacobs and Weissert, 1987, p. 77). Crystal (1982) has further established that it is nursing home care that has been the fastest growing cost in the health care system, increasing in recent years about 18-20 per cent annually. Therefore, those concerned with the human and financial costs of institutional care have concluded that wholesale institutionalization is no longer the solution in meeting the long-term care needs of the chronically ill and disabled elderly (Callahan et al., 1981; Estes, 1981; Warren, 1981).

THE ROLE OF FAMILY IN LONG-TERM CARE

After years of policy debate about the role of the family in providing long-term care, it is a truism that the family is and has been the primary source of care for the frail and/or disabled elderly (Achenbaum, 1988; Callahan et al., 1980; Doty, 1986). Nearly three-quarters of the disabled older persons who live in the community rely solely on family and friends while most of the remainder depend upon a combination of family care and paid help (Liu et al.,

1986; Soldo, 1983). "The number of disabled elderly persons in the community is perhaps twice the number in institutions, and yet only a quarter of these individuals are receiving formal care" (Weiner, 1988, p. 10). Provisions made by families have been and remain "the primary line of defense against the vicissitudes of late life" (Achenbaum, 1988, p. 27).

Consequently, policy makers are beginning to explore strategies for bolstering and strengthening the informal support system to help ensure that elderly persons are maintained in the community as long as possible. The avoidance or delay of institutionalization is seen as a way to curtail the spiraling costs of these services (Wetle, 1985).

Over the past decade, several studies have documented the important role of family and friends in providing long-term care to dependent elders. Much of this literature has focused on the composition of the informal caregiving network and the responsibilities and time commitment required for this activity. Some researchers (Cantor, 1983; Horowitz and Dobrof, 1982) have described the variety of sources for care including spouses, children, their relatives, friends, and neighbors. Others (Brody, 1981; 1985; 1986; Stoller, 1983) have focused on the role of adult children, daughters in particular, in providing care to elderly parents.

Many articles have addressed the problem of "caregiver burden;" that is, the social, emotional, and financial costs associated with the caregiving experience. Several studies (Brody, 1981; Stephens and Christianson, 1986; Stoller, 1983) have described the burden caregiving imposes on the family and provided evidence that family support is threatened by the stress engendered by caregiving and by the continuing need to meet other family and work responsibilities.

These studies have shed light on the nature and magnitude of the informal care system and have raised questions about the capacity of informal caregivers to continue providing the bulk of long-term care. However, if formal community long-term care services may strengthen and enhance the caregiving capacity of informal supports as Kane (1987) has written,

> *The challenge is to enhance organized long-term care services for persons living in the community without eroding family care and the private purchase of help.*

> *A cost-effective long-term care program must supple-
> ment and augment rather than simply replace personal
> family initiatives (p. 61).*

The flaw in the argument for the provision of community care is, according to Weissert (1985), "that it asks society to begin paying for something that it is now getting free" (p. 48). Yet, the issue is more complex than suggested by Weissert, particularly for caregivers who may be absorbing the physical, emotional, and financial costs of community care, thereby obscuring the true cost-savings potential that may be available when community care and institutional care are compared. Rather, the issue is, as suggested by Litwak, how might informal care and formal support services be used as a cooperative continuum in humanely and cost-effectively meeting the dependency needs of the frail elderly in the community and, perhaps, delaying or avoiding institutionalization? The focus of this study, adult day care, is one of the emerging programs offering services to the frail elderly client and respite for the caregiver in a community setting.

COMPETING IDEOLOGIES

The aging of the population has exacerbated the debate among competing ideologies for the delivery of social services. These ideologies profess belief in either the overriding value of cost effect- iveness or the primacy of the right to quality of life, often using the phrase "humane care." Recurrently, this is projected as a dichotomy: On the one side, the institutional bias of long-term care (controlled through limited government funding), and, on the other, the depen- dent elder's desire to remain in the community (controlled by the presence, ability, and willingness of caregivers) provide the poles of this contention. The body of doctrines or beliefs held by each has its roots in history. This lack of consensus for the delivery of social services strains social well-being.

Litwak's somewhat recent theory asserting the complementary nature of informal networks and formal organizations (This theory is explained, in depth, in the second section of Chapter 2, Comple- mentary Functions) integrates the underlying goals inherent in the values of both those who prize cost-effectiveness, and those who prize humaneness. The values of cost-effectiveness and humaneness, therefore, need not be seen as a dichotomy (Kane and Kane, 1987). Indeed, the humaneness and warmth provided by primary groups are as essential to the effective achievement of most long-term care goals as is the rationalistic approach of bureaucratic organizations (Litwak, 1978).

As the aged become less independent, they increasingly turn to informal systems for assistance with their dependency needs (Shanas, 1979a,b). It is only when assistance from the family is unavailable, or kin and "significant others" can no longer absorb the burden of assistance (because of excessive time and/or money commitments, or lack of requisite skill) that older persons and their families turn to formal organizations for help (Cantor and Little, 1985). Cantor (1980) has characterized this manner of selecting assistance as the hierarchical compensatory theory of social supports.

But, the primacy of the kin network in assisting older people does not devalue the role of formal social services. Litwak, in his theories of shared functions and balanced coordination, postulates that the dependency needs of elders are best met if there is a proper balance between formal services and informal supports, with each system performing the tasks for which it is most suited. Ideally an older person should be able to access the element of care most appropriate for a particular time and needed function (Litwak, 1978; Litwak and Meyer, 1966; Sussman, 1977). Thus the social support system of elders can be viewed as an amalgam of kin, friends, and societal services, each having different roles and differing relative importance at various phases in the dependency continuum of old age.

It, therefore, becomes critical to have information about how the formal service system and the informal primary network may complement one another in meeting the dependency needs of the frail elderly in the community and delaying or possibly avoiding long-term institutional care. Such an organizing framework is necessary in order to evaluate the extent to which current and future policies will efficiently and humanely address the needs of our aging population. For this reason, this analysis attempts to contribute to the expansion of the currently undeveloped knowledge base from which community service delivery might be conceptualized. If informal supports are to continue to be a principal mode of social care for older people, serious consideration must be given to methods of assisting family, friends, neighbors, and other informal groups in their efforts (Cantor and Little, 1985).

> ". . . (P)ublic monies are more likely to be spent for medical/technical services than for social services; more likely to pay for institutional services in hospitals and nursing homes than for services that keep elders in their own homes; and are more likely to pay for later more intrusive interventions than earlier interventions that support the client, family, and other informal supports." (Wetle, 1985, p. 33).

Despite the significance of primary supports in maintaining the dependent elderly in the community and avoiding unnecessary institutionalization, little is known about how formal community services may complement the primary or informal network in doing this. Litwak's theory, as it applies to the aged, has not previously been tested in a community program setting except for the nursing home. The purpose of this study is to address this knowledge gap by:

(1)   describing the differences in the structures of the formal and informal systems;

(2)   documenting the dependency needs of the target population; i.e., those at-risk of institutionalization;

(3)   identifying the services provided, over time, by each organization, i.e., the formal system and the informal network; and,

(4)   specifying the complementary functions of these services.

Providing a program data base for choosing among alternative models of long-term care for the expenditure of public funds is essential if professionals wish to pay more than lip service to promoting cost-effective, humanistic long-term care services for the frail elderly[1].

To summarize, this study will look at adult day care program variables within the context of Cantor's theory of compensatory social supports and Litwak's theory of complementary roles between bureaucratic organizations and community primary groups in order to analyze the delivery of adult day care as it relates to community care and caregivers' needs. In this study, adult day care is considered to be both a subsystem of the larger comprehensive formal community care service system for dependent older adults as well as a system of care and a core service for the informal network of caregivers through the provision of respite.

---

[1] *In the past twenty years, America has witnessed an impressive proliferation of what are now termed alternative institutions. They are important sociologically insofar as they depart radically from established modes of organization. Owing their legacy to the anti-authority movement of the 1960s, alternative institutions may be defined by their resolve to build organizations parallel to, but outside of, established institutions to fulfill social needs without recourse to internal bureaucracies, or external direction (Rothschild-Whitt, 1979). These participatory-democratic organizational forms attempt to blend humane and cost-effective perspectives; however, "little research has been devoted to this social development" (Rothschild-Whitt, 1979). Therefore, the ability of democratic-participatory organizations to deliver humane and cost-effective services is yet to be determined. In any event, the question this study seeks to investigate is not whether variant organizational structures can deliver humane, cost-effective services but whether the hierarchical, bureaucratic organization can be used to complement humane, cost-effective human service delivery.*

8.   *Adult Day Care: Formal & Informal Systems of Care*

END NOTES - CHAPTER 1

Achenbaum, W. Andrew. "Historical Perspectives on Public Policy & Aging." Generations, XII, No 3 (Spring 1988), pp. 27-29.

Brody, Elaine M. "Parent Care as a Normative Family Stress." The Gerontologist, 25, No 1 (1985), pp. 19-29.

Brody, Elaine, M. "Women in the Middle and Family Help to Older People." The Gerontologist, 21, No 5 (1981), pp. 471-480.

Brody, Elaine M. and C. Schoonover. "Patterns of Care for the Dependent Elderly When Daughters Work and When They Do Not." The Gerontologist, 26, No 4 (1986), pp. 372-381.

Callahan, James J. et al. "Responsibility of Families for Their Severely Disabled Elders." Health Care Financing Review (Winter 1980), pp. 29-48.

Callahan, James J. and Stanley S. Wallack, eds. Reforming the Long Term Care System. Lexington, MA: D. C. Heath & Company, 1981.

Cantor, Marjorie. "The Informal Support System, Its Relevance in the Lives of the Elderly." In Aging and Society. Eds. E. Borgotta and N. McClusky. Beverly Hills, CA: Sage Publications, 1980, pp. 111-146.

Cantor, Marjorie. "Strain Among Caregivers: A Study of Experience in the United States." The Gerontologist, 23, No 6 (1983), pp. 597-603.

Cantor, Marjorie and Virginia Little. "Aging and Social Care." In Handbook of Aging and the Social Sciences. Eds. Robert Binstock and Ethel Shanas. New York: Van Nostrand Reinhold Co., 1985, pp. 745-781.

Crystal, Stephen. America's Old Age Crisis. New York: Basic Books, 1982.

Doty, Pamela. "Family Care of the Elderly: The Role of Public Policy." The Milbank Quarterly, 64, No 1 (1986), pp. 34-75.

Estes, Carroll L. and Charles A. Harrington. "Fiscal Crisis, Deinstitutionalization, and the Elderly." American Behavioral Scientist, 24, No 6 (1981), pp. 811-826.

Horowitz, A. and Rose Dobrof. "The Role of Families in Providing Long-Term Care to the Frail and Chronically Ill Elderly Living in the Community." Final Report Submitted to the Health Care Financing Administration Grant #18-P-97541/2-02. New York: Brookdale Center on Aging of Hunter College, (1982).

Hudson, Robert B. "Renewing the Federal Role." Generations, XII, No 3 (Spring 1988), pp. 23-26.

Jacobs, B. and William Weissert. "Financing Long-Term Care." Journal of Health, Politics, Policy and Law, 12, No 1 (Spring, 1987), pp. 77-95.

Jennings, Bruce, Daniel Callahan and Arthur Caplan. "Ethical Challenges of Chronic Illness." Hastings Center Report, Special Supplement, (February/March 1988), pp. 1-16.

Kane, Rosalie and Robert Kane. Long-Term Care: Principles, Programs, and Policies. New York: Springer Publishing Co., 1987.

Kane, Rosalie. "Long-Term Care." In Encyclopedia of Social Work, Vol 2. 18th edition, Silver Spring, MD: National Association of Social Workers, 1987, pp. 59-72.

Litwak, Eugene. "Agency and Family Linkages in Providing Services." In Reaching People: The Structure of Neighborhood Services, Vol 3. Social Service Delivery Systems: An International Annual. Eds.

D. Thursz and J. Vigilante. Beverly Hills, CA: Sage Publications, 1978, pp. 59-95.

Litwak, Eugene. "Part II-Theoretical Bases for Practice." In <u>Maintenance of Family Ties of Long-Term Care Patients: Theory and Guide to Practice</u>. Rose Dobrof and Eugene Litwak. Rockville, MD: National Institute of Mental Health, 1977b, pp. 80-116.

Litwak, Eugene and H. Meyer. "A Balance Theory of Coordination Between Bureaucratic Organizations and Community Primary Groups." <u>Administrative Science Quarterly</u>, 11 (1966), pp. 31-58.

Liu, K., K. G. Manton and B. M. Liu. "Home Care Expenses for the Disabled Elderly." <u>Health Care Financing Review</u>, 7, No 2 (1985) pp. 51-58.

Rothschild-Whitt, Joyce. "Conditions for Democracy: Making Participatory Organizations Work." In <u>Co-Ops, Communes and Collectives in Social Change in the 1960s and 1970s</u>. Ed. J. Case and R. C. R. Taylor. New York: Pantheon Books, 1979.

Shanas, Ethel. "The Family as a Social Support System in Old Age." <u>The Gerontologist</u>, 19, No 2 (1979b), pp. 169-174.

Shanas, Ethel. "Social Myth as Hypothesis: The Case of the Family Relations of Old People." <u>The Gerontologist</u>, 19, No 1 (1979a), pp. 3-9.

Siegel, Jacob S. and Cynthia M. Taeuber. "Demographic Dimensions of an Aging Population." In <u>Our Aging Society</u>. Eds. Alan Pifer and Lydia Bronte. New York: W. W. Norton & Co., 1986, pp. 79-110.

Soldo, Beth J. and J. Myllyluoma. "Caregivers Who Live with Dependent Elderly." <u>The Gerontologist</u>, 23, No 6 (1983), pp. 605-611.

Stephens, Susan A. and Jan B. Christianson. <u>Informal Care of the Elderly</u>. Lexington, MA: D. C. Health and Company, 1986.

Stoller, E. P. "Parental Caregiving by Adult Children." *Journal of Marriage and the Family*, (November 1983), pp. 851-858.

Sussman, Marvin. "Bureaucracy and the Elderly Individual: An Organizational Linkage Perspective." In *Family Bureaucracy and the Elderly*. Eds. E. Shanas and M. Sussman. Durham, NC: Duke University Press, 1977.

Sussman, Marvin. "The Family Life of Old People." In *Handbook of Aging and the Social Sciences*. Eds. Robert Binstock and Ethel Shanas. New York: Van Nostrand Reinhold Co., 1976.

Torres-Gil, Fernando M. "Process, Politics, & Policy." *Generations*, XII, No 3 (Spring 1988), pp. 4-9.

Warren, Carol A. B. "New Forms of Social Control: The Myth of Deinstitutionalization." *American Behavioral Scientist*, 24, No 6 (1981), pp. 724-740.

Weiner, Joshua. "A Look at Policy Choices." *Perspective on Aging*, XVI, No 6 (November/December, 1987), pp. 10-11.

Weissert, William. "Rationales for Public Health Insurance Coverage of Geriatric Day Care: Issues, Options and Impacts." *Journal of Health Politics*, Policy and Law, 3, No 4 (Winter 1979), pp. 555-556.

Weissert, William. "Seven Reasons Why It Is so Difficult to Make Community Based Long-Term Care Cost Effective." *Health Services Research*, 20, No 4 (1985), pp. 423-433.

Wetle, Terrie. "Long-Term Care: A Taxonomy of Issues." *Generations*, X, No 2 (1985), pp. 30-34.

CHAPTER 2

CONTEXT AND THEORETICAL PERSPECTIVES

*"When we try to pick out anything by
itself, we find it is tied to everything
else in the universe."*
                                        John Muir

The objectives of this chapter are to trace the development of formal and informal long-term care delivery for the dependent aged, examine the relationship of these systems to the theory of complementary roles between the informal network and formal organization, and to consider its application to adult day care. Therefore, the philosophical, theoretical and empirical perspectives underlying the phenomena of concern to this study, namely the concepts of formal and informal community long-term care, adult day care, and complementary functions of the formal and informal networks are described. The chapter's review of the literature, including previous adult day care program studies, is in three parts and includes an examination of the following:

(1)   the role of formal and informal supports in community long-term care;

(2)   the complementary functions of formal and informal supports in long-term care; and,

(3)   adult day care.

COMMUNITY LONG-TERM CARE

Definitions and a description of long-term care, its public importance, and a profile of the long-term care user will be followed by a discussion of the role of the family (i.e., informal supports) and the institution (i.e., formal supports) in providing long-term care to the dependent elderly. The steady tension that exists in all human service endeavors between incentives to serve people properly, and the need to conserve scarce resources is depicted. This is followed by a profile of future demographic trends to underscore the burgeoning national preoccupation with long-term care issues. Recent long-term care efforts will then be described and discussed in relation to their current impact on the dependent elderly and their caregivers. This will be enhanced by a portrayal of caregiver willingness to bring dependent elders into their home, caregiving stress, reasons for institutionalization, and government policies promoting family care. Finally, respite services will be discussed.

Definitions and Description of Long-Term Care:
     Weiler and Rathbone-McCuan (1978) defined long-term care as "the external support systems needed by the aged to maintain life at a satisfactory level of quality, whether in community-based facilities, at home, or in institutions" (p. 3).
     Padula (1983) described community long-term care services as including:

> *homemaker, home health, home-delivered meals or eating together programs, transportation, senior centers, housing and flexibly designed services to assist with dressing, escort, evening or weekend sitters or friendly visitors (p. 9).*

This author also described three relatively new services developing on the long-term care continuum: respite services, hospices for the dying, and Centers for Independent Living for severely handicapped people. Adult day care is a service providing respite to caregivers (Respite Care for the Frail Elderly, 1983; Strang and Neufeld, 1990).
     Eustis et al. (1984) has summarized the public importance of long-term care:

> *Long-term care (informal help, health and social services, special housing) for functionally impaired older persons is a topic of concern for almost every older person, most multigeneration families, numerous*

> *service organizations, and public agencies at every level of government. Reduced ability to function physically, mentally, and socially—one of many losses potentially associated with old age—may leave the individual in need of substantial assistance (p. 1).*

Previously referring only to institutionalization, long-term care now includes a continuum of services for the care of older persons that most often begins in the community. With the goal of preventing institutionalization until it is absolutely necessary and appropriate, long-term care provides a range of services to supplement losses that threaten independent living (Brown and O'Day, 1981).

Users of Long-Term Care:

Harkins (1981) described users of long-term care as "those who are depending on at least one other person for their daily maintenance because they are unable to perform these tasks by themselves" (p. 1).

The typical user of long-term care services usually has three or more chronic health conditions, experiences more illness days, and rates their general health as fair to poor (Harkins, 1981). Harkins (1981) reported long-term care users were "older, more likely to be black, poorer, less well educated, and less likely to be currently married than those not utilizing long-term care" with limitations in activities of daily living the single most important factor (p. 9).

At present, there is no generally accepted definition of "at-risk of institutionalization" (Kirwin, in press). However, Weissert (1979) and Knox (no date, p. 5) have used the number of impairments and caregiver status as indicators of "at-risk;" and, Stanley Brody (1987) using instruments developed by Katz (1963) and Lawton (1969) defines "at-risk" as the presence of five to six deficiencies in the activities of daily living (ADL). Most old people in institutions have five or six ADL deficits (Soldo and Manton, 1985). A six year study by the Harvard Medical School ("Factors Correlated," 1983) suggested that five variables were positively related to long-term care institutional admission: advancing age, use of ambulatory aids, mental disorientation, solitary living, and use of assistance in performing activities of daily living.

　　While the definition of the term at-risk of institutionalization is unclear, so is the definition for activities of daily living. The activities encompassed by the term ADL are not consistent. Kane and Kane (1981) list 13 ADL (p. 27-28); whereas, Stephens and Christianson (1986) list 6 ADL—bathing, dressing, toileting, getting out of bed or a chair, continence, and eating—(p., 19). Kerson and Kerson (1985) define ADL as "Specific activities encountered during the normal daily routine—bed, eating, hygiene, dressing, utilities, communication, locomotion, toileting" (p. 301). Activities such as shopping, cooking, cleaning, and laundry are generally considered instrumental activities of daily living (IADL) (Doty, 1986, p. 35).

　　Yet, "Frailty, functional deficit, and chronic illness do not directly determine likelihood of institutionalization. A lesson of the (Channeling) demonstration is that there needs to be a link between the nursing home-eligibility process and community-based care systems in order to properly target clients for such care" (Eisenberg and Amerman, 1988, p. 22). That is, the availability of community centered services and caregiver preference for service also must be factored into the at-risk of institutionalization assessment (Doty, 1986).

The Role of the Family in Long-Term Care of Elders:

　　According to recent national surveys conducted by the Department of Health and Human Services (the 1979 Health Interview Survey and the 1982 National Long-Term Care Survey and Informal Caregivers' Survey), informal caregiving by family and friends is currently the dominant mode, by far, of providing long-term care services to functionally disabled elderly. Nearly one-quarter (22.9 percent) of all United States elderly aged 65 and older are functionally disabled. That is, they require assistance from another person with personal care, with mobility, or with instrumental activities of daily living, or they require nursing care of the sort provided by visiting nurses or by nursing home staff (Doty, 1986, p. 35). Only one in five of these elders with long-term care needs is cared for in a nursing home; the remaining four-fifths can go on living in the community primarily because family and friends provide all or most of the assistance they require (Kane and Kane, 1987). Nearly three-quarters of the elderly disabled who live in the community rely solely on family and friends for the assistance they require. Most of the remainder rely on a combination of family care and paid help. Only a small minority (9 percent in the 1979 Health Interview Survey, 5 percent in the 1982 National Long-Term Care Survey and Informal Caregivers Survey) received all their care from paid providers. Moreover, three-quarters of all such noninstitutional paid care is privately financed by elders themselves and their relatives; only 26 percent is government financed (U. S. Bureau of the Census 1983). According to the National Center for Health Services, there are more than 7 million unpaid caregivers in the United States caring for an ill relative or friend (Felder, 1988, p. 7).

The above referenced 1979 and 1982 survey results replicated earlier survey findings that many impaired elders living in the community and receiving family assistance are as disabled as nursing home residents and, as such, could meet medical and functional disability criteria for nursing home admission if they chose to apply (Shanas, 1979a). Clearly, family care enables many impaired elderly to remain in the community when, without such support, they would require nursing home placement (Smyer, 1980). Conversely, elders without close kin are statistically over-represented among nursing home residents (Doty, 1986, p. 36). According to one area study by Brody, Poulshock, and Masciocchi (1978), 50 percent of nursing home residents are childless and 20 percent have no immediate living family; but, no national figures are available.

Because the availability of families willing to provide long-term care services is such a pivotal factor in preventing or postponing nursing home placement for many impaired elderly, policy makers have reason to be concerned about the potential fiscal consequences of any decrease in families' willingness to provide this care.

Trends in Institutional Use:

It is widely believed, by many policy makers and members of the public, that families today are becoming less willing than families were historically to care for elderly impaired family members at home

(Crystal, 1982; Doty, 1986). Prominent family-care researchers Ethel Shanas (1979b) and Elaine Brody (1981) refer to this belief as the myth of abandonment because there is little scientific evidence to support it and, indeed, much evidence to the contrary. Elaine Brody (1985) has advanced a psychosocial theory to account for the prevalence of the myth of abandonment among the general public despite the fact that more and more people are having personal experience caring for disabled elderly relatives. Indeed, Brody's theory includes the assertion that providing informal long-term care to elderly relatives is becoming a "normative" event. However, based on Doty's (1986) experience in government, policy makers differ from the general public, in justifying their belief that families are increasingly abandoning care of dependent elders to institutions by citing what at first glance appear to be convincing statistics. Doty demonstrates that closer examination of these data reveals that this alleged trend rests largely on a misinterpretation of the fact that elders' use of nursing home care has increased dramatically over the past half-century, and especially, over the past 25 years. A study of historical patterns in institutionalization rates of the elderly carried out for the 1980 Under Secretary's Task Force on Long-Term Care found, however, that most of the growth in the percentage of elderly aged 65 and older in nursing homes is due to two factors unrelated to family caregiving: (1) the shift from use of mental hospitals (and, earlier almshouses and homes for the aged) to nursing homes, and (2) the greater percentage of elderly in older age groups (75 and older) that have traditionally had higher use rates for nursing home care (U. S. Department of Health and Human Services, Assistant Secretary for Planning and Evaluation, 1981).

The Task Force's analysis of institutionalization rates among elders found that, from 1950 to 1970, the proportion of the population aged 65 to 79 in institutions remained almost constant. In contrast, the institutionalization rate of the elderly aged 80 and older increased more than 50 percent over the same period.

There are several theories as to why, from 1950 to 1970, the nursing home use rate increased so dramatically among the elderly aged 80 and older. One theory is that advances in medical science increased the survival rates of individuals at higher levels of chronic disease and disability (Gruenberg, 1977; Butler, 1983). In addition, the gap in longevity increases between men and women (e.g., as of 1977 white females aged 65 could expect to live an average of 18.5 years longer as compared to 13.9 years for white males) (U. S. Bureau of the Census, 1983) has produced larger numbers of very elderly widows than existed in the past. Larger numbers of widows coupled with higher divorce rates and trends toward lower fertility also may mean that the elderly aged 80 and older not only are more disabled than they were 20 to 30 years ago but have fewer family members available to provide informal care (Doty, 1986). And, Crystal (1982) estimates that 10 to 15 percent of recent increases in nursing home use are because today's elderly have fewer children than their parents did.

Future Impact of Demographic Trends:

It is also worth noting that, as life expectancy increases, the age at which elders are likely to become dependent on adult children for assistance increases. As a result, the impaired elderly in need of informal long-term care are more and more likely to have children who are themselves past retirement age. Currently, 10 percent of the population aged 65 and older have children who are also aged 65 or older (Doty, 1986). Doty has reported on studies that suggest that the aging of a child is a precipitating factor for institutional placement; that willingness to take an older relative into one's home is negatively correlated with age; and that older children reported more negative feelings and greater emotional strain associated with caregiving.

Another factor that affects both the willingness and the availability of family members to provide long-term care services informally to elders in their or the elder's home is the compatibility of giving such care with other roles. Since most of the family care of impaired elders not provided by spouses has traditionally been provided by middle-aged adult daughters and daughters-in-law, many experts believe that the increasing trend toward women in the labor force is likely to decrease the capacity of these traditional caregivers to meet the care needs of impaired elderly relatives (Brody, 1985). Currently, 51 percent of adult women are working outside the home and three-quarters of these women work full time (U. S. Bureau of the Census, 1983). Sixty percent of women aged 45 to 54 work outside the home (Brody, 1981).

Competing demands, child rearing, and employment in particular, have been considered potential sources of stress in providing long-term care to the dependent elderly (Stone et al., 1987). Many caregivers have also cited neglect of familial responsibilities as a major concern (Rathbone-McCuan, 1976).

It is suggested by research findings (Cantor, 1983; Creedon, 1987), that many working caregivers experience conflict between the demands of employment and their elder care responsibilities. Studies of the degree to which employment impinges on caregiving have produced equivocal results. Soldo and Myllyluoma (1983) analyzed aggregate data and identified female labor force participation as a significant factor influencing rates of institutionalization of elderly persons. Findings from several community studies, however, show that employment status is not related to the total amount of help provided (Brody, 1981; Cantor, 1980). Stoller (1983) observed gender differences in the impact of employment on level of parental caregiving. Although being employed decreased the average level of a son's assistance by 20 hours per month, employment was not a significant predictor of caregiver hours among daughters.

Clearly, working women cannot themselves provide hands-on care during the hours when they are at work, but the income they receive from working may increase their ability to finance paid care. "(F)amilies in which both spouses are working may choose to pay others to provide some or all the care that they themselves would have provided had they had more time available" (Doty, 1986, p. 40).

Willingness to Bring Elderly Relatives into One's Home:
Demographic factors that may be decreasing the availability of family members to provide informal care, have thus far been reviewed. This section will focus on the willingness of family to provide informal care, in particular, the willingness of family members to provide the amounts and types of care similar to that provided in nursing homes (Crystal, 1982). This means the willingness of family members to bring an elderly disabled parent to live with them when they become heavily dependent for help with personal care needs: bathing, dressing, eating, toileting, or when they become so mentally

confused as to require constant supervision.

Historical studies have documented that shared living arrangements between parents and adult children have never been a preferred cultural pattern in this country (Achenbaum, 1978; Fischer, 1978). Indeed, even in Colonial times, many families "boarded out" their elderly relatives. So long as adult children were willing to assume the financial responsibility of supporting elderly relatives, rather than leaving it to the church or the county, "boarding out" was viewed as a perfectly acceptable way to avoid the potential family tensions that might arise from three-generational shared living arrangements (Haber, 1983). Elders themselves have strong preferences for independent living and strong desires not to be a burden (Louis Harris and Associates, Inc., 1982).

According to the Horowitz and Dobrof (1982) study of family caregiving patterns in New York, shared living arrangements among family caregivers and elderly care receivers were more prevalent among the never married (e.g., unmarried daughters and their elderly mothers and never married siblings), lower income, and nonemployed persons. Such arrangements were also found to be unrelated to ethnic tradition when income was controlled. The only characteristic of those receiving care that showed a statistically significant association with the locus of family caregiving was functional ability. Elderly persons living in their children's or other relatives' homes had higher dependency, ADL scores than those who remained in their own homes.

In sum, the evidence suggests that until the impaired elderly become highly dependent in terms of personal care needs (such as bathing, dressing, feeding, toileting) both they and their children or other family caregivers prefer to maintain separate living arrangements. Since most family caregivers live within an hour—and most live within a half hour's travel time from those they care for—separate living arrangements can generally be maintained, if income permits, while the elder primarily requires assistance with instrumental activities of daily living, e.g., shopping, cleaning, cooking, laundry (Shanas, 1979b).

The Horowitz and Dobrof (1982) study of family caregivers in New York examined the willingness of family members already involved in providing long-term care services to an elderly relative to bring the elders into their home. In this study, 27 percent of the adult children caregivers and 15 percent of other relatives (primarily siblings) were already providing assistance to the older person in their home. This study showed that the major barriers to willingness to bring elderly disabled into the home were emotional ones. On the one hand, there was the resistance of elders toward giving up their home and moving in with relatives; on the other hand, there were the family caregivers' concerns about interpersonal tensions and conflicts.

Among Horowitz and Dobrof's sample of New York caregivers, familial responsibility was the most frequently mentioned reason for providing long-term care assistance to an elderly relative; this motivation was spontaneously cited by 58 percent of the caregivers. The second most common motivation mentioned was love (51 percent), followed by reciprocity (e.g., acknowledgment of past assistance received), which was cited by 17 percent. These findings confirm other research that suggests that family caregiving is motivated primarily by three factors: love and affection felt toward the individual; a sense of gratitude and desire to reciprocate caregiving or other help that was previously provided by the impaired elderly person to the spouse or adult child; and, allegiance to a more generalized societal norm of spousal or filial responsibility, i.e., the family caregiver is responding to what they believe to be society's expectations concerning morally correct or approved behavior (Cantor and Little, 1985).

Stresses of Caregiving:

When studied, caregivers often express feelings of worry, burden, frustration, being "tied down," and complain of social isolation due to friendship patterns being interrupted and mobility impaired (Springer and Brubaker, 1984). Conflicting family obligations also can cause psychological strain. Responsibilities to parents may take precedence over responsibility to spouse, children, or others because the former is seen as the more pressing need. Still, this is usually felt as a forced choice (Stephens and Christianson, 1986). Stephens and Christianson have reported that there may be a marked impact for the worse on marital and other family relationships of an adult child who is the principal caregiver of an elderly parent.

All these stresses were found among the family members of persons applying for nursing home care in the Virginia PreAdmission Screening Study (Arling and McAuley, 1983). In this study, the family members of the nursing home applicants were asked about the changes in their lives that had taken place during the six months prior to the decision to seek institutional placement. Forty-three percent said that they had to consider their impaired elderly relatives in planning activities with others. Forty-two percent said they had less time for themselves. Forty-one percent reported mental anguish or worry. Thirty-one percent reported that their social or recreational activities decreased. Twenty-eight percent said that they had less time with their spouse or children. The social and emotional stresses were more pervasive than interference with work or financial strains, which were reported by only 11 percent and 10 percent of family members.

Although the literature on family caregiving repeatedly cites stress and "burnout" on the part of the caregiver as causes of institutionalization of elderly relatives, very little is actually known about how this process operates. The relation between emotional stress and the decision to institutionalize an elderly relative is a complicated one because some research suggests that it is precisely the caregivers who are emotionally closest to the impaired person and most committed to providing care who experience the greater stress (Cantor, 1983). Spouses, in particular, show a strong tendency to maintain caregiving whatever the social and emotional costs and stop only when deterioration in their health physically prevents them from providing the services (Doty, 1986).

As Johnson and Catalano (1983) point out, other adaptive mechanisms are available besides institutionalization for coping with stress. In their eight month follow-up of dependent elderly discharged from hospitals, Johnson and Catalano found that children were more likely than spouses to turn to formal supports (use of physicians and social workers for advice, and employment of paid homemakers) or to seek assistance from other family members.

Reasons for Institutionalization:

A review of the research literature suggests that the single most common precipitating factor in family decisions to institutionalize an impaired elderly relative is the elderly individual's worsening health. For example, in one recent study (Smallegan, 1985) of 288 new admissions to 28 nursing homes in Michigan and North Carolina, the most frequently reported reason for institutionalization was a deterioration in the patient's condition. Sixty-four percent of the patients had become less well shortly before admission. Deterioration in health status was serious enough so that two-thirds of the patients were admitted directly from a hospital. The most common medical conditions precipitating admission were: frequent falls (27 percent), general debility (25 percent), confusion (21 percent), fractures (14 percent), stroke (13 percent), incontinence (13 percent), and difficult behavior (13 percent). All but 7 of the patients in this study had been receiving some informal long-term care from family members prior to admission. Of those patients with children (N=212), more than 86 percent had received care from them before institutionalization. Fifteen percent of patients had received home care from relatives (spouse, children, others) for more than 5 years prior to admission. Weissert and Scanlon (1983), using a data set formed by combining the 1977 National Health Interview Survey and the 1977 National Nursing Home Survey, found that personal care dependency was among the most important determinants of residency in a nursing home among the aged (Jacobs and Weissert, 1987).

Other studies of families' decisions to seek institutional placement for elderly impaired relatives or to consider seriously seeking such placement (Zarit, Reever, and Bach-Peterson, 1980; Lebowitz, 1978) have cited as major motivations the following: caretakers' lack of time for themselves and other family members due to the constant burden of caregiving, difficulty in dealing with incontinence or confusion and behavioral problems associated with senility, inability to meet the physical demands of caring for someone with severe paralysis, and caretaker fatigue due to sleep disturbances when relatives require care during the night. In some cases, a change for the worse in the caregiver's own health status was a precipitating factor in the decision to institutionalize someone (Springer and Brubaker, 1984). In addition, Doty (1986) found that lack of privacy and insufficient space were major reasons given for not taking a dependent elder into one's home who otherwise requires institutional placement.

Government Policies to Promote Family Care:

The total nursing home industry costs, and the cost to government, have more than doubled each five years for the last two decades (Crystal, 1982). The implementation of Medicare and Medicaid in the late sixties caused a jump to 70 percent in the proportion that was publicly financed, falling to 42 percent in 1972 after Medicare cutbacks. The proportion rose again to about the 55 percent level in the late seventies, with Medicaid as the main source (Crystal, 1982, p. 70).

Crystal further documents that between 1973 and 1979, the increase in total public and private nursing home expenditures was 148 percent, versus a 64 percent increase in the consumer price index. Nursing home care has been the fastest growing cost in the health system, increasing in recent years about 18 to 20 percent annually.

In spite of the extensive government participation, nursing home costs can be devastating to individuals. The impoverishment resulting from nursing home costs reduces the chances of leaving the nursing home and reestablishing life outside, even if health improves after a convalescent period; and in fact few patients who stay for more than a few weeks ever return to the community. The lack of incentive for the nursing home to help patients move out, the absence of public social services serving this function, and the complexity of reestablishing housing arrangements and needed services all contribute to the very low rate of return to community life. If arrangements were made to maintain and pay for the patient's home during a convalescent period, and if needed assistance was available, Crystal (1982) believes that more people probably would leave nursing homes than actually do. As regulators put increasing pressure on hospitals to discharge patients once the need for acute care is passed, we may need to organize ourselves better to use nursing homes on a short-term basis as well as for "permanent placement" (Crystal, 1982, p. 72).

The burden of long-term care is particularly difficult because of the great cost of extended stays. "Even the middle-class elderly end up using Medicaid" (Crystal, 1982, p. 72). Largely because of nursing home expenses, the average elderly Medicaid recipient in 1976 used (in addition to Medicare reimbursements) almost six times the cost of services used by the average child on Medicaid under age six, and 5.4

times the cost of services used by Medicaid recipients between the ages of six and twenty (Crystal, 1982). The sense that expenditures are out of control, claims Crystal, has led to severe Medicaid cuts in most states.

The financial impact of nursing home placement on a spouse remaining in the community can be very severe, particularly if the institutionalized spouse was the source of income for the household. The Health Care Financing Administration (1981) has reported that this can force the noninstitutionalized spouse to enter an institution as well.

Respite Services:

Respite care provides time out for both the frail elder and their caregiver. In-home and out-of-home respite may involve overnight placement or a day service such as adult day care. Respite is seen as a "practical, prophylactic and therapeutic remedy" for easing the burden of caregiving (Respite Care for the Frail Elderly, 1983). Many experts believe that families would be better able to tolerate the long-term stress of caring for a disabled elderly person—particularly one afflicted with Alzheimer's disease or some other form of dementia or one with heavy personal care assistance needs—if they were able to obtain periodic respite (Strang and Neufeld, 1990). Respite care could take many different forms ranging from a temporary stay in a nursing home while the family takes a vacation to a few hours per week of "sitter" service so that the principal caregiver of an elder who cannot be left alone can have some regular time off. Doty (1986) suggests that adult day care programs also can provide respite for family members when the individual requiring care has heavy personal care needs or must have constant surveillance at night and on weekends. "Reliance on day care also may be the only potentially affordable means for working caregivers to manage home care of Alzheimer's or other mentally impaired, heavily dependent elderly" (Doty, 1986, p. 55).

According to Rathbone-McCuan (1976) day care often represents a "last ditch" effort to maintain an elderly person at home. A more recent evaluation of a day care program for Alzheimer's patients concluded that such a program can provide an alternative to nursing homes as relief to families caring for a person suffering from Alzheimer's disease or a related disorder in the home (Sands and Suzuki, 1983). Other researchers have voiced the same conclusion (Blaser, 1983; Meltzer, 1982; Rathbone-McCuan and Coward, 1985; Saperstein, 1987; Zaki, 1982).

While the above studies suggest that "supportive formal services can reduce the stress on the caregiver, it is yet unclear whether they will prevent or delay institutionalization" (Doty, 1986, p. 56). If one assumes that social service programs, by providing instrumental assistance, will permit the caregiver to attend to the elderly person's emotional needs and that such emotional support can be crucial in preventing or delaying deterioration in physical function-ing, institutionalization also may be delayed or prevented (Springer and Brubaker, 1987). In a study by Sager (1978) of hospital patients who were to be discharged to nursing homes, the discharge planner believed that three-fourths of the families would have been willing to maintain the patient at home if supportive outside services had been available. In another study, Eggert et al. (1977) found that family willingness to provide home care to an elder following a hospitaliza-tion dropped from 70 percent following the first hospitalization to 38 percent following the second hospitalization; the authors speculated that families; initial willingness or capacity to provide home care "appears to be significantly eroded over time when, as it may be assumed, the burden is not shared by supplementary social provisions" (p. 110).

In summary, through the complementing care of informal supports and institutional systems, the social service of adult day care may prove both humane and cost-effective thereby satisfying both government and consumer (i.e., client and caregiver needs), and providing care options through a continuum of choices ranging from total family care to long-term institutional residency. Social services are defined as,

> *organized societal approaches to the amelioration or eradication of those conditions which are viewed at any historical point of time as unacceptable and for which knowledge and skills can be applied to make them more acceptable. Such services, therefore, are based*

upon scientific knowledge and humanistic values out of which are defined the roles, responsibilities, and acceptable conditions for the individual family, community, and society (Beattie, 1976, p. 619).

Funding for this continuum would range from family support to local and federal government support depending on client levels and sources of income (i.e., social security, pensions, personal resources) to private insurance and public support through long-term care policy initiatives now being advocated by government representatives (Stone et al., 1987).

There is a pressing need to match the growing demands of an aging population with resources that, we now know are limited (i.e., family caregivers, local and federal government dollars, community preferences, and private abilities) to generate alternative options. The biting question is how do we serve people adequately, equitably, and efficiently with these limited resources? As Kane and Kane (1987) have stated,

> *Perhaps the greatest challenge of all is to temper our passion for cost-effectiveness with a continuing concern about the purpose of the effort. The overriding goal of any long-term care program is to provide the necessary care in a humane fashion, respecting the preferences and dignity of the recipients. The ultimate test of such care is whether it is indeed decent. Is it the sort of care one would want for oneself or one's parents? Does the service come with so many strictures that more is taken away (in terms of dignity and freedom) than is given (p. 374)?*

"Instead of regarding family and public responsibility for the aged's care as a duality," Noelker and Townsend (1987) suggest "it seems more efficacious to view them as having complementary functions" (p. 59). Several social scientists have, in fact, proposed models conceptualizing the nature of the relationship between the aged's informal and formal support systems in this manner (Cantor, 1979; Litwak, 1985; Sussman, 1977).

COMPLEMENTARY FUNCTIONS OF FORMAL AND INFORMAL SUPPORTS IN LONG-TERM CARE

One major issue currently under review by policy makers and researchers is the role of the formal sector in supporting informal caregivers, and the proper mix of informal and formal services required to meet the needs of noninstitutionalized elderly care recipients (S. Brody et al., 1978; Callahan et al., 1980; Litwak, 1985). Litwak and his associates (Dobrof and Litwak, 1977; Litwak and Figueira, 1970) have insisted that dependency needs of an older person may be met effectively by a balance between formal services and informal supports—by their shared function. The informal system, according to these authors, is better adapted to perform the non-uniform aspects of care; that is, those that are simple, idiosyncratic, unpredictable[1] or those that result from contingencies (Litwak, 1985). The formal care system, Litwak postulates, is better able to handle those aspects of care that require technical knowledge and predictable resources (1985). According to this theory, the care of an elderly person requires the involvement and coordination of both sectors.

---

[1] *Litwak (1985) gives the example of an older man who has a stroke and becomes paralyzed in the middle of the night. "Who is to help him? There are a number of specialists who can do something for him, such as the internist, the surgeon, the anesthesiologist, the nurse, the ambulance driver and the hospital intake clerk. But the likelihood of any such specialist's being present in this man's home at the time of the stroke is small. If this stroke victim is to survive, someone must be by his bedside, or within hearing distance, who can either take him to the hospital or call an ambulance" (p. 11). This is, of course, an extremely unpredictable event. For less extreme unpredictability, Litwak suggests that formal organizations generally attempt to reduce these events to routine tasks and then gain efficiency more through a division of labor and task simplification than through technical knowledge (p. 13). An example of this is the teaching of the Heimlich Maneuver or CPR to community classes through the Red Cross.*

In this section of the literature review, the theoretical history and assumptions of primary groups and/or informal networks, and bureaucracies or formal systems will be reviewed. (See Chapter 3 for definitions of these terms.) Whereas Cooley's sociological theory of primary groups and Weber's theory of the organization underpin this discussion, it is particularly the differences in structure and motivation each theorist presented and how these are incorporated in Litwak's theory which will be discussed here. Finally, Litwak's theory of shared functions detailing the importance of each of these different organizational structures in the delivery of long-term care services will be discussed in relation to their potential impact on dependent elderly and their caregivers.

The Primary Group:
    In Social Organization (1909), Cooley defined primary groups in the following manner:

> *By primary groups I mean those characterized by intimate face-to-face association and cooperation. They are primary in several senses, but chiefly in that they are fundamental in forming the social nature and ideals of the individual. The result of intimate association, psychologically, is a certain fusion of individualities in a common whole, so that one's very self, for many purposes at least, is the common life and purpose of the group. Perhaps the simplest way of describing this wholeness is by saying that it is a 'we'; it involves the sort of sympathy and mutual identification for which 'we' is the natural expression. One lives in the feeling of the whole and finds the chief aims of his will in that feeling (p. 23).*

That is, the structure of primary groups, according to Cooley, involves "intimate face-to-face association and cooperation" as opposed to rules and regulations. The individuals in these groups are motivated by a "fusion of individualities in a common whole." The self, for many purposes, is identical to "the common life and purpose of the group."

The most important spheres of this intimate association and cooperation, Cooley asserts, are the family, the play-group of children, and the neighborhood or community group of elders (p. 26). This definition of primary groups is similar to Cantor's (1979), Dono's (1979), and Litwak's (1985) description of informal networks where members are selected by elders from among kin, friends, and neighbors. These are universal, belonging to all times and all stages of development; and accordingly a chief basis of what is universal in human nature and human ideals (1909, p. 24).

Furthermore, Cooley states that,

> *Primary groups are primary in the sense that they give the individual his earliest and completest experience of social unity, and also in the sense that they do not change in the same degree as more elaborate relations, but form a comparatively permanent source out of which the latter are ever springing (1909, p. 26-27).*

Primary groups are the "chief sphere of sympathy and mutual aid" (Cooley, 1909, p. 25). Nevertheless, "primary groups themselves are subject to improvement and decay, and need to be watched and cherished with a very special care" (p. 33). While the structure and motivation that prevail in the primary group are assumed to be enduring, Cooley suggests that these groups may vary in their degree of constancy and, for this reason, are to be "cherished with a very special care" presumably to preserve their valuable structure and motivation which are built on ideals of loyalty, truth, service, and kindness.

Simmel (1956), on the other hand, theorized that a too cooperative, consensual, and integrated society would show "no life process." His analysis of conflict suggested that solidarity and unification and continuity are promoted by conflict. This source of conflict, according to Simmel, lies in our innate and biological makeup.

Primary ideals are loyalty and kindness (Cooley, 1909, p. 37). "Among the ideals inseparable from loyalty are those of truth, service, and kindness, always conceived as due to the intimate group rather than to the world at large" (p. 38-39). These motivations may help explain why families endure in their caregiving responsibilities at the sacrifice of their personal, emotional, physical, and financial needs.

> *One is never more human, and as a rule never happier, than when he is sacrificing his narrow and merely private interest to the higher call of the congenial group. Without doubt the natural genesis of this sentiment is in the intimacy of face-to-face cooperation. It is rather the rule than the exception in the family, and grows up among children and youth so fast as they learn to think and act to common ends (Cooley, 1909, p. 38).*

Nonetheless, Cooley cautions that,

> *It is a mistake to suppose that the person is, in general, better than the institution. Morally, as in other respects there are advantages on each side. The person has love and aspiration and all sorts of warm, fresh, plastic impulses, to which the institution is seldom hospitable, but the latter has a sober and tried goodness of the ages, the deposit, little by little, of what has been found practicable in the wayward and transient outreachings of human idealism. The law, the state, the traditional code of right and wrong, these are related to personality as a gray-haired father to a child (1909, p. 322).*

On the other hand, "an institution is a mature, specialized and comparatively rigid part of the social structure. It is made up of persons, but not of whole persons; each one enters into it with a trained and specialized part of himself" (Cooley, 1909, p. 319). Thus Cooley indicated concern that this imbalance, especially at the level of government, could create a negative impact on society.

> *The most general defect of government is that which goes with its good qualities. Just because it is the most ancient and elaborate machine we have, it is apt to be*

too mechanical, too rigid, too costly and inhumane. As the most institutional of institutions it has a certain tendency toward formalism, and is objectionable on grounds of red-tape, lack of economy and remoteness from the fresher needs of the people (Cooley, 1909, p. 404).

The solution to this Cooley wrote "is that wholesome relation between individuality and the institution in which each supports the other, the latter contributing a stable basis for the vitality and variation of the former" (Cooley, 1909, p. 350). How this would be accomplished Cooley does not say. In the nineteen forties and fifties, the previously underutilized theoretical framework provided by Cooley, received increased attention (Coser, 1957).

Whereas the sociology between World Wars had been preoccupied with the decline in intimate interpersonal relationships, nearly a whole generation has recently rediscovered a countercurrent from the past. Its spokesmen postulate the universality and indestructibility of primary groups (p. 293).

The importance of informal groups emerged in all areas of modern life. As Litwak has documented, researchers pointed out its major role in the heartland of the contractual instrumental arena, the world of business (Homans, 1950; LaRocco et al., 1980; Roethlisberger and Dickson, 1947; Pennings, 1975; Simmel, 1956; Whyte, 1956). Others pointed out that primary group ties are essential for understanding the effectiveness of combat troops (Shils and Janowitz, 1948). Still others pointed out that the mass media could not operate effectively without supporting primary groups (Katz and Lazarsfeld, 1955); the importance of primary groups in preserving health (Cobb, 1976; Berkman and Syme, 1979) and in education (Blau, 1981) have also been emphasized. Some have even argued that the noninstrumental, affective ties of primary groups are possibly growing stronger in modern society (Anderson, 1977; Fischer et al., 1977). In any case, the utility of primary groups for the management of problems of older people has become a dominant theme of contemporary researchers in aging (Brubaker, 1987; Cantor, 1979; Dobrof et al., 1977; Dono et al., 1979; Doty, 1986; Shanas et al., 1968; Sussman, 1977).

The German writer Ferdinand Tönnies (1855-1936), assumed that what he called the "Gemeinschaft"—quite like Cooley's primary group—was on the wane and would be superseded everywhere by the "Gesellschaft" or impersonal contractual type of relationship (Coser, 1957; Poplin, 1979). Tönnies' general point of view—briefly, that modern man is moving irreversibly away from the warmth of tribal life in small isolated communities to cold urban anonymity—was formulated in a dozen different ways by many observers. For instance, the German sociologist, Max Weber, referred to the bureaucratization, depersonalization, and routinization that he saw all about him as an "iron cage" (Giddens, 1971, p. 242).

What is important is that these investigators have not just been saying that informal groups exist; they have been saying that informal groups are essential for the achievement of the goals of formal organizations. Barnard, as early as 1938, affirmed that the attitudes, institutions, and customs of informal society affect and are partly expressed through formal organization.

> *They are interdependent aspects of the same phenomena—a society is structured by formal organizations, formal organizations are vitalized and conditioned by informal organization. What is asserted is that there cannot be one without the other. If one fails the other disintegrates (1962, p. 120).*

In sum, primary groups "form a comparatively permanent source" of "intimate face-to-face association and cooperation." They are our "chief sphere of sympathy and mutual aid" and we are cautioned to cherish them with a "very special care." Cooley cites the primary ideals of loyalty, truth, service, and kindness. Primary groups have "vitality and variation," i.e., "love and aspiration and all sorts of warm, fresh, plastic impulses." The concept of primary group motivation for Cooley is deontological (Frankena, 1963) compared to Parsons' utilitarian system idea of pattern variables where motivation is a complex schema of cognitive, cathectic, and evaluative components (Parsons, 1951; 1960).

The Bureaucracy:

Weber attempted to define a "pure type" of bureaucratic organization by abstracting what he considered the most characteristic features of bureaucracy.   "He hoped thus to furnish a kind of 'measuring rod' which could direct and guide future investigators of specific bureaucratic structures. By providing an ideal construct of the pure form of bureaucracy, Weber sought to permit subsequent research to measure departures from the model" (Coser, 1957, p. 433).

Bureaucracy, as defined by Weber, is a permanent structure with a system of rational rules, fashioned to meet calculable and recurrent needs by means of a normal routine (Gerth and Mills, 1946, p. 245). The structure of the bureaucracy, as defined by Weber, is, therefore, bound by rules and regulations. Its motivation derives from the fact that, "The bureaucracy seeks to secure the official position, the orderly advancement, and the provision for old age" (p. 242). That is, motivation is economic and rational rather than affiliative and affective as was seen to be the case with primary groups.   The following characteristics of bureaucracy stress rationality, organization, rules of procedure, and training (Gerth and Mills, 1946, p. 327-329):

(1) There is the principle of fixed and official jurisdictional areas, which are generally ordered by rules, that is by laws or administrative regulations.

(2) The principles of office hierarchy and of levels of graded authority mean a firmly ordered system of super- and sub-ordination in which there is a supervision of the lower offices by the higher ones.

(3) The management of the modern office is based upon written documents ("the files"), which are preserved in their original or draught form.

(4) Office management, at least all specialized office management—and such management is distinctly modern— usually presupposes thorough and expert training.

(5) When the office is fully developed, official activity demands the full working capacity of the official, irrespective of the fact that his obligatory time in the bureau may be firmly delimited.

(6) The management of the office follows general rules, which are more or less stable, more or less exhaustive, and which can be learned.

Weber contended that these bureaucratic characteristics would result in the following for the position of the official:

Office holding is a 'vocation.' This is shown, first, in the requirement of a firmly prescribed course of training, which demands the entire capacity for work for a long period of time, and in the generally pre- scribed and special examinations which are prerequi- sites of employment (Gerth and Mills, 1946, pp. 329- 330).

That is "education produces a system of special examinations and the trained expertness that is increasingly indispensable for modern bureaucracy" (p. 240). Furthermore, Weber voiced his belief that,

Bureaucracy inevitably accompanies modern <u>mass democracy</u> in contrast to the democratic selfgovernment of small homogeneous units. This results from the characteristic principle of bureaucracy: the abstract regularity of the execution of authority, which is a result of the demand for 'equality before the law' in the personal and functional sense—hence, of the horror of 'privilege' and the principled rejection of doing business 'from case to case' (Gerth and Mills, 1946, p. 331).

Yet, we have seen that in primary groups, it is generally the case-by-case, or face-to-face relationship that allows for the meeting of idiosyncratic needs. And, while Weber argued that to maximize technical knowledge, it was necessary for people to be hired and fired based on their technical knowledge, by contrast, in primary groups, people are assessed based on their ability to handle everyday problems (Litwak, 1985, p. 8).

Using a historical perspective, Weber cautioned that the general cost-efficiency of bureaucracy is initially truncated when these organizations replace the limited but formerly freely given service, under feudalism, with a paid administrator.

> *Bureaucratization and democratization within the administration of the state therefore signify and increase the cash expenditures of the public treasury. And this is the case in spite of the fact that bureaucratic administration is usually more 'economical' in character than other forms of administration. Until recent times—at least from the point of view of the treasury—the cheapest way of satisfying the need for administration was to leave almost the entire local administration and lower judicature to the landlords of Eastern Prussia. The same fact applies to the administration of sheriffs in England. Mass democracy makes a clean sweep of the feudal, patrimonial, and—at least in intent—the plutocratic privileges in administration. Unavoidably it puts paid professional labor in place of the historically inherited avocational administration by notables (Gerth and Mills, 1946, p. 331).*

Activities, in order to be cost-effective, usually involve, to some degree, a division and organization of human services in the interest of production (Gerth and Mills, 1946, p. 218). Weber argues that this is often obvious for "A mere glance at the facts of economic action reveals that different persons perform different types of work and that these are combined in the service of common ends" (p. 219). Furthermore,

> . . . '(O)rganization' is a technical category which designates the ways in which various types of services are continuously combined with each other and with non-human means of production. Its antithesis is one

> *of two things; either intermittent activity or that which
> is discontinuous from the technical point of view, as is
> true empirically of every household (Gerth and Mills,
> 1946, p. 221). . . . The case where there is little
> division of labour because of the low technical level is
> typical of primitive household economies.   There. .
> .every individual performs every function as the occa-
> sion arises. (p. 225).*

Weber maintained that the demand for a hierarchical
organization with a highly trained staff, producing cost-efficient
products or services through the rational division of labor is built
upon a developed technology.

That is, bureaucratic organizations are hierarchical organizations rationally designed to coordinate the work of many individuals
in the pursuit of large-scale administrative tasks (Coser, 1957, p. 433).
"The bureaucratic structure is organized to handle uniform tasks using
an ever-developing technology, vast resources, and extensive lines of
communication, buttressed by the ideology of merit and the model of
rationality" (Sussman, 1977, p. 6). Technical knowledge is the area in
which bureaucratic organizations generally operate. They seek to
dispense technical information in a rational manner. Consequently,
they are particularly well equipped to deal with similar or uniform
situations. The idiosyncrasies of families can create havoc within a
bureaucratic organization (Brubaker, 1987).

Brubaker provides a vivid illustration of the uniform nature
of bureaucracies that can be seen in the forms presented to families
at the time of initial client contact. These forms are standardized so
that the bureaucracy receives the same information from all families.
Still, each family may have some unique piece of information that may
be crucial to the situation but it is not received because the form fails
to request family-specific information. If families are not aware of
the need to inform the bureaucracies of this family-specific information, it may not become a part of the planning process.

"There is little doubt that bureaucracies are needed to provide
long-term care to older persons and their families" (Brubaker, 1987,
p. 17). Older persons' long-term care needs may require technical
knowledge and sophisticated equipment that is beyond the scope of

the family. And, not all older persons, especially the oldest-old (Shanas, 1979a,b), have families who can care for them. Although the bureaucracy is necessary, clearly the family is also an important part of the long-term care process. Many dependent older persons live within a community setting because they have family members who are willing to provide assistance on a daily basis (Brody and Brody, 1987; Callahan et al., 1981; Cantor, 1980; Cantor and Little, 1985, Doty, 1986). Indeed, if the family did not provide this support, it is likely that our institutional care system would be overwhelmed (Brubaker, 1987; Kane and Kane, 1987).

In sum, Weber in defining the "ideal type" of bureaucracy described a permanent, hierarchical, rational structure with a system of rules that usually presupposes thorough and expert training. This structure is fashioned to meet calculable and recurrent needs by means of a normal routine. The motivation is economic or utilitarian, rather than affiliative or deontological. The structure "is usually more 'economical' . . . than other forms of administration" and it "is organized to handle uniform tasks using an ever-developing technology."[2]

Finding a balance between the rational and nonrational activities of human behavior is a fundamental issue of society. It is also the central problem of long-term care. The basic question is how best to coordinate available resources to assure a dependable and efficiently delivered continuum of humane care to dependent adults and, simultaneously, maintain social integration, the normative commitments of informal networks, and their motivation to participate in providing care. Cooley and Weber provided ideal typologies for the analysis of primary groups or informal networks, and bureaucracies or formal organizations. They are appropriate for use in this study: Litwak's theory rests on both foundations seeking a synthesis of the two conceptual models. Like the theories of Cooley and Weber, Litwak's theory is an ideal-type construct providing modal points for approximating but never achieving the ideal. Also, Litwak's

---

[2] *While this is true of the whole structure, it may not be true at the point of delivery of a service such as adult day care where staff may relate to individuals in a primary-like way (Litwak, 1985; Mintzberg, 1979).*

theory is connected to a population whose care is currently receiving much attention.   Therefore, his suggested theoretical model is potentially practical and useful for practitioners in service delivery and program development in the field of long-term care for dependent adults.

As Mintzberg (1979) and others have suggested, organizational structure may be configured as a continuum.   Using Mintzberg's structural configurations (simple structure, machine bureaucracy, professional bureaucracy, divisionalized form, and adhocracy), Weber's ideal-type of bureaucracy is most similar to a machine bureaucracy. However, the organizations included in this study are most similar to professional bureaucracies since they employ professional social workers, nurses, and trained therapists.   Litwak, like Mintzberg, refers to the synthesis of professional and bureaucratic organization models as professional bureaucracies (Litwak, 1977a).   Some may counter that these disciplines are semi-professional or not professional at all (Gustafson, 1982; Toren, 1969; Wilensky, 1964).   Different organizational configurations vary in structure, motivation, hierarchy, etc.   For example, Etzioni (1958) has identified coercion, material sanction, and social or symbolic motivators in addition to Weber's economic motive.

Therefore, the line between informal networks and formal systems may, at times, be blurred; and, in fact, the formal organizations participating in this study are in many ways substituting for the informal network.   They are likely to be more similar in structure to primary groups than either the machine or the professional bureaucracy.   Litwak acknowledges this (1985).

Weber's and Cooley's specification of the nature of "ideal-type" concepts, and their usage in the social sciences, is logically rooted from a general epistemological standpoint (Giddens, 1971).

> *The ideas that are used in the social sciences cannot be derived directly from reality without the intrusion of value-presuppositions, since the very problems which define the objectives of interest are dependent upon such presuppositions.   Thus the interpretation and explanation of a historical configuration demands the construction of concepts that are specifically delineated for that purpose which, as in the case of the objectives*

of the analysis itself, do not reflect universally 'essential'
properties of reality. . . . An ideal type is constructed by
the abstraction and combination of an indefinite
number of elements that, although found in reality, are
rarely or never discovered in this specific form
(Giddens, 1971, p. 141).

Theory of Shared Functions:
      The theory of shared functions of bureaucracies and primary groups relates the underlying structural dimensions of these two variant forms of social organizations to the tasks that each can most effectively perform (Dobrof and Litwak, 1977; Dono et al., 1979; Litwak, 1977b; 1978; 1985; Litwak and Figueira, 1970). Primary groups described in terms of small size, noninstrumental and diffuse role relations, continuous face-to-face contact, affectivity, and long-term commitments, are structurally best able to handle "nonuniform tasks" (Litwak, 1985). These, as described by Litwak, include unanticipated events; those that are subject to many contingencies; and, those that do not require anything more than everyday socialization to master. What characterizes such tasks is the inability to effectively complete them using technically trained experts or large numbers of people. When confronted with such problems, the primary group member is more likely to be available for unpredictable events; more familiar with the contingencies of the situation; and, more motivated to act under conditions of uncertainty where objective evaluation and instrumental rewards are not available or possible. Examples of nonuniform tasks from medicine include the application of first aid in an emergency, the provision of everyday food and medication for those ill at home, and the monitoring of a proper diet (Dono et al., 1979).
      Illustrative of the kind of technical tasks the bureaucracy can best handle in medicine are the diagnosis of malignancies that require x-rays or laboratory tests and surgery, and illnesses that require continuous 24-hour long-term care (Litwak, 1985).

The question must still be answered as to how impor-
tant these nonuniform events are. The answer is that

> *they are as important as the uniform ones, the reason*
> *being that most tasks consist of both types of events,*
> *and failure in one type would lead to failure in the*
> *other. Medical care requires doctors to handle techni-*
> *cal problems, while primary groups provide emergency*
> *first aid, initial diagnoses, and preventive care. How*
> *else can one explain the Berkman and Syme (1979)*
> *findings that people with informal networks live longer?*
> *The importance of nonuniform tasks is espe-*
> *cially obvious in dealing with older people who can no*
> *longer handle those nonuniform tasks that the average*
> *person manages (e.g., shopping, housecleaning, cooking,*
> *dressing, bathing, etc.) (p. 15-16).*

Litwak echoes Barnard (1962), Selznick (1948), and other organizational theorists when he states that "the effectiveness of large-scale organizations depends on a close alliance with informal organizations" (p. viii). While the basic thesis of shared functions is axiomatic, Litwak's theory presses forward to suggest why and how this coordination might be operationalized.

> *. . . (I)n a modern society one must have both large*
> *scale formal organizations and small primary groups*
> *(i.e., family, neighbors, friends) to manage most tasks*
> *. . . . The large scale organization cannot perform*
> *effectively without close cooperation with strong prima-*
> *ry groups, and primary groups cannot function without*
> *formal organizations (Litwak, 1985, p. 1).*

The reason formal organizations and primary groups manage different aspects of the same tasks Litwak contends, is that they have very different, and often contradictory, structures, i.e., hierarchical or face-to-face relationships. To make his argument, Litwak avoids distinguishing variant organizational structures and bases his premises on the Weberian ideal-type bureaucracy using simplifying assumptions (1985, Chapter 6). The primary group puts much greater stress on motivating people by affection and duty, while the formal organization emphasizes impersonal economic incentives (Litwak, 1985). These two types of groups need each other because they manage complementary aspects of the same goal (Litwak, 1978; 1985). Again, Litwak's theoretical framework (1985) builds upon the sociological theories of ideal-type primary groups and organizations provided by Cooley (1909) and Weber (1947). His emphasis on complementary roles optimally suggests a synchronous fit between the tasks each support network can provide in the long-term care of dependent elders. Indeed, Litwak, Meyer, and Hollister (1977) say these social systems "must coordinate their behavior if they are to effectively achieve their goals" (p. 122). Yet, reality is complex, few relationships between people or organizations are ever neat and uncomplicated. In long-term care for the dependent elderly, the tasks performed by formal organizations often are the same as would be undertaken by informal networks. The nursing home as a substitute for family care is an obvious example of this.

In the past, social scientists and humanists believed that a dilemma arose from the need to choose either the highest standards of living caused by formal organizations and by science and technology, or the humanistic values of affection that are stressed by family and friendship groups (Litwak, 1985). A choice seemed necessary because the organizations appeared to have opposing structures. The formal organization required segmental ties, impersonal, objective evaluations, and economic motivations, while families required permanent ties, effective, loving evaluations, and diffused relations (Litwak, 1985, p. 7). As Cooley (1909) and Barnard (1962) insisted, however, that "choice" was theoretically inconceivable. By limiting his theoretical approach to the strictly Weberian construct and avoiding the complexity of myriad organizational models and primary group vagaries, Litwak tends to appear prescriptive and polemic. The question is, when used at the empirical level do his ideas work? This study will attempt to find out.

Litwak attempted to infuse empirical life into his theoretical constructs through the study of shared functions between the nursing home and caregivers for the dependent elderly (Dobrof and Litwak, 1977; Litwak, 1985); through the application of his theory to education and public health (Litwak, Meyer, and Hollister, 1977); and, the study of structures and functions of primary groups (Litwak and Szelenyi, 1969). In "Primary Group Structures and Their Functions:

Kin, Neighbors, and Friends" (1969), it was hypothesized that, because of differences in structures, neighbors could best handle immediate emergencies; kin, long-term commitments; and friends, idiosyncratic interests. With Figueira in 1970 and with Falbe in 1982, Litwak presented the theory and policy implications for his idea of shared function or the complementary aspects provided by informal and formal groups in goal attainment. When motivated by societal values, the formal organization may take on activities for which there is little knowledge or where tasks are uniform. Then, according to Litwak and Figueira (1970), the formal organization tends to more nearly resemble the family creating a closer working relationship than is normally common between these systems. With Kulis (1982), Litwak provided a framework for classifying tasks and structures fashioning a continuum from the traditional organization theorists (Weber) to network theorists (Blau, Mintzberg, Etzioni, Litwak). As early as 1966 Litwak with Meyer was formulating a balance theory of coordination between bureaucratic organizations and community primary groups. This theoretical construct, however, is an extension of the theory of shared functions and is not tested in this study.

In Helping the Elderly (1985) Litwak most concisely and clearly presented the theory of shared functions. Most goals, this theory asserts, have one component that can be best handled by people with specialized training and another that requires everyday experience and continual contact to handle.

Litwak (p. 10) asks what kind of activity cannot be handled better by a person with trained skills? He responds by suggesting that part of the answer is to understand what is meant by "nontechnical knowledge."

> *What is meant is knowledge learned through everyday socialization in the primary groups (e.g., the first spoken language, getting dressed, preparing food, administering first aid, shopping, driving a car, etc.). By contrast, technical knowledge is learned in special schools or on-the-job training in a formal organization (p. 10).*

Litwak, using ideal-type constructs that he referred to as

"simplifying assumptions" (1985, Chapter 6), provided three reasons why a person with advanced technical training "is not able to manage all activities better than the person who has only learned through his or her primary groups or minor forms of technical training" (p. 10): the presence of unpredictable events, too many contingencies, and tasks that are not easily subdivided.

> *(1) . . . For extremely unpredictable events, detailed experts often cannot be used because (a) they cannot be trained in time to make a difference; or (b) they cannot be brought to the scene in time to make a difference; and (c) their work cannot be easily supervised, ...*
> *(2) . . . When the number of contingencies is greater than the technologies' capacities to coordinate them, then technical knowledge generally cannot be used effectively because (a) the technical experts cannot be coordinated in time to make a difference; or (b) personnel are insufficient to permit the training of all the technical experts needed, so that large gaps in service occur; and (c) it is difficult to supervise their work . . . .*
>
> *(3) . . . Using technical knowledge for tasks that cannot benefit from a division of labor generally involves slower decision making processes because (a) nothing is gained by use of the experts; and (b) the costs of coordination, such as costs of communication, selection, training, and evaluation, slow up decision making (p. 10).*

In summary, Litwak's argument is that three conditions (unpredictability, too many contingencies, and tasks not easily subdivided) are basic to everyday life and, generally, cannot be handled by technical knowledge alone. For the unpredictable accident, for instance, it is rarely the professional who is first on the scene. Litwak refers to these conditions and the tasks characterized by them as "non-uniform" situations, events, or tasks. He argues that there are non-uniform tasks which are most effectively managed by primary groups and these cannot be eliminated in the foreseeable future (pp. 10-11). Therefore, the Red Cross instructs community members about proper procedures for medical emergencies such as choking, heart attacks, and loss of consciousness. That is, the Red Cross can simplify a non-uniform medical emergency by making the initial intervention uniform and assuring the possibility of immediate non-technical assistance until more highly trained technicians, or professionals, can take over.

"The very division of labor," states Litwak, "that permits the development of specialized knowledge requires that the experts only deal with people in segmental, specialized circumstances, and not have continual face-to-face contact with them" (p. 11). "By contrast" continues Litwak, "primary groups (such as marital dyads, neighbors, friends, or relatives) have as one of their major objectives the continual face-to-face proximity of their members" (p. 11). For handling tasks that are typically unpredictable and do not require large numbers, the primary group's small size and continual face-to-face contact is superior to the formal organization's stress on rules and hierarchy (p. 12). To handle the problem of many contingencies and unpredictability, the formal organization must reduce them to routine tasks and then gain efficiency more through a division of labor known as task simplification than through technical knowledge (p. 13).

It should be noted, however, that the major services provided for the aged by formal organizations are designed to replace activities that are normally handled by primary groups. This is what programs for homemakers, or delivery of hot meals, or nursing homes, or adult day care are doing (p. 13). In this manner, formal organizations are providing respite or time away for caregivers.

In addition, there is in all human services programs, a steady tension between incentives to <u>serve</u> clients appropriately, and the need to <u>conserve</u> scarce resources (Eisenberg and Amerman, 1988, p. 22). Other writers also concerned with providing humanistic service to clients while assuring the efficient conservation of resources have voiced their conviction in the efficacy of complementary informal and formal interaction (Brubaker, 1987; Callahan et al., 1981; Capitman, 1987; Chappell, 1985; Kane and Kane, 1987; Sussman, 1977).

Litwak's theory of shared functions while empirically tested in the milieu of education (Litwak and Meyer, 1974), the nursing home (Dobrof and Litwak, 1977), and in an organizational analysis of home care services for older people (Kaye, 1982), has not, to this writer's knowledge, been tested in a community-based program such as adult day care. Litwak and Meyer (1974), for example, reported that while raising the reading level of the child was clearly a well defined task of the elementary schools, families and neighborhood groups played a part by helping with the non-uniform aspects of the task. Most staff and families agreed that the families are responsible for teaching the child basic vocabulary and language skills, for the modeling process that teach the child the importance of reading even before the child can read, for coaching to supplement the school, for teaching the child how to deal with educational bureaucracy, and for supervising the child to ensure that peer groups will re-enforce positive attitudes toward school.

While there is an extensive body of literature on variant organizational structures (Mintzberg [1979] nicely synthesizes much of this work), and on intra-and inter-organizational relations (Heyde-brand, 1973, Part II), little has been written on the division of labor between the formal organization and the informal, familial network. Litwak attempts to sort out which system is more likely to perform which tasks most efficiently. If tasks are predictable, that is, capable of routinization and require technical knowledge, Litwak asserts that formal organizations are the most efficient. On the other hand, if tasks are unpredictable and require only everyday knowledge, the close-at-hand primary group is most efficient.

If this theoretical construct holds up under empirical testing at the community level, perhaps Litwak offers an "out" to several current concerns such as the high economic cost of long-term institutional care for the dependent elderly; the high personal cost of long-term caregiving to this population; and, the historic tension between efficiency and humanism in social services. The question is, does Litwak offer a viable theory or do his prescriptive and polemic ideal typologies fail to meet the test of complex organizations interacting with complex caregiving at the community level?

ADULT DAY CARE

To meet the current and future needs of dependent elders, the long-term care system must be both cost-effective and humane. One relatively new service in the continuum of long-term care is adult day care. In the first section of the literature review adult day care in the United States is defined and described. While the historical development of adult day care is not documented in this review, the reader should know that pioneering efforts in day care treatment were first developed in Moscow about 1920 (Bilitski, 1985, p. 106). In the remaining sections of this adult day care review, program definitions, legislation, funding sources, models of adult day care, program research, and the relationship between area agencies on aging and social models of adult day care are described. Adult day care in Pennsylvania, as it has been documented in the literature, is included.

Adult Day Care in the United States:

Although day care for the elderly does not exist in all countries, it is an integrated concept in community care systems in several European countries, having evolved from the geriatric psychiatric concept of comprehensive care (McCuan & Elliott, 1977; Padula, 1983). The first program in the United States similar to geriatric day care in Europe began in 1947 under the guidance of the Menninger Clinic (Adult Day Care, 1983; Mehta, 1975, p. 281). In 1974, the federal government provided support for a state-of-the-art paper on adult day care. There were fewer than 15 locations from which programs could be selected for study (Robins, 1981). In 1984, there were more than 900 such programs (Kirwin, 1986). In a 1985 national survey conducted for the National Institute on Adult Daycare, a unit of the National Council on the Aging, questionnaires were mailed to 1400 adult day care centers throughout the country. More than 800 centers responded (Von Behren, 1986). On an average day, 14,748 persons were receiving care at these centers with a total enrollment of 27,176, more than double the number identified in 1980 (Crossman, 1987).

While this rapid growth is, in part, a reflection of escalating interest in the development of long-term care alternatives in the community, it is significant that these programs developed despite the absence of any national policy to support this idea and without a permanent funding base. "The growth of adult day care in the United States has truly been a grass-roots effort, arising out of the concern of local communities for the quality of life and the care of their elders" (Crossman, 1987, p. 3).

Adult day care was slow to develop in the United States. Weiler and Rathbone-McCuan (1978) attributed this to the Medicare and Medicaid health programs of 1965 that supported and encouraged institutionalization. Reimbursements were provided for hospital or nursing home services rather than outpatient community health services. During this period, there were many nursing homes constructed as pressure mounted to move chronic patients from hospitals into nursing homes to make room for acute cases (Supplement to the Encyclopedia of Social Work, 1983). It was at this time that funds authorized under the Hill-Burton legislation that paid for hospital construction became available to build nursing home facilities (Eustis, Greenberg and Patten, 1984, p. 17). This source of funding linked institutional long-term care with provision of medical and nursing care. Today, caution Estes and Harrington (1981, p. 822), "A major concern of aging advocates is that states may move to curtail, limit, or reduce the number of nursing home services, while at the same time failing to assure alternative services at the local level."

Several factors have influenced the growth of the adult day care movement in the 1980s: (1) the expense involved in maintaining people in institutions (Crystal, 1982); (2) the social value attributed to promoting humaneness in caring for the frail elderly (Chappell, 1979; Grimaldi, 1979); and, (3) recognition of caregiver burden (Greene, 1985; Hooyman, 1986; Mace and Rabins, 1982; Strang and Neufeld, 1990). All have refocused care onto deinstitutionalization (Chappell, 1979). Goldstein (1983) has suggested that adult day care programs did not evolve in response to society's commitment to older people as much as in recognition of their needs (p. 157). Indeed, it was in response to the fact that institutionalization was not cost-effective and the public's growing awareness that dependent elders are heterogeneous that helped promote the development of day care.

A refocus in the demarcation between health care and social models of program orientation may have been another factor. An example of this is the growing emphasis on social service case management as opposed to crisis oriented health care since the passage of the Older American Act Amendments of 1978 (Kane and Kane, 1987). The increased number of elderly in the United States and its continued projected growth also may have been other factors. The arrival of consumerism, too, may have influenced the movement as well as decentralization of government where the responsibility of caring for elders has been shifted back to the family and community (Zones, 1987).

Hooyman (1986) described two overall program purposes: (1) adult day care centers can provide meaningful activities and (2) respite for families of frail elders. By providing services, Wilson (1984) indicates that adult day care centers: assist impaired older people in maintaining their usual place of residence, thereby avoiding unnecessary institutionalization. Ohnsorg (1981) supports Wilson's assertion that all adult day care programs "have a common denominator: to provide a noninstitutionalized support system for persons who would otherwise have difficulty in maintaining their independent living status in the community setting" (p. 18). Padula (1983), envisioning adult day care as part of a system or continuum of long term care, offered the following program definition in Developing Adult Day Care:

> Day care . . . means any program which provides
> personal care, supervision and an organized program of
> activities, experiences and therapies during the day in a
> protective group setting. Day care offers an individual-
> ized plan of care designed to maintain . . . impaired
> persons at, or to restore them to, optimal capability of
> self care" (p. 13).

The goal is to avoid "inappropriate or premature institutinalization" (p. 8). Indeed, John Melcher (D-Montana), Chairman of the Senate Special Committee on Aging has called day care "a more humane and cost-effective alternative to nursing homes and hospitals" (April 18, 1988).

Adult Day Care Legislation:

The National Council on the Aging was founded in 1950 committed to the principle that the nation's older people are entitled to lives of dignity, security, physical, mental and social well-being, and to full participation in society (Public Policy Agenda 1988-1989, 1988). The National Institute of Adult Daycare (NIAD) was created in 1979 for three purposes: (1) to promote adult day care as a long-term care component, (2) to develop adult day care standards and guidelines for high quality adult day care, by offering idea and experience exchange, and (3) to provide training and consultation (Padula, 1983).

Federal assistance for adult day care was first provided in 1970, when the Medicaid Program and Administration on Aging awarded grants to the following program sites: (1) On Lok in San Francisco; (2) Burke Rehabilitation Center in New York; (3) YMHA program in Montefiore Hospital, New York; and, (4) Levindale Day Care Program in Baltimore (Robins, 1980). Zawadski has documented that Medicaid remains the primary source of program funding ("Number of Adult Day Care Centers Increasing . . .," 1990). However, not all states—including Pennsylvania—have applied for the Medicaid waiver that allows for the funding of community programs such as adult day care.

A White House Conference on Aging was held in 1971. It emphasized the need to coordinate services for dependent elders and maintain them at home for as long as possible (Pratt, 1972). In 1973, an amendment to the Older Americans Act of 1965 created area agencies on aging in each state, designed to improve and coordinate elderly services (Ficke, 1985). The Older Americans Act has placed major "emphasis on the older person's right to choose living arrangements, medical care, and lifestyle" (Streib, 1983, p. 43). Congress has reaffirmed its support for Older Americans Act programs 12 times through amendments and reauthorization actions. Reauthorization, in 1987, continued a trend of setting total funding authorization at about $1 billion (Public Policy Agenda 1988-1989, p. 12).

In 1974, the Department of Health, Education and Welfare provided funds for the "development and evaluation of a particular model of day care which for convenience at that time was called the health model" (Robins, 1980, p. 2). At the same time Public Law

92-603 mandated establishment of an experimental program to provide day care services. Eligible individuals were enrolled in the supplemental medical program under Title XVIII and XIX of the Social Security Act (Robins, 1980). Sponsored by the National Center for Health Services Research and Public Law 92-603, in 1974, the TransCentury Corporation conducted a national study of 10 adult day care programs. This study has been widely cited in the literature, and is known as the TransCentury Study (Weissert, 1975). At the time of the Trans-Century Study, only 18 adult day care programs were identified in the United States (Weissert, 1978).

In 1975 Title XX of the Social Security Act was enacted to help prevent institutionalization (Lowy, 1980, p. 156). Later in 1981, this social services funding stream was incorporated into the Social Services Block Grant (Lee and Benjamin, 1983).

In 1976, under the Department of Health, Education, and Welfare, the concept of adult day care was studied as an alternative to long-term institutionalization. Adult day care was considered cost-effective, yet no national policy emerged (Burris, 1981). Weissert (1978) conducted a comparative study of the costs of adult day care versus nursing homes, and concluded that adult day care was less costly. However, Grimaldi (1979) rebutted Weissert's finding, suggesting the emergence of adult day care programs would result in many more people using the program than would normally go to a nursing home. Thus, the result would be an increase in costs (Grimaldi, 1979, p. 164). However, while

> . . . (C)ost-effectiveness analysis may play a minor role in generating popular support to expand the spectrum of long-term care services. More important will be a strong social mandate to allocate additional resources to improve the quality of life of the elderly (Grimaldi, 1979, p. 164).

In 1980, the Subcommittee on Health and Long-Term Care of Select Committee on Aging "recommended the establishment of a national policy on day care, with funds for planning, and a comprehensive restructuring of funds to better implement the day care concept" (Aaronson, 1983, p. 35). This and subsequent recommendations of the 1980s were still-born. "The 1980s have seen the election of a national administration committed to dismantling many public programs and entitlements and reducing the scope of federal government" (Torres-Gil, 1988, p. 6). In this political milieu, new policy initiatives have languished.

The 1981 White House Conference on Aging, recognized adult day care as part of the long-term care continuum. Six of the 14 issue committees addressed adult day care in their recommendations. Recommendations relevant to adult day care included: (1) self-care programs in adult day care; (2) Medicare coverage of adult day care through amendment of Title XVIII of the Social Security Act; (3) reimbursement of programs to be established by the Health Care Financing Administration for development of day hospital services for acute and rehabilitative services; (4) adoption of a basic national social policy for long-term care allowing people to choose from among several different services, such as adult day care; (5) creation of a community-based continuum of care facilitated through passage of Title XXI of the Social Security Act or expansion of Title XVIII and XIX of Social Security Act; (6) tax credit for families using adult day care; (7) support services to include adult day care; and (8) tax exemptions for those who care for elderly in their homes. This conference provided potent energy to the growing long-term care community-based service of adult day care ("White House," 1982).

The Economic Recovery Act, effective January 1, 1982, and the 1981 Omnibus Budget Reconciliation Act provided economic incentives for adult day care. The Economic Recovery Act allowed families with elderly dependents who use adult day care to claim tax credit. The Omnibus Budget Reconciliation Act allowed states to request a waiver allowing Medicaid coverage for day care services (Padula, 1981). States also may request waivers for Medicaid reimbursement for other community-based services as in-home care, respite care, and homemaker services. The purpose of these acts is to prevent institutionalization ("Adult Day," 1983).

In 1986, landmark legislation was introduced by Congressman Leon Panetta (D-California) calling for Medicare reimbursement for adult day care (Crossman, 1987). It was re-introduced in the 1987 session of Congress as HR 550. The bill had 80 co-sponsors, evidence of a nationwide grass-roots effort led by adult day care advocates. A

Senate companion bill (S.1839) was introduced and there was sufficient interest among legislators to conduct a congressional hearing April 18, 1988 (Crossman, 1987; Larmer, 1988). The 1987 reauthorization of the Older Americans Act contains an amendment providing $36 million over five years to fund up to two meals and a snack daily for certain participants in state-licensed adult day care centers (Melcher, 11/12/87).

The trend to assist in meeting the community long-term care needs of dependent elders can be seen in the legislation of the past 12 years. As Kay Larmer, Chair of the National Institute on Adult Day Care (1988) has written, at an average daily cost of $31 for 6 to 8 hours of client care and caregiver respite, adult day care is less costly than paid care in the home at $8-10 per hour, or residency in a skilled nursing home at $68-$100 per day. Therefore, day care services may provide new hope in addressing some problems of the elderly. Yet, in the absence of an overarching national policy, an uncoordinated variety of sources fund variant models for day care services (Bilitski, 1985).

Funding Sources:

There are a variety of funding sources for adult day care. Among the 14 sources of funding included in the National Institute of Adult Daycare's 1985 survey responses are: participant fees, Medicare, Medicaid, Title III of the Older Americans Act, Community Development Block Grants, United Way, and other state, county or federal funds (Von Behren, 1986, p. 23). This survey also reported 10 different licensing agencies. Not only was there extensive variability in the scope, quality and uniformity of standards by these agencies, but state definitions for program criteria also varied.

A multitude of funding sources, as well as a lack of clear policy has resulted in a variety of program models. This may not necessarily be detrimental, as the idea of adult day care is still evolving. What is important is that the various models be analyzed, monitored, and evaluated, followed by a dissemination of information.

Models of Adult Day Care:

Cited by Aaronson (1983) and Koenen (1980), Weissert (1976) has identified two types of adult day care programs currently existing in the United States:

(1) Model I Programs - Model I, or health-oriented programs, are associated with health care institutions or ambulatory settings and draw participants from them. These programs have a strong health care orientation and seek physical rehabilitation as a treatment goal. Participants in this group typically have suffered a stroke or have other chronic disabling problems. They may have been previously institutionalized, but have become sufficiently recovered to be released from in-patient status provided that follow-up treatments are available on an ambulatory basis. The program provides such services as meals and counseling, social work services, physical and occupational therapy, and periodic medical evaluation.

(2) Model II Programs - Weissert (1976) refers to Model II programs as a "pot pourri." "Program goals suggest social rehabilitation, maintenance, alleviation of social isolation, nutrition, recreation, and health care services" (p. 425). Weissert points out that the delivery of health services, unlike in Model I programs, is not stressed in these programs.

In identifying target populations for adult day care, Aaronson (1983) and Koenen (1980) include those who are at-risk of acute or long-term care if they do not receive the specialized services provided by a day care program. Koenen described those at-risk as persons "who are mentally, physically, or socially and/or emotionally impaired, and need day health services to maintain or improve their level of functioning, so that they can remain in, or return to, their own homes" (p. 219). According to the same author, other prospective clients are those who cannot be left alone or unattended, and whose caregivers need some relief from their 24-hour-a-day task.

In the literature, there are other program divisions: Robins (1981) suggested four program distinctions encompassing varying levels of health and service needs. Weiler and Rathbone-McCuan (1978) also proposed four taxonomies. O'Brien (1982b) refined Robins' models to relate to a "progression from greater to lesser participant disability from Model I to Model IV" (p. 240).

While there are variant models of adult day care, they often are based on an identified community need (Weiler and Rathbone--McCune, 1978). Others are developed with "funding" purposes and constraints in mind (Kane and Kane, 1987). Many have developed erratically, as an alternative to institutionalization (Goldstein, 1983). Goldstein adds that each model does meet some of the needs of the long-term care frail elderly. The division between these theoretical constructs, however, has blurred according to a recent national survey (Von Behren, 1988).

Adult Day Care Research:

"Embryonic stage best characterizes research about adult day care" (Bilitski, 1985, p. 122). There are few experimental studies, most are still in the process of trying to characterize adult day care programs and client characteristics. A few studies have had national samples, but many are reports from selected states and single sites. The major foci of the studies have been descriptive, a few comparative, and several evaluative.

Adult day care research has been synthesized and widely reported by Paul Harder, Janet Gornick, and Martha Burt (1983); and by Margaret Stassen and John Holahan (1981) all of the Urban Institute. Joan Scialli Bilitski (1985) provided a thorough and extensive overview of adult day care research in her doctoral dissertation completed at West Virginia University. Peter Kemper's review of 30 years of community care demonstrations (1987) included many studies previously evaluated by Harder et al. and Stassen et al. Weiler and Rathbone-McCuan's earlier (1978) review of program research is also of interest. Because the writings of these authors summarize the major findings and critical commentary on previous adult day care studies, these studies are but briefly mentioned in this review:

(1) The Mosholu-Montefiore Day Care Center - One of the earliest adult day care centers described and evaluated (matched comparison groups) in the literature, Mosholu-Montefiore, a geriatric Model I day program located in the northwest Bronx, was a federally funded program opened in 1972 under the auspices of a consortium of agencies.

(2) Adult Day Care in the U. S.: A Comparative Study - prepared for the National Center for Health Services Research by the

TransCentury Corporation in 1975 in which Weissert compared ten adult day care programs.

(3) The On Lok Senior Health Services - A free-standing, independent program in San Francisco's North Beach/Chinatown area, this program opened in 1973 as an Administration on Aging research and demonstration project (matched comparison groups using cross-sectional and longitudinal techniques).

(4) The Levindale Adult Treatment Center - The Levindale Adult Treatment Center was one of the earliest day care centers in the United States. Located in Baltimore, Maryland, it opened in 1970, three years before On Lok. It was the only one of the federally funded programs that had been in operation prior to the awarding of the federal research and development monies in 1972. The methodology included four unmatched group comparisons (Weissert, 1975; 1976; 1977; 1979; Harder et al., 1983; 1986; Kostick, 1972; Stassen and Holahan, 1981).

(5) The Section 222 Day Care Experiments - Section 222 of the 1972 Amendments of the Social Security Act provided funds to several adult day care programs for demonstration purposes. Four of these programs were evaluated by the National Center for Health Services Research: (1) a trio of contracted hospital day care facilities in San Francisco; (2) the Center for Creative Living in Lexington, Kentucky; (3) the Burke Rehabilitation Center in White Plains, New York; and, (4) the St. Camillus Health and Rehabilitation Center in Syracuse, New York. The reports summarizing the results of this demonstration were published in stages between 1975-1981 (Weissert, 1975; 1976; Weissert, Wan, and Livieratos, 1979; Weissert, 1981). This research (an experimental study design with a randomized assignment method) is probably the most often cited—and the most methodologically controversial—research on adult day care conducted in this country (Harder et al., 1986; 1983; Stassen and Holahan, 1981).

More recent research has been conducted at the state level rather than at the individual program level. These include:

(1) Adult Day Health Care in California - With the 1978 passage of the California Adult Day Health Care (ADHC) Act and Medi-Cal Law, California became the first state to offer this outpatient alternative to institutional long-term care as a mandated Medicaid benefit (Capitman, 1982; Stassen and Holahan, 1981; Harder

et al., 1983).

(2) Georgia's Alternative Health Care Project - This was a demonstration project, funded by the U. S. Health Care Financing Administration and administered through Georgia's Department of Medicaid Assistance. (Harder et al., 1983; Skellie, Mobley and Coan, 1982).

(3) Nursing Home Pre-admission Screening and Adult Day Care in Virginia - The Virginia Center on Aging, a private research institution, published in 1983 an extensive empirical analysis of adult day care clients served in adult day centers across the state during the previous year. (Virginia Center on Aging, 1983; Arling, Harkins and Romaniuk, 1982; 1984; Harder et al., 1983).

(4) Adult Day Care in Washington State - The Washington State Association of Adult Day Centers conducted a recent survey of day care utilization in the state (U. S. Congress 1980; Harder et al., 1983).

In addition to the above mentioned program level and state wide evaluations, the National Institute of Adult Day Care (NIAD), a membership unit of the National Council on Aging (NCOA), conducted a national survey of member agency programs in the late fall of 1985 as a follow-up to their 1982 survey. In October 1986, a preliminary report summarizing the findings was published. Of approximately 1400 mailed survey forms, 847 responses were received (Von Behren, 1986). In summarizing the findings no attempt was made to distinguish between Model I (health oriented) and Model II (social oriented) programs nor between publicly and privately funded programs.

The average adult day care participant, based on survey respondents, was Caucasian, female, 73 years old with an average income of $478 per month and lived with their spouse, relatives or friends. One out of two needed supervision.

It is interesting that 85 percent of the responding program staff indicated that they aimed to provide an alternative to premature or inappropriate institutionalization. Sixty-three percent sought to maximize functional capacity. An objective for 55 percent of the respondents was the provision of respite for caregivers. While 53 percent strove to provide psychosocial supportive services to program participants.

Questions regarding physical impairments or at-risk of institutionalization were not asked.

Adult Day Care Research in Pennsylvania:
The Pennsylvania Council on Aging (Adult Day Care, 1983, p. 2) stated that

> *(T)he target population for adult day care is those persons who are mentally, physically, socially, and/or emotionally impaired and who require supervision and regular health services in order to sustain or improve their present level of functioning so they can remain in the community.*

Application for the Medicaid waiver under Public Law 92-603 mandating extended services by the Department of Health, Education and Welfare (now the Department of Health and Human Services) was not applied for by the state of Pennsylvania. Therefore, programmatic funding in the state came from the private sector, the Social Services Block Grant, and Title III of the Older Americans Act. These funding streams favored the development of a Model II, or social model, of adult day care. In this section of the review the following studies are cited: (1) Vintage, Inc.; (2) Fayette County Adult Day Care Center; (3) Watkins Avenue Senior Center Adult Day Care Program; and, (4) the Delaware County Adult Day Care Study. Each studied program received area agency on aging funding and each was a social model of day care.

(1) A report by Vintage, Inc., a program that began operations in 1981, was presented by Rhodes (1982). The purpose of the Rhodes' study was to answer two questions: (1) who was the appropriate client that benefitted from adult day care; and, (2) who was the appropriate staff (p. 3)? Data included descriptions of services; services needed; staff tasks; costs with recommendations for staffing patterns to maximize the match between needs and services (based on budget constraints), and client health characteristics of 24 of the most active clients.

Two study samples were used for comparative purposes. The

first sample consisted of 24 of the most active clients and the second sample consisted of 15 new clients who joined the adult day care program half way through the study. Rhodes (1982) compared the two phase groups with regional and state socio-demographic variables. Client characteristics were compared with the TransCentury Study. While the TransCentury Study was of a Model I program, Vintage was a Model II type (Rhodes, 1982, p. 24).

With respect to the TransCentury Study, Vintage clients were older (78 years), and none of the Vintage clients lived alone. Vintage had twice as many clients with a form of dementia, ranking higher than any other adult day care program in the TransCentury Study. Vintage was "similar in terms of wheelchair use, activities of daily living assistance, and blindness" (Rhodes, 1982, p. 27); but Vintage ranked low in relation to incidence of fractures; hypertension and mental disorders. The average number of medical conditions was 2.5 (p. 20).

During the first 8 months of operation, it was found that all clients had families who cared for them in the home and that many of these clients suffered from some sort of dementia. Rhodes (1982) concluded, "Professions that are able to examine and treat the physiologic, sensoriperceptual, and interactional factors that contribute to confusion and dementia, become of primary import in this type of model" (p. 104).

(2) Fayette County Adult Day Care Center - A descriptive study and a process evaluation study of the Fayette County Adult Day Care Center in Uniontown, Pennsylvania were conducted in 1982 and 1983 respectively (Bilitski, 1985). The descriptive study served as a pretesting tool. Impact or product evaluation occurred after a three year period (1985). Two major program goals were: (1) to prevent institutionalization of at-risk elderly community residents (Bilitski, 1985); and, (2) to promote satisfying lifestyles through maximizing personal resources of the at-risk elderly (Bilitski, 1985).

There were 24 adult day care clients who participated in the descriptive study (Bilitski, 1985). The major population served in both reports was clients from foster and domiciliary care, where these constituted 58.3% and 54.5% of the sample. This was much higher than the reported 2%-8% reported in the literature (Bilitski, 1985). Because of the small client population in this local process evaluation, the positive results reported by Bilitski cannot be generalized; but, the inclusion of client and caregiver perspectives in this study is noteworthy.

(3) <u>Watkins Avenue Senior Center Adult Day Care Program</u> - In response to a Pennsylvania Department of Aging Request for Proposal, the Department of Leisure Services of Upper Darby Township submitted a successful proposal in August 1983 that funded the start-up of an adult day care program within the Watkins Avenue House Senior Center (Kirwin, 1986). This was the first program in Delaware County to receive funds from the County's area agency on aging.

To provide a comprehensive summary report to the Department of Aging, secondary analysis, survey-interview procedures, and participant observation were used to collect quantitative and qualitative data in the least intrusive manner. This multi-method approach, common in field work, increased the objectivity and reliability of the results while sacrificing control and representativeness. The brevity of the Department of Aging contract period (seven months) meant that program implementation and evaluation needed to proceed simultaneously. The evaluation of the Watkins Avenue House adult day care program was, therefore, a process evaluation lacking generalizability. Even with established but small programs, for evaluative purposes, it remains difficult to distinguish ideas, methods, and those persons using them.

This program, as reported by Kirwin (1986) after a year of operation, grew to 35 unduplicated clients. While Alzheimer's disease is now the fourth major disease of the aged, among the Watkin's program's participants it ranked first with 13 of the participants reporting the presence of Alzheimer's disease; 9 arthritis; 8 stroke paresis; 5 diabetes; and, 4 cardiac problems. All clients had at least 1 impairment. Fourteen of the 35 had 2 impairments. One client had 3 impairments. For 17 of the 35 participants, their spouse was the primary caregiver (p. 65).

This demonstration project showed that the integration of 2 aging services such as a senior center and an adult day care program may allow for a back and forth flow of participation as needs and abilities allow. The average time per day spent in the senior center by an adult day care participant was 4 hours. This was seen as beneficial to the clients' maintenance of independence and to the cost-effectiveness of the more staff intensive single service adult day care facility. The provision of transportation services was seen as a vital link between isolation at home and socialization and access to services available through senior center adult day care programs.

(4) Adult Day Care in Delaware County - Kirwin (1988) reporting on an analysis of three suburban Delaware County adult day care programs (N=64) supported previous studies that suggested a low use of services by the multi-impaired elderly. This was true even for the multi-impaired who had been attending adult day care programs for over 17 months. This finding positively correlated with an intact informal social support system and the absence of a life history of mental illness.

In this study Kirwin examined the relationships between: (1) the range of services used by these clients; (2) the range of client impairments; and, (3) the range of relationships of primary caregivers to clients. The studied programs were targeted to clients at-risk of institutionalization and, therefore, these clients were perceived to be among the frailest community members. "At-risk" was determined by the client's need for assistance in performing four or more of the activities of daily living (Katz, 1963; Lawton and Brody, 1969).

In summary, the program evaluations that have been cited varied enormously by program model, institutional affiliation, service capability, staffing, client group, and funding. There were also significant methodological differences among the studies. The common element found was that the evaluators attempted to discover the consequences and costs of providing day care to dependent elders. Neither client nor caregiver preference was a major study variable. In reviewing previous programmatic studies in Adult Day Care: Supplement or Substitute? (1983), Harder et al., concluded that while the benefits of the program are demonstrable, and adult day care may indeed prolong lives, it has not saved money. The critical policy issue is, how much is this service worth? Criteria on which to base this value decision, however, have not been offered.

Additional problems in comparing adult day care program studies include the fact that different programs offered different services to clients, making program comparison infinitely more difficult. While all the cited programs targeted clients at-risk of institutionalization, the predictive capability of doing this was very low (Weissert 1979, p. 559). Furthermore, operational definitions for such terms as "at-risk of institutionalization," "activities of daily living," and "caregiver burden" are not uniformly used by researchers (Kirwin, in press).

In reviewing the status of program research Weiler and Rathbone-McCuan (1978), concluded that too much data was collected resulting in poor analysis and interpretation. There were poor sample sizes to test for significance, with controls difficult to establish, and there was difficulty in controlling for the long-term care networking system costs. But, they believed the studies did provide many answers to guide policy in a broad sense.

Stassen and Holahan (1981) in discussing Section 222 adult day care experiments suggested that: (1) adult day care generally enhanced and effected positive participant outcomes; (2) adult day care does not appear to have affected in-patient hospital service utilization; (3) to a very limited extent, adult day care substituted for nursing home care and some ambulatory services; and (4) adult day care appeared to increase the total cost of care, as many people who normally would not have used skilled or intermediate care, were using adult day care (Stassen and Holahan, 1981).

Nonetheless, despite the possibility of increased costs to long-term care, adult day care and other community-based programs may enhance well-being and therefore be desirable. "This is the most convincing argument for expanding long-term care services" (Stassen and Holahan, p. 230). The cited authors reported a reduction in mortality (increased longevity) in some studies, increased cognitive functioning, social activity and satisfaction. There were no clear improvements in functional ability.

Several long-term care policy research implications regarding future demonstration projects were presented by Stassen and Holahan (1981):

(1) There is a need to describe and compare costs of community-based services for individuals with varying levels of health. These costs must be comprehensive considering program costs, Medicare, and Medicaid costs for comparative purposes.

(2) Start-up costs for demonstration projects are generally

very high during the initial years of programs and these "bias the cost upwards" (p. 229). Ongoing program costs must be considered as well as start-up costs.

(3) Community-based programs have not identified and targeted their services to those who are potential nursing home patients. Thus many who use the services are add-ons to long-term care rather than substituting for the at-risk population. This has increased long-term care costs.

(4) The effect on elderly patients, families, and community well-being needs to be studied.

The authors reflected the heart of the issue of cost benefits versus well-being benefits of community-based services including adult day care, when they contended that "the issue of whether the improvement in outcomes are worth the costs of expanded benefits is a political or social judgment" (Stassen and Holahan, 1981, p. 228).

The reviewed adult day care evaluations were empirical and based on limited scientific notions of controls and statistical analysis.

There may be other useful perspectives to use to analyze social programs. While it is not the purpose of this study to compare diverse perspectives or research strategies, it is important to note their existence. C. Wright Mills, for instance, in The Sociological Imagination (1959), contends that physical science often fails to solve the problems of social affairs. This is so, asserts Mills, because the problems of social science, when adequately formulated, must include both troubles and issues, both biography and history, and the range of their intricate relations (p. 226). Within that range, Mills insists, the life of the individual and the making of societies occur; and within that range the sociological imagination has its chance to make a difference in the quality of human life in our time. Often, empirical studies get caught up in methodology without the benefit of the biographies and histories of the people being studied. Life involves quantitative and qualitative factors.

There was little to no information regarding shared functions between formal and informal systems evidenced in the cited studies. A need exists, therefore, to describe conceptually how informal networks and formal organizations relate in the provision of long-term care through the emerging models of adult day care. A base line of formal and informal system characteristics as seen in adult day care programs not only would assist funding sources in measuring program cost-efficiency by revealing the relevant variables, but with a multidimensional approach focusing on quality of life, adult day care may be seen to facilitate successful aging and support for caregivers. As Rhodes (1982) has written

> *Adult Day Care is based on the premise that the elderly maintain their mental and physical well being longer and at higher levels of functioning in the community and home-integrated milieu as opposed to institutional settings. Support services are geared to maintaining and stabilizing the elder to prevent premature institutionalization (pp. 1-2).*

END NOTES - CHAPTER 2

Aaronson, Linda. "*Adult Day Care: A Developing Concept.*" *Journal of Gerontological Social Work*, 5, No 3 (Spring 1983), pp. 35-47.

Achenbaum, W. Andrew. *Old Age in the New Land*. Baltimore, MD: Johns Hopkins University Press, 1978.

Adult Day Care: A Community-Based Long-Term Option. Harrisburg, PA: Pennsylvania Council on Aging, 1983.

Anderson, M. "*The Impact on the Family Relationships of the Elderly of Changes Since Victorian Times in Governmental Income-Maintenance Provision.*" In *Family, Bureaucracy, and the Elderly*. Ed. E. Shanas and M. B. Sussman, Durham, NC: Duke University Press, 1977, pp. 36-59.

Arling, Greg, Elizabeth B. Harkins and Michael Romaniuk. "*Adult Day Care and the Nursing Home: The Appropriateness of Care in Alternative Settings.*" *Research on Aging*, 6, No 2 (June 1984), pp. 225-242.

Arling, Greg, Elizabeth Harkins, and Michael Romaniuk. *Adult Daycare in Perspective: A Comparison of the Adult Daycare Study and the Study of the Virginia Nursing Home Pre-Admission Screening Program*. Richmond, VA: Virginia Center on Aging, 1982.

Arling, Greg and W. J. McAuley. "*The Feasibility of Public Payments for Family Caregiving.*" *The Gerontologist*, 23, No 3 (1983), pp. 300-306.

Barnard, Chester I. *The Functions of the Executive*, Cambridge, MA: Harvard University Press, 1962.

Beattie, W. M., Jr. "*Aging and the Social Sciences.*" *In Handbook of Aging and the Social Sciences*. Eds. R. H. Binstock and E. Shanas. New York: Van Nostrand Reinhold Co., 1976, pp. 619-642.

Berkman, L. J. and L. S. Syme. *"Social Networks, Host Resistance, and Mortality: A Nine-Year Follow-Up Study of Alameda County Residents." American Journal of Epidemiology, 190, No 4 (1979), pp. 186-204.*

Bilitski, Joan Scialli. *"Assessment of Adult Day Care Program and Client Health Characteristics in U. S. Region III." Diss. West Virginia University, 1985.*

Blaser, Peg R. *"Illinois Adult Day Care Parallels National Trend." Perspective on Aging, XII, No 3 (May/June, 1983), pp. 20-23.*

Blau, Z. S. *Black Children/White Children: Competence, Socialization, and Social Structure. New York: The Free Press, 1981.*

Brody, Elaine M. *"Parent Care as a Normative Family Stress." The Gerontologist, 25, No 1 (1985), pp. 19-29.*

Brody, Elaine, M. *"Women in the Middle and Family Help to Older People." The Gerontologist , 21, No 5 (1981), pp. 471-480.*

Brody, Elaine and Stanley Brody. *"Aged: Services." In Encyclopedia of Social Work, Vol 1, 18th edition. Silver Spring, MD: National Association of Social Workers, 1987, pp. 106-127.*

Brody, Stanley. *"Strategic Planning: The Catastrophic Approach." The Gerontologist, 27, No 2 (1987), pp. 131-138.*

Brody, S. J., S. W. Poulshock and C. F. Masciocchi. *"The Family Caring Unit: A Major Consideration in the Long Term Support System." The Gerontologist, 18, No 6 (1978), pp. 556-561.*

Brown, Charlane and Mary O'Day. *"Services to the Elderly." In Handbook of the Social Services. Eds. Neil Gilbert and Harry Specht. Englewood Cliffs, NJ: Prentice-Hall, Inc., 1981.*

Brubaker, Timothy. *Aging, Health and Family: Long Term Care. Beverly*

Hills, CA: Sage Publications, 1987.

Burris, K. "Recommending Adult Day Care Centers." *Nursing and Health Care*, 2, No 8 (1981), pp. 437-441.

Callahan, James J. et al. "Responsibility of Families for their Severely Disabled Elders." *Health Care Financing Review* (Winter 1980), pp. 29-48.

Callahan, James J. and Stanley S. Wallack, eds. *Reforming the Long-Term Care System*. Lexington, MA: D. C. Heath & Company, 1981.

Cantor, Marjorie. "The Informal Support System, Its Relevance in the Lives of the Elderly." In *Aging and Society*. Eds. E. Borgatta and N. McClusky. Beverly Hills, CA: Sage Publications, 1980, pp. 111-146.

Cantor, Marjorie H. "Neighbors and Friends: An Overlooked Resource in the Informal Support System." *Research on Aging*, 1, No 30 (1979), pp. 434-463.

Cantor, Marjorie. "Strain Among Caregivers: A Study of Experience in the United States." *The Gerontologist*, 23, No 6 (1983), pp. 597-603.

Cantor, Marjorie and Virginia Little. "Aging and Social Care." In *Handbook of Aging and the Social Sciences*. Eds. Robert Binstock and Ethel Shanas. New York: Van Nostrand Reinhold Co., 1985, pp. 745-781.

Capitman, John A. *Evaluation of Adult Day Health Care Programs in California Pursuant to Assembly Bill 1611, Chapter 1066, Statutes of 1977*. Sacramento, CA: Office of Long Term Care and Aging, Department of Health Services, May 1982.

Capitman, John et al. "Public and Private Costs of Long-Term Care for Nursing Home Pre-Admission Screening Program Participants." *The Gerontologist*, 27, No 6 (1987), pp. 780-787.

Chappell, Neena. "Social Supports and the Receipt of Home Care Services." The Gerontologist, 25, No 1 (1985), pp. 47-54.

Chappell, Neena and Margaret J. Penning. "The Trend Away From Institutionalization." Research on Aging, 1, No 30 (September 1979), pp. 361-387.

Cobb, S. "Social Support as a Moderator of Life Stress." Psychosomatic Medicine, 38 (1976), pp. 300-314.

Cooley, Charles Horton. Social Organization. New York: Charles Scribner's Sons, 1909, pp. 23-28.

Coser, Lewis A. and Bernard Rosenberg, editors. Sociological Theory: A Book of Readings. New York: The MacMillan Company, 1957.

Creedon, Michael A., ed. Issues for an Aging American: Employees and Eldercare: A Briefing Book. Bridgeport, CT: University of Bridgeport, Center for the Study of Aging, 1987.

Crossman, Linda. "Adult Day Care: Coming of Age." The Aging Connection, 8, No 4 (August/September 1987), pp. 1, 3.

Crystal, Stephen. America's Old Age Crisis. New York: Basic Books, 1982.

Dobrof, Rose and Eugene Litwak. Maintenance of Family Ties of Long-Term Care Patients: Theory and Guide to Practice. Rockville, MD: National Institute of Mental Health, 1977, pp. 1-79.

Dono, John, C. M. Falbe, B. L. Kail, E. Litwak et al. "Primary Groups in Old Age." Research on Aging, 1, No 4 (1979), pp. 403-433.

Doty, Pamela. "Family Care of the Elderly: The Role of Public Policy." The Milbank Quarterly, 64, No 1 (1986), pp. 34-75.

Eggert, G. et al. "Caring for the Patient with Long-Term Disability."

Geriatrics, 32 (1977), pp. 102-114.

Eisenberg, David and Emily Amerman. *"A New Look at the Channeling Demonstration,"* Part II. *Perspective on Aging*, XVII, No 1 (1988), pp. 20-23.

Estes, Carroll L. and Charles A. Harrington.   *"Fiscal Crisis, Deinstitutionalization, and the Elderly."* *American Behavioral Scientist*, 24, No 6 (1981), pp. 811-826.

Etzioni, Amitai. *"Industrial Sociology: The Study of Economic Organizations."* *Social Research*, 25, No 3 (1958), pp. 303-324.

Eustis, Nancy N., Jay N. Greenberg and Sharon K. Patten. *Long-Term Care for Older Persons: A Policy Perspective*. Monterey   CA: Brooks/Cole Publishing Company, 1984.

"Factors Correlated With Entering Long-Term Care Institutions." *NIAD News*, 3, No 1 (1983), p. 5.

Felder, Leonard.   *"Caregiver Support Programs Spreading Nationwide."* *The Aging Connection*, IX, No 2 (April/May 1988), p. 7.

Fengler, Alfred P. and Nancy Goodrich. *"Wives of Elderly Disabled Men: The Hidden Patients."* *The Gerontologist*, 19, No 2 (1979), p. 175.

Fischer, C. S., R. M. Jackson et al., ed. *Networks and Places: Social Relations in the Urban Setting*. New York: The Free Press, 1977.

Fischer, David Hackett. *Growing Old In America*. New York: Oxford University Press, 1978.

Frankena, William L. *Ethics*. New Jersey: Prentice-Hall, Inc., 1973.

Frankfather, D. L. et al. *Family Care of the Elderly*. Lexington, MA: Lexington Books, 1981.

Gerth, H. H. and C. Wright Mills. *From Max Weber: Essays in Sociology.* New York: Oxford University Press, 1946.

Giddens, Anthony. *Capitalism and Modern Social Theory.* London: Cambridge University Press, 1971.

Goldstein, R. "Adult Day Care: Expanding Options for Service." *Journal of Gerontological Social Work,* 5, Nos 1-2 (Fall/Winter 1983), pp. 157-168.

Greene, V. *Strengthening Informal Caregiver Effectiveness through Stress Reduction Counseling: Training and Policy Implications.* Tucson, AZ: University of Arizona, 1985.

Grimaldi, P. L. "The Costs of Adult Day Care and Nursing Home Care: A Dissenting View" [Commentary]. *Inquiry,* 16, No 2 (Summer 1979), pp. 162-166.

Gruenberg, E. M. "The Failures of Success." *The Milbank Memorial Fund Quarterly, Health and Society,* 55 (1977), pp. 3-24.

Gustafson, James M. "Professions as 'Callings.'" *Social Service Review,* 56 (December 1982), pp. 503-515.

Haber, C. *Beyond Sixty-Five: The Dilemma of Old Age in America's Past.* Cambridge: Cambridge University Press, 1983.

Harder, W. Paul, Janet C. Gornick and Martha R. Burt. *Adult Day Care: Supplement or Substitute? Draft Report.* Washington, DC: The Urban Institute, 1983.

Harder, W. Paul, Janet Gornick and Martha Burt. "Adult Day Care: Substitute or Supplement?" *The Milbank Quarterly,* 64, No 3 (1986), pp. 414-441.

Harkins, E. *Social and Health Factors in Long-Term Care: Findings from the Statewide Survey of Older Virginians.* Virginia Office on Aging, 1981.

Health Care Financing Administration, *Data on the Medicaid Program: Eligibility, Services, Expenditures.* Baltimore: Medicaid/Medicare Management Institute, 1979.

Heydebrand, Wolf V. *Comparative Organizations: The Results of Empirical Research.* Englewood Cliffs, NJ: Prentice-Hall, Inc., 1973.

Homans, George C. *The Human Group.* New York: Harcourt, Brace and Company, 1950.

Hooyman, Nancy and Wendy Lustbader. *Taking Care.* New York: The Free Press, 1986.

Horowitz, A. and Rose Dobrof. "The Role of Families in Providing Long-Term Care to the Frail and Chronically Ill Elderly Living in the Community." *Final Report Submitted to the Health Care Financing Administration Grant #18-P-97541/2-02.* New York: Brookdale Center on Aging of Hunter College, 1982.

Jacobs, B. and William Weissert. "Financing Long-Term Care." *Journal of Health, Politics, Policy and Law,* 12, No 1 (Spring, 1987), pp. 77-95.

Johnson, C. and D. J. Catalano. "A Longitudinal Study of Family Supports to Impaired Elderly." *The Gerontologist,* 23, No 6 (1983), pp. 612-618.

Kane, Rosalie and Robert Kane. *Assessing the Elderly.* Lexington, MA: Lexington Books, 1981.

Kane, Rosalie and Robert Kane. *Long-Term Care: Principles, Programs, and Policies.* New York: Springer Publishing Co., 1987.

Katz, E. and P. F. Lazarsfeld. *Personal Influence.* Glencoe, IL: The Free Press, 1955.

Kaye, Lenard W. "Home Care Services for Older People: An Organization-

al Analysis of Provider Experience." Diss. Columbia University, 1982.

Katz, Sidney, Amasa Ford et al. "Studies of Illness in the Aged." Journal of the American Medical Association, 185 (1963), pp. 914-919.

Kemper, Peter, Robert Applebaum et al. "Community Care Demonstrations: What Have We Learned." Health Care Financing Review, 8, No 4 (Summer 1987), pp. 87-100.

Kerson, Toba S. and Lawrence A. Kerson. Understanding Chronic Illness. New York: The Free Press, 1985.

Kirwin, Patricia M. "Adult Day Care: An Integrated Model." In Social Work and Alzheimer's Disease. Ed. Rose Dobrof. New York: Haworth Press, 1986, pp. 59-71.

Kirwin, Patricia M. "Correlates of Service Utilization Among Adult Day Care Clients," Home Health Care Services Quarterly, 9, No 3 (1988), pp. 103-115.

Kirwin, Patricia M. "You Heard What I Said, but Do You Know What I Meant?" Generations, (in press).

Knox, Rita and Lester Marks. "Program Report: Day Center for the Elderly." Mosholu-Montefiore Community Center, Bronx, NY, No Date.

Koenen, Robert E. "Adult Day Care: A Northwest Perspective." Journal of Gerontological Nursing, 6, No 4 (1980), pp. 218-221.

Kostick, Abraham. "A Day Care Program for the Physically and Emotionally Disabled." The Gerontologist, 12, No 2 (Summer 1972, Part 1), pp. 134-137.

Larmer, Kay. Memorandum. National Council on the Aging, Washington, DC, March 29, 1988.

La Rocco, J., J. S. House and J. R. French, Jr. "Social Support, Occupational Stress, and Health." Journal of Health and Social Behavior, 21, No 3 (September 1980), pp. 202-218.

Lawton, M. Powell and Elaine Brody. "Assessment of Older People: Self-Maintaining and Instrumental Activities of Daily Living." The Gerontologist, 9, No 3 (Autumn 1969), pp. 179-186.

Lebowitz, B. "Old Age and Family Functioning." Journal of Gerontological Social Work, 2 (1978), pp. 111-118.

Lee, Philip and A. E. Benjamin. "Intergovernmental Relations: Historical and Contemporary Perspectives." In Fiscal Austerity and Aging. Eds. Carroll L. Estes, Robert J. Newcomer and Associates. Beverly Hills, CA: Sage Publications, 1983, pp. 59-81.

Litwak, Eugene. Helping the Elderly. New York: The Guilford Press, 1985.

Litwak, Eugene. "Models of Bureaucracy which Permit Conflict." In Human Service Organizations. Eds. Yeheskel Hasenfeld and Richard English. Ann Arbor, MI: University of Michigan Press, 1977a.

Litwak, Eugene. "Part II-Theoretical Bases for Practice." In Maintenance of Family Ties of Long-Term Care Patients: Theory and Guide to Practice. Eds. Rose Dobrof and Eugene Litwak. Rockville, MD: National Institute of Mental Health, 1977b, pp. 80-116.

Litwak, Eugene. "Reference Group Theory, Bureaucratic Career, and Neighborhood Primary Group Cohesion." Sociometry, 23 (1960), pp. 72-84.

Litwak, Eugene and Cecilia Falbe. "Formal Organizations and Community Primary Groups: Theory and Policy of Shared Functions as Applied to the Aged." Conference on Organizational Theory and Public Policy, State University of New York at Albany, April 1-2, 1982a.

Litwak, E. and J. Figueira. "Technical Innovation and Ideal Forms of Family Structure in an Industrial Society." In *Families in East and West: Socialization Process and Kinship Ties.* Eds. R. Hill and R. Konig. Paris: Mouton, 1970, pp. 348-396.

Litwak, E. and S. Kulis. *Networks, Primary Groups, and Formal Organizations: Alternative Principles for Matching Group Structures with Tasks Among the Aged.* New York: Columbia University Center for the Social Sciences (Preprint Series No 88), 1982b.

Litwak, E. and H. Meyer. "A Balance Theory of Coordination Between Bureaucratic Organizations and Community Primary Groups." *Administrative Science Quarterly,* 11 (1966), pp. 31-58.

Litwak, Eugene and H. Meyer. *School, Family, and Community: The Theory and Practice of School-Community Relations.* New York: Columbia University Press, 1974.

Litwak, E., H. Meyer and C. D. Hollister. "The Role of Linkage Mechanisms Between Bureaucracies and Families: Education and Health as Empirical Cases in Point". In *Power Paradigms and Community Research.* Ed. R. J. Liebert and A. W. Imershine. Beverly Hills, CA: Sage Publications, 1977, pp. 121-152.

Litwak, Eugene and Ivan Szelenyi. "Primary Group Structures and Their Functions: Kin, Neighbors, Friends." *American Sociological Review,* 34, No 4 (1969), pp. 465-481.

Louis Harris and Associates, Inc. *Priorities and Expectations for Health and Living Circumstances: A Survey of the Elderly in Five English-Speaking Countries.* A study for the Commonwealth Fund. New York: Harris and Associates, 1982.

Lowy, Louis. *Social Policies and Programs on Aging.* Lexington, MA: Lexington Books, 1980.

Mace, Nancy L. and Peter V. Rabins. *The 36-Hour Day: A Family Guide to Caring for Persons with Alzheimer's Disease, Related Dementing Illness and Memory Loss in Later Life*. Baltimore, MD: Johns Hopkins University Press, 1982.

McCuan, Eloise and M. Elliott. "Geriatric Day Care in Theory and Practice." *Social Work in Health Care*, 2 (1977), pp. 153-170.

Mehta, N. and C. Mack. "Day Care Services: An Alternative to Institutional Care." *Journal of the American Geriatric Society*, 23, No 6 (1975), pp. 280-283.

Melcher, John. "Toward Expanded Adult Day Care." Senate Special Committee on Aging. News Release, April 18, 1988.

Meltzer, Judith W. *Respite Care: An Emerging Family Support Service*. Center for the Study of Social Policy: Washington, DC: Administration on Aging. National Conference on Social Welfare, June, 1982.

Mills, C. Wright. *The Sociological Imagination*. New York: Oxford University Press, 1959.

Mintzberg, Henry. *The Structuring of Organizations*. Englewood Cliffs, NJ: Prentice-Hall, Inc., 1979.

Noelker, Linda and Alven Townsend. "Perceived Caregiving Effectiveness." In *Aging, Health, and Family: Long-Term Care*. Beverly Hills, CA: Sage Publications, 1987, pp. 58-79.

"Number of Adult Day Care Centers Increasing, but Payment is Slow." *Hospitals*, November 5, 1990.

Ohnsorg, Dorothy W. "The Role of Therapy in Adult Day Care." *National Institute of Adult Day Care News*, 3, No 2 (Spring 1983).

Padula, Helen. *Developing Adult Day Care: An Approach to Maintaining Independence for Impaired Older Persons*. Washington, DC:

National Council on the Aging, 1983.

Padula, Helen. "Toward a Useful Definition of Adult Day Care." Hospital Progress, (March 1981), pp. 42-45.

Parsons, Talcott. "Pattern Variables Revisited: A Response to Robert Dubin." American Sociological Review, 25 (1960), pp. 467-482.

Parsons, Talcott. The Social System. Glencoe, IL: The Free Press, 1951.

Pennings, J. "The Relevance of the Structural-Contingency Model for Organizational Effectiveness." Administrative Science Quarterly, 20 No 3 (1975), pp. 393-410.

Poplin, Dennis. Communities: A Survey of Theories and Methods of Research, 2nd. edition. New York: Macmillan Publishing Co., 1979.

"Public Policy Agenda 1988-1989 of the National Council on the Aging, Inc." Perspective on Aging, XVII, No 2 (March/April 1988), entire issue, 40 pp.

Rathbone-McCuan, Eloise. "Geriatric Day Care: A Family Perspective." The Gerontologist, 16 (1976), pp. 517-521.

Rathbone-McCuan, E. and Raymond T. Coward. "Respite and Adult Day Care Services." In Handbook of Gerontological Services. Ed. Abraham Monk. New York: Van Nostrand Reinhold, 1985, pp. 457-482.

Respite Care for the Frail Elderly. A Summary Report on Institutional Respite Research and Operations Manual. Albany, NY: The Center for the Study of Aging, Inc., 1983.

Rhodes, Linda M. A Weissert Profile and Functional Task Analysis of Vintage, Inc. Adult Day Care (Pittsburgh, PA). Washington, DC: TransCentury Corporation, January 1982.

Robins, Edith. *"Adult Day Care: Growing Fast But Still for Lucky Few."* *Generations*, (Spring 1981), pp. 22-23.

Robins, Edith. *Directory of Adult Day Care Centers*. Washington, DC: U. S. Department of Health and Human Services, Health Care Financing Administration, 1980.

Roethlisberger, F. J. and William J. Dickson. *Management and the Worker*. Cambridge, MA: Harvard University Press, 1947.

Sager, A. *Learning the Home Care Needs of the Elderly: Patient, Family, and Professional Views of an Alternative to Institutionalization*. Final Report to the Administration on Aging, Grant No 90-A-10-26. Washington, DC: Government Printing Office, 1978.

Sands, D. and T. Suzuki. *"Adult Day Care for Alzheimer's Patients and Their Families."* *The Gerontologist*, 23, No 1 (1983), pp. 21-23.

Saperstein, A. R. and E. Brody. *"What Types of Respite Services Do Family Caregivers of Alzheimer's Patients Want."* Revised version of paper presented at the Annual Meeting of the Gerontological Society of America. Washington, DC, November 1987.

Shanas, Ethel. *"The Family as a Social Support System in Old Age."* *The Gerontologist*, 19, No 2 (1979b), pp. 169-174.

Shanas, Ethel. *"Social Myth as Hypothesis: The Case of the Family Relations of Old People."* *The Gerontologist*, 19, No 1 (1979a), pp. 3-9.

Shanas, E., P. Townsend, D. Wedderburn, H. Friis, P. Milhaj and J. Stehouwer, eds. *Old People in Three Industrial Societies*. New York: Atherton Press, 1968.

Shils, E. A. and M. Janowitz. *"Cohesion and Disintegration in the Wehrmacht in World War II."* *Public Opinion Quarterly*, 12, No 2 (Summer 1948), pp. 280-315.

Simmel, Georg. Conflict and the Web of Group Affiliation. Trans. K. H. Wolff. Glencoe, IL: Free Press, 1956.

Skellie, F. Albert, Melton Mobley and Ruth Coan. "Cost-Effectiveness of Community-Based Long Term Care: Current Findings of Georgia's Alternative Health Services Project." American Journal of Public Health, 72, No 4 (1982), pp. 353-358.

Smallegan, M. "There Was Nothing Else to Do: Needs for Care Before Nursing Home Admission." The Gerontologist, 25, No 4 (1985), pp. 364-369.

Soldo, B. J. and K. G. Manton. "Health Services Needs of the Oldest Old." The Milbank Memorial Fund Quarterly, 63 (1985), pp. 286-319.

Soldo, B. J. and J. Myllyluoma. "Caregivers Who Live with Dependent Elderly." The Gerontologist, 23, No 6 (1983), pp. 605-611.

Springer, Dianne and Timothy Brubaker. Family Caregivers and Dependent Elderly. Beverly Hills, CA: Sage Publications, 1984.

Stassen, Margaret and John Holahan. Long-Term Care Demonstration Projects: A Review of Recent Evaluations. Washington, DC: The Urban Institute, February 1981.

Stephens, Susan A. and Jan B. Christianson. Informal Care of the Elderly. Lexington, MA: D. C. Health and Company, 1986.

Stoller, E. P. "Parental Caregiving by Adult Children." Journal of Marriage and the Family, (November 1983), pp. 851-858.

Stone, Robyn et al. Caregivers of the Frail Elderly: A National Profile. Washington, DC: U. S. Department of Health and Human Services, 1987.

Stone, Robyn et al. "Caregivers of the Frail Elderly: A National Profile." The Gerontologist, Vol 27, No 5 (1987), pp. 616-626.

Strang, Vicki and Anne Neufeld. *"Adult Day Care Programs A Source for Respite." Journal of Gerontological Nursing, 16, No 11 (November 1990), pp. 16-20.*

Supplement to the Encyclopedia of Social Work, 17th edition, 1983-1984. Silver Spring, MD: National Association of Social Workers, 1983, pp. 19-24.

Sussman, M. *"Bureaucracy and the Elderly Individual: An Organizational Linkage Perspective." In Family Bureaucracy and the Elderly. Eds. E. Shanas and M. Sussman. Durham, NC: Duke University Press, 1977.*

Toren, Nina. *"Semi-Professionalism and Social Work: A Theoretical Perspective." In The Semi Professions and Their Organization. Ed. Amitai Etizioni. New York: The Free Press, 1969, pp. 142-195.*

Turner, Jonathan H. *The Structure of Sociological Theory. Chicago, IL: The Dorsey Press, 1986.*

U. S. Bureau of the Census. *"America in Transition: An Aging Society." Current Population Reports, special studies, series P-23, No 128. Washington, DC: Government Printing Office, 1983.*

U. S. Congress. *"Adult Day Care Programs: Hearings Before the Subcommittee on Health and Long Term Care of the Select Committee on Aging." House of Representatives. Washington, DC: Government Printing Office, April 23, 1980.*

U. S. Department of Health and Human Services. *1979 Health Interview Survey. Washington, DC: Government Printing Office, 1979.*

U. S. Department of Health and Human Services. *1982 National Long-Term Care Survey and Informal Caregivers Survey. Washington, DC: Government Printing Office, 1981.*

U. S. Department of Health and Human Services. *Assistant Secretary for*

Planning and Evaluation. <u>Working P{apers on Long-Term Care</u> <u>Prepared for the 1980 Under-Secretary's Task Force on Long-</u> <u>Term Care,</u> *Washington, DC, 1981.*

Virginia Department of Aging. "Study of the Public and Private Cost of Institutional and Community-Based Long-Term Care." Richmond, VA, 1983.

Von Behren, Ruth. <u>Adult Day Care: A Program of Services for the</u> <u>Functionally Impaired.</u> *Washington, DC: National Council on Aging, National Institute on Adult Daycare, July 1988.*

Von Behren, Ruth. <u>Adult Day Care in America: Summary of a National</u> <u>Survey.</u> *Washington, DC: National Council on Aging, National Institute on Adult Daycare, October 1986.*

Weber, Max. <u>The Theory of Social Economic Organizations.</u> *Eds. and translation A. M. Henderson and T. Parsons. New York: Oxford University Press, 1947.*

Weiler, P. G. and E. Rathbone-McCuan. <u>Adult Day Care: Community</u> <u>Work with the Elderly.</u> *New York: Springer Publishing Co., 1978.*

Weissert, William. <u>Adult Day Care in the United States: A Comparative</u> <u>Study: Final Report,</u> *Washington, DC: TransCentury, 1975.*

Weissert, William G. "Adult Day Care Programs in the United States: Current Research Projects and a Survey of 10 Centers." <u>Public</u> <u>Health Reports,</u> *92 (January/February 1977), pp. 49-56.*

Weissert, William G. "Costs of Adult Day Care: A Comparison to Nursing Homes." <u>Inquiry,</u> *15, No 1 (1978), pp. 10-19.*

Weissert, William. "Rationales for Public Health Insurance Coverage of Geriatric Day Care: Issues, Options and Impacts." <u>Journal of</u> <u>Health Politics, Policy and Law,</u> *3, No 4 (Winter 1979), pp. 555-556.*

Weissert, William. "Toward a Continuum of Care for the Elderly: A Note of Caution." Public Policy, 29, No 3 (Summer 1981), pp. 331-340.

Weissert, William. "Two Models of Geriatric Day Care: Findings from a Comparative Study." The Gerontologist, 16, No 5 (1976), pp. 420-427.

Weissert, W. and W. Scanlon. "Determinants of Institutionalization of the Aged." Working Paper No 1466-20. Washington, DC: The Urban Institute, 1983.

Weissert, William, Thomas Wan and Barbara Livieratos. Effects and Costs of Day Care and Homemaker Services for the Chronically Ill: A Randomized Experiment: Executive Summary. Washington, DC: National Center for Health Services, U. S. Dept. of Health, Education and Welfare, January 19, 1979.

White House Conference on Aging, "Adult Day Care - Related Recommendations." NIAD NEWS, 2, No 1 (1982), pp.6-7.

Whyte, W. H. The Organization Man. New York: Simon and Schuster, 1956.

Wilensky, Harold L. "The Professionalization of Everyone?" The American Journal of Sociology, LXX, No 2 (September 1964), pp. 137-158.

Wilson, Albert J. Social Services for Older Persons. Boston: Little, Brown and Company, 1984.

Zaki, Gamal and Sylvia Zaki. Day Care as a Long-Term Care Service. Brown University: Rhode Island College Gerontology Center, 15 February 1982.

Zarit, Steven H. et al. "Relatives of the Impaired Elderly: Correlates of Feelings of Burden." The Gerontologist, 20, No 6 (1980), p. 649.

Zones, Jane et al. "Gender, Public Policy and the Oldest Old." <u>Ageing and Society</u>. 7 (1987), pp. 275-302.

CHAPTER 3

METHODOLOGY AND DEFINITION OF TERMS

"Seek simplicity and distrust it."
Alfred North Whitehead

The purpose of this chapter is to present the study design. An overview of the design and its rationale will be discussed first. The sections that follow define the key terms indicating how they will be measured; explain the details of data collection and the sampling plan; provide the sample response; set forth the study variables; specify the hypotheses; and outline the procedures for data analysis.

STUDY DESIGN - OVERVIEW AND RATIONALE

This study was an analysis of area agency on aging funded adult day care programs in the three southeastern Pennsylvania counties of Chester, Delaware, and Philadelphia (N=14). The purpose of the study was to both describe and explain the complementary roles performed by adult day care programs and primary groups in meeting the community long-term care dependency needs of the frail elderly. The results, in revealing how tasks are divided between the informal caregiving network and the formally organized program of adult day care, may contribute to enriching the currently undeveloped knowledge base from which community service delivery might be conceptualized. In many respects the study can be approached on two levels. First, it can be considered exploratory in nature. The process and context of the interdependence of formal and informal caregiving for participants of the community long-term care service of adult day care has received relatively little attention in gerontological and social welfare research. Research is still in the stage of identifying the salient variables and describing the characteristics of the program's population and the phenomena of family care.

However, the general knowledge base on formal and informal caregiving patterns, has allowed for the prior specification of some critical factors and the formation of selected hypotheses to be tested (Brubaker, 1987; Dobrof and Litwak, 1977; Horowitz and Dobrof, 1982; Litwak, 1985; Kane and Kane, 1987; Springer and Brubaker, 1984; Stone, 1987). Therefore, the second level of approach more appropriately classifies the research as an explanatory survey. Its main purpose is to explain the variation found in the caregiving roles between formal organizations and informal networks.   This dual approach is not uncommon. As Finestone and Kahn (1975) note: ". . . many studies are at some point between the 'pure' points which have been given names . . . it is common for a particular research undertaking to begin with one level . . . and go on to another level."

The questions posed in this study dictated that the complementary nature of the caregiving relationship be approached from both the formal and informal caregivers' points of view. Therefore, the populations of interest consisted of caregivers of adult day care participants (N=79), adult day care participants (N=79), adult day care directors (N=14), and area agency on aging program managers (N=3) to triangulate the measurement.   Additionally, program participant data from area agency on aging files (N=159) was collected. The programs included in this study received some or all of their funding from area agencies on aging. Area agencies on aging were established by a 1973 amendment to the Older Americans Act of 1965.   Area agencies are informally referred to as the "aging network" (Ficke, 1985).[1] Given the range of data required and the

---

[1] *"An area agency on aging (AAA) is a public or nonprofit private agency or office designated by the state to carry out the Older Americans Act at the sub state level." (Ficke, 1985, p. 63). "...an AAA serves both as the advocate and visible focal point in its planning and service area to foster the development of more comprehensive and coordinated service systems to serve older individuals" (Ficke, 1985, p. 63). The Older Americans Act of 1965 and its amendments is the major categorical social services and nutrition services program provided in federal law for America's elderly, i.e., those persons over the age of 60 (Ficke, 1985, p. v). The Older Americans Act serves as the common thread which binds the membership of the nation's 57 State Units on Aging together.   The Pennsylvania Department of Aging is one of these 57 state units. There are*

sensitive nature of these data, the availability of an appropriate subset of data from a recent evaluation of adult day care programs in the state of Pennsylvania performed for the Pennsylvania Department of Aging was indeed propitious.[2]

In sum, this analysis used a subset of a larger study to examine quantitative and qualitative data from formal and informal sources regarding the division of tasks between these systems in providing long-term community care to the frail elderly. Following the section defining the key terms, the specifics of the procedures will be discussed.

DEFINITION OF TERMS

Key terms in this study are, At-Risk of Institutionalization, Formal Organizations, Informal Networks, Cost-Effectiveness, Adult Day Care Program Models, Technical Knowledge, Predictable Events, and Division of Tasks. This section provides the operational definitions for these terms.

At-Risk of Institutionalization:

At this time, there is no agreed-upon social indicator for identifying clients at-risk of institutionalization (Clark, 1987; Kirwin, in press). Weissert (1979, p. 559) has used the number of client impairments as an indicator for being at-risk. However, the number

---

51 AAA in Pennsylvania funded by the state unit. In 1986-87 31 AAA funded adult day care programs.

[2] *In September of 1987, the Bryn Mawr College Graduate School of Social Work and Social Research was awarded funding by the Pennsylvania Department of Aging for an 18 month study to evaluate the state's adult day care programs funded by area agencies on aging for fiscal year 1986-87 (Kaye and Kirwin, 1989; Kirwin, 1989).*

of impairments may be a meaningless indicator if the degree of impairment is not included in decision-making. The number of client deficits in activities of daily living may be a more meaningful indication of at-risk. "The number of activities of daily living (ADL) deficits is emerging in study after study as the key to overall need for service as a part of the continuity of care" (S. Brody, 1987). "Forty-six percent of those over the age of 75 have major limitations in their abilities to perform activities of daily living" (U. S. Senate, 1984).

Targeting those at-risk of institutionalization by ADL and IADL (instrumental activities of daily living) deficits was at the heart of 30 years of long-term demonstration projects evaluated by Peter Kemper and his associates (1987). In their report of this meta-analysis, Kemper and associates considered such activities as eating, bathing, and dressing to be ADL. Cooking and shopping; continence; and lack of cognitive impairment, which was determined by responses to 10 questions about the respondents' age, the day of the week, the name of the U. S. President, etc., were classified as IADL.

Definitions of ADL and IADL, however, may vary according to the particular assessment instrument used by the evaluator (Kirwin, in press). For instance, Clark, in examining the Department of Health and Human Services funded demonstration known as the National Long Term Care Channeling Demonstration, stated that ADL "typically include eating, transferring, dressing, bathing, toileting, and continence." Assessment instruments often combine categories such as bathing and shaving, or walking and getting around. In addition, toileting and continence may be considered as an aspect of physical health rather than as an ADL. This is true for the area agency on aging file assessment instruments used in this study.

Operational definition: High at-risk, is defined as the presence of deficits in 3 of 4 ADL as measured by the area agency on aging file assessment instruments used in this study: bathing/shaving, walking/getting around, dressing, eating (S. Brody, 1987; Soldo and Manton, 1985) and in at least 1 IADL (Kemper et al., 1987). Moderate at-risk is defined as the presence of deficits in 1 to 2 ADL and in at least 1 IADL. A participant with no ADL deficits, is considered to be at low risk of institutionalization.

Formal Organizations:

The most common formal definition of an organization is a collection of people engaged in specialized and interdependent activity to accomplish a goal or mission. Typically, organization theorists define their interest as "large, complex organizations" that are sizable, specialized, and highly interdependent collectivities (Gortner, 1987, p. 2).

The term *Bureaucracy* is used to identify a particular type of organizational structure. The definition of bureaucracy offered by Weber (1947) is the most authoritative and still serves as the point of departure for contemporary organizational theory (Gortner, 1987). Based on historical and contemporary study of several great social and economic institutions, including the Prussian military, the Roman Catholic church, and the Chinese civil service, Weber identified a number of specific characteristics of organizational structure and personnel policy that set the bureaucratic institution apart from all other less neutral, stable, and expert means of administering the law and coordinating the intricate activities of vast numbers of people in a predictable and efficient manner.

The characteristics of bureaucracy that Weber noted included the specialization of function, the requirement that the hiring and promotion of officials be based solely on expertise, that authority be exercised through a centralized, hierarchical chain of command with an intricate system of rules to cover all possible actions and to minimize discretion (Weber, 1947).

As Gortner (1987) demonstrated, it is necessary to distinguish public organizations, with which this study is concerned, from the whole universe of formal organizations. By public organizations we mean government agencies, that is, organizations created to be agents of some unit of government. "Public organizations are part of government and have as their purpose the administration of law" (Gortner, 1987, p. 3). This, Gortner asserts, sets them apart from privately owned firms and nonprofit organizations, which are accountable to owners or boards of directors that are not government entities.

This is a purely legal distinction with implications
concerning the purpose, requirements, and character of

the organization. Public oversight and accountability for example, while a prominent and necessary feature of public organizations, is nonexistent, or limited and temporary, in firms and nonprofit organizations (Gortner, 1987, p. 3).

Operational definition: For this study, the terms formal organization, formal systems, and bureaucracies refer to area agencies on aging and the adult day care programs they fund. The area agencies on aging for Chester and Delaware Counties are government offices. The area agency on aging for the county of Philadelphia is a private non-profit agency; but, nearly 100% of its funding is from governmental agencies to whom it is accountable.

Informal Network:

The informal network or support system is distinguishable from the formal or organizational support system by virtue of its individualistic and nonbureaucratic nature and by the fact that members of this informal network are selected by the elderly from among kin, friends, and neighbors (Cantor, 1979; Dono, 1979; Litwak, 1985). A support system is successful if it fulfills three major needs: socialization, the carrying out of the tasks of daily living, and assistance during times of illness or crisis (Cantor, 1979).

Operational definition: The informal network for this study's population is the combination of kin, friends, and neighbors providing care to the frail elder as recorded in area agency on agency adult day care client files and identified by clients and caregivers through the interview process.

Cost-Effectiveness:

"Cost-effectiveness and cost-benefit methodologies were developed by economists as ways of rationalizing government expenditures, so as to achieve the maximum desired effect for the minimum required cost" (Robinson, 1986, p. 134). There is no single, "correct" and simple effectiveness analysis. And, "Although effectiveness is one of the most crucial issues to determine in any evaluation of day care, it is the most difficult" (Weiler and Rathbone-McCuan, 1978, p. 134). The limitations of cost-benefit and cost-effectiveness analyses are acknowledged by "even the strong advocates of cost-benefit analyses" (Rossi and Freeman, 1982, p. 271). "Values are reflected in expectations for outcomes that underlie problem recognition" (McKillip, 1987, p. 15). Cost-effectiveness is a value most often expressed by large institutions. As portrayed in The Mean Season (Block et al., 1987), cost-effectiveness as an expected outcome of social services contrasts with the consumer's desire for humane care. This lack of consensus jeopardizes social well-being.

Operational definition: Cost-effectiveness is defined as the ratio of total cost of all area agency on aging services provided to adult day care clients during fiscal year 1986-1987 to the Medicaid rates for county nursing home residency for the sampled population during the same period. At this time, there is no acceptable method for computing the amount of cost externalized by government programs. That is, there is no way to measure the emotional, physical, or familial cost of caregiving. This study's measure of cost-effectiveness is further qualified as it does not attempt to measure the additional public costs which may be hidden in government income, transportation, shelter, food, or health benefits not recorded in the examined social service records for this population. However, the major alternative to community care, the nursing home, also has additional fees for residential care which are not reflected in the stated per diem. These expenses vary by facility, diagnosis, individual care requirements, and facility.

Adult Day Care Program Models:

Adult day care is a community-based program offering a "blend of psychosocial and health services that exist in a variety of balances" (O'Brien, 1982, p. 3). It serves older adults who, to some degree, are currently incapable of total independent living, yet do not require 24-hour institutional care. Services relate to health restoration, rehabilitation, maintenance and/or socialization. Adult day care goals include preventing institutionalization, enhancing quality living in the community, and providing assistance to family members or caregivers (Von Behren, 1986). Adult day care exists on the long-term care continuum of services for the elderly. Funding for adult day care centers may come from a variety of sources, with multi-source funding being the rule (Von Behren, 1986). Area agencies on aging have increased support to adult day care since the Older Americans Act amendments of 1978 which emphasized the least-restrictive-environment concept (Wilson, 1984).

Weissert (1976) has described two models of day care (p. 425). The models differ in their goal orientation, and participant profile. Model I adult day care is a physical rehabilitation program:

> *Participants need professionally administered rehabilitative physical, occupational, and speech and hearing therapy. They exhibit multiple chronic conditions, and functional impairments including a high incidence of being wheelchair-bound and a high incidence of paralysis and stroke. Most require assistance in walking, some require assistance in wheeling, and many require assistance in toileting or they are frequently incontinent. A substantial proportion are under 65 years old, reflecting a tendency to have entered the health care system following a major physical breakdown such as a stroke or fall resulting in disabling fractures (p. 425).*

> *Model II programs are a pot-pourri:*

> *Program goals suggest social rehabilitation, maintenance, alleviation of social isolation, nutrition, recreation, and health care services. But health services delivery is not particularly stressed as it is in Model I. There is no typical class of Model II participants. Ages vary widely between the late 50s and over 90 and 100 years of age, and all ages in between. A few participants need rehabilitative therapy, some are very disoriented, a few are at times disruptive and abusive in their behavior, some are wheelchair-bound, and some exhibit no problems with independent functioning and suffer few diagnosed chronic conditions (Weissert, 1976, p. 425).*

Operational definition: The universe of adult day care programs funded by area agencies on aging in the counties of Chester,

Delaware, and Philadelphia were included in this study. This included 14 programs: 4 in Chester County; 4 in Delaware County; and, 6 in Philadelphia County. Program models in this study were identified using a 23-item list. This list is a modified version of a Program Services list used by the National Institute of Adult Day Care in their 1985 national survey of programs (Von Behren, 1986, p. 32). Items in the list were to be checked if the service was provided by staff or a contractor. The items for the List of Program Model Characteristics were:

	Staff	Contractor
a. Social Services	_____	_____
b. M. D. (assessment)	_____	_____
c. M. D. (treatment)	_____	_____
d. Psychiatry	_____	_____
e. Podiatry	_____	_____
f. Dentistry	_____	_____
g. Nursing	_____	_____
h. Diet Counseling	_____	_____
i. Physical Therapy	_____	_____
j. Occupational Therapy	_____	_____
k. Speech Therapy	_____	_____
l. Recreational Activities	_____	_____
m. Art Therapy	_____	_____
n. Music Therapy	_____	_____
o. Exercises	_____	_____
p. Reality Therapy	_____	_____
q. Transportation (home-Center)	_____	_____
r. Transportation (other)	_____	_____
s. Meals (at Center)	_____	_____
t. Toileting	_____	_____
u. Field Trips	_____	_____
v. Other_____		
w. Other_____		

Where at least 2 of the following: b, c, d, f, g, i, j, or k were checked in either the "staff" or the "contractor" column, the program was considered a Model I using Weissert's description. For the purpose of defining program model the activity may have been provided by either the program staff or by an independent contractor.

Model II, using the above 23-item list, was defined as a program *not* providing more than 1 of the above cited services. Table 3.1 presents the results of this analysis.

TABLE 3.1
RESULTS OF ADC PROGRAM[1]
MODEL CHARACTERISTICS/ACTIVITIES[2]
(N=13)

ACTIVITY	%	|	1	2	3	4	5	6	7	8	9	10	11	12	13
a. Social Services	100.0		S	S	S	M	S	S	S	S	S	S	M	M	M
b. M.D. (assessment)	30.8					M							M	M	M
c. M.D. (treatment	30.8					M							M	M	M
d. Psychiatry	30.8					M							M	M	M
e. Podiatry	46.2			S	S	M							M	M	M
f. Dentistry	38.5					M							M	M	M
g. Nursing	92.3		S	S	S	M		S	S	S	S	S	M	M	M
h. Diet counseling	77.9		S	S		M	S		S	S	S	S	M	M	M
i. Physical therapy	46.2		S	S		M			S				M	M	M
j. Occuptn'l therapy	61.6		S	S	S	M			S			S	M	M	M
k. Speech therapy	38.5		S			M			S				M	M	M
l. Recrtn'l activities	100.0		S	S	S	M	S	S	S	S	S	S	M	M	M
m. Art therapy	84.6		S		S	M	S	S	S	S	S		M	M	M
n. Music therapy	100.0		S	S	S	M	S	S	S	S	S	S	M	M	M
o. Exercises	100.0		S	S	S	M	S	S	S	S	S	S	M	M	M
p. Reality therapy	84.6		S	S	S	M		S		S	S	S	M	M	M
q. Trnsprt'n to cntr	92.3		S		S	M	S	S	S	S	S	S	M	M	M
r. Trnsprt'n-other	61.5		S		S	M	S		S			S	M	M	M
s. Meals (at center)	100.0		S	S	S	M	S	S	S	S	S	S	M	M	M
t. Toileting	100.0		S	S	S	M	S	S	S	S	S	S	M	M	M
u. Field trips	92.3		S	S	S	M	S	S	S	S		S	M	M	M

[1] *Chester County programs*

    1 = Coatesville Area Senior Center
    2 = Manatawny Adult Day Care
    3 = New Beginnings
    4 = Pat's Adult Day Care

Delaware County programs

    5 = Crozer Chester Medical Center
    6 = Squire Intell'ly Impaired Adult Day Care
       Program
    7 = Squire Rehab. Adult Day Care Program
    8 = Watkins Avenue Senior Center

Philadelphia County programs

    9 = Community Senior Respite Center
    10 = Interac, Inc.
    11 = Pennsylvania Hosp. Adult Day Health Center
    12 = Philadelphia Geriatric Center
    13 = Primary Community Health Care, Inc.

[2] *Where at least 2 of the following services are provided, the program is considered to be a Model I or medical model program: b, c, d, f, g, i, j, or k. These programs are indicated with the letter "M." "S" indicates the program is a Model II or social model of adult day care.*

Technical Knowledge:
"Technical knowledge means all knowledge which requires training above and beyond that of everyday socialization" (Dobrof and Litwak, 1977, p. 87). Two attributes of the formal organization, it will be recalled, are its specialization of function and the requirement that the hiring and promotion of officials be based solely on expertise. Technical knowledge is learned in special schools or on-the-job training in a formal organization" (Litwak, 1985, p. 10).

Operational definition: Technical knowledge in this study was measured by a 7-item ranking probe first used by Kaye (1982). Items in the probe were measured on a 3-point scale. The items for the Ranking of Technical Knowledge were:

What have been the major ways in which you feel you have learned what you know about caregiving? (Please rank the 3 major ways in which you have learned what you now know where 1 = the most important way, 2 = the second most important way, etc.)

Classes at school   _____
Training programs offered by community organizations   _____
On-the-job experience   _____
Discussions with supervisors   _____
Discussions with other caregivers   _____
Personal experiences   _____
Other **(Write in)**_____

Caregiving skills acquired through classes at school, on-the-job experience, and/or through community training organizations were considered technical knowledge. Caregiving skills acquired through discussions with supervisors and/or other caregivers, or through personal experiences were not considered technical knowledge. Table 3.2 presents the results of the Ranking of Technical Knowledge.

TABLE 3.2
RESULTS OF RANKING OF TECHNICAL KNOWLEDGE
BY CAREGIVERS AND ADC PROGRAM STAFF

	Caregivers (N = 18)					ADC Staff (N = 13)				
	1	2	3¹	Total	%	1	2	3¹	Total	%
TECHNICAL KNOWLEDGE										
Classes at school	1			1	3.13	2	1	2	5	13.16
Training programs	1			1	3.13			3	3	7.89
Sub-total				2	6.26				8	21.05
NON-TECHNICAL KNOWLEDGE										
On-the-job experience	4	4		8	25.00	6	3	3	12	31.58
Discussions with supervisor			1	1	3.13	2	5	3	10	26.32
Discussions with caregiver	1	1	2	4	12.50	1	2	3	6	15.79
Personal experiences	10	4		14	43.75	1			1	2.63
Other²	3			3	9.38		1		1	2.63
Sub-total				30	93.76				30	78.95
Total				32	100.02³				38	100.00

[1] 1 = most important way of learning about caregiving.
   2 = second most important way of learning about caregiving.
   3 = third most important way of learning about caregiving.

[2] Under "other" caregivers listed program staff, staff at a geriatric hospital, tv, and reading. One adult day care staff member cited nursing experience.

[3] Percent is greater than 100 due to rounding.

Predictable Events:
    Predictable events, that is tasks which are repetitive and can be anticipated, lend themselves to standardization. Such activities can be prepared for beforehand knowing that they will have to be performed at a given point in time in a particular way.

> *For extremely unpredictable events detailed experts often cannot be used because (a) they cannot be trained in time to make a difference; or (b) they cannot be brought to the scene in time to make a difference; and (c) their work cannot be easily supervised . . . (Litwak, 1985, p. 10).*

Litwak refers to unpredictable tasks as nonuniform situations, and he argues "that nonuniform tasks are most effectively managed by primary groups . . . ." (Litwak, 1985, p. 10-11). In uncertain situations, bureaucracies, in contrast to primary groups have more difficulty in responding quickly (Sussman, 1977). When the tasks people perform are well understood, predictable, routine, and repetitive, a bureaucratic structure is the most efficient (Perrow, 1979, p. 162).

Operational definition: To measure predictable, routine, or uniform events—these terms are considered synonymous in this study—Aiken and Hage's (1968) Index of Routinization of Technology (a 6-item index measuring the degree of routineness of work activities) was used to operationalize this concept. A modified version of this index was also used by Kaye (1982) in analyzing home care services for older people. Five statements were scored on a 4-point true-false scale reversed for one question to minimize the potential for response set. They were:

	Definitely True 1	Some- what True 2	Some- what False 3	Definitely False 4
I do the same job in the same way every day.	_____	_____	_____	_____
One thing I like about caregiving is the variety of the work.	_____	_____	_____	_____
In providing care there is some- thing new happening every day.	_____	_____	_____	_____
Every day there is something different to do.	_____	_____	_____	_____

	Highly Non-Routine 1	Some- what Non- Routine 2	Some- what Routine 3	Highly Routine 4
How would you describe your caregiving routine?	_____	_____	_____	_____

	Definitely True	Some- what True	Some- what False	Definitely False
It is easy to predict what kinds of help the client will need.	___	___	___	___

A sixth question which asked the respondent to assess the overall routineness of their job was scored 1=highly non-routine, 2=somewhat non-routine, 3=somewhat routine, and 4=highly routine. Table 3.3 presents the results for items in the Index of Routinization of Technology for adult day care programs and for caregivers. The potential score range was from 1 (low routineness) to 6 (high routineness). The Cronbach alpha for the program scale was .86 based on 3 cases and 6 items reflecting a high level of internal reliability. The mean for the scale was 2.11 with a standard deviation of .51. For caregivers, the Cronbach alpha was .42 based on 20 cases and 6 items. The mean for the scale was 2.70 with a standard deviation of .53.

In the state-wide study, from which this subset was selected (Kaye and Kirwin, 1989), the Cronbach alpha for the program scale was .74 based on 23 cases and 6 items. The mean for the scale was 2.20 with a standard deviation of .49. For caregivers in the larger study, the Cronbach alpha was .68 based on 65 cases and 6 items. The mean for the scale was 2.68 with a standard deviation of .65.

Division of Tasks:
Weber implied a second basis (other than technical knowl-edge) for the formal organization's effectiveness. The formal organization can subdivide complex tasks into smaller units and by doing so make each subunit simpler to do. As a result the total task can be done faster, more reliably, and with less cost. This may be called "task simplification" by a division of labor. The classic illustration of this is the assembly line. However, as Litwak (1985) states,

> *The rationale behind task simplification is especially important for the aged, because many formal organiza-*

tions such as nursing homes, are fundamentally seeking to replace everyday family tasks by task simplification and not by technical knowledge (p. 9).

TABLE 3.3
FREQUENCIES FOR ADC PROGRAM AND CAREGIVER INDEX
OF ROUTINIZATION OF TECHNOLOGY[1]

	ADC Programs (N=13) Mean S.D.	Caregivers (N=20) Mean S.D.
I do the same job in the same way every day.	2.15 .69	3.25 1.07
One thing I like about caregiving is the variety of the work.	1.79 .60	2.70 1.17
In providing care there is something new happening every day.	1.85 .69	1.95 1.00
Every day there is something different to do.	1.85 .55	2.05 1.15
How would you describe your caregiving routine?	1.77 .72	2.90 1.02
It is easy to predict what kinds of help the Client will need.	2.54 .88	3.35 .88
SUMMARY SCORE	2.11 .51	2.70 .53

[1] The range for this scale is 1 (highly non-routine) to 4 (highly routine).

Tasks usually performed by the informal network have been delineated by Stephens and Christianson in Informal Care of the Elderly (1986) which was based on data collected for an evaluation of the National Long-Term Care Demonstration (more commonly known as the "channeling demonstration"). This study generally confirmed the findings of previous research.

Of the categories of in-home care provided to elderly care recipients, medical care was the least frequently mentioned by the primary caregivers in the channeling study. In contrast, almost all primary caregivers provided help with at least 1 ADL or other household task. Almost 90 percent helped with shopping, nearly 80 percent with meals and housework, and almost 75 percent with managing money. Help with medications, and help with chores were less frequently mentioned, but were still provided by over half of the primary caregivers. Personal care was also provided frequently—more than 70 percent of the primary caregivers performed at least one personal care task, over 50 percent provided help with dressing, and a somewhat smaller percentage helped with bathing and getting out of bed or a chair.

The type of personal care least frequently provided was help with eating (22 percent of the caregivers reported providing this assistance). Almost 40 percent of the caregivers helped regularly with toileting and with problems associated with incontinence. Slightly more than 40 percent provided supervision for personal safety. Help with transportation and with arranging services and benefits was provided by more than half of the caregivers. The majority of caregivers helped with more than one caregiving task, and over 80 percent kept company with the care recipient above and beyond the time they devoted to other caregiving tasks (p. 34).

Operational definition: This study was interested in examining the division of tasks between the informal network and the formal organization. Task division was operationalized by the Task Frequency Index, a modified version of a 20-item index previously developed by Kaye (1982). Index items were measured on a 5-point progression. The items for the Task Frequency Index were:

	Very Often 1	Often 2	Sometimes 3	Seldom 4	Never 5
Meal planning &/or preparation	___	___	___	___	___
Serving a meal	___	___	___	___	___
Marketing or shopping	___	___	___	___	___
Household cleaning	___	___	___	___	___
Laundry	___	___	___	___	___
Escort	___	___	___	___	___
Companionship	___	___	___	___	___
Personal help w bathing, eating/dressing/ toileting	___	___	___	___	___
Simple nursing tasks	___	___	___	___	___
Budgeting assistance	___	___	___	___	___
Teaching nutrition	___	___	___	___	___
Helping with family problems	___	___	___	___	___
Recreational activities	___	___	___	___	___
Minor home repairs	___	___	___	___	___
Friendly visiting	___	___	___	___	___
Identifying client needs	___	___	___	___	___
Speaking on behalf of clients at community offices	___	___	___	___	___
Providing emotional support	___	___	___	___	___
Paying bills, writing letters	___	___	___	___	___
Other (Write in)	___	___	___	___	___

Table 3.4 presents the results for items in the Task Frequency Index as measured independently by caregivers and adult day care programs. The potential score range was from 1 (very often performed) to 5 (never performed). The alpha for the index of caregiver responses was .77 based on 11 cases and 19 items with a mean of 1.73

and a standard deviation of .55. The alpha for the index of adult day care program responses was .60 based on 9 cases and 19 items with a mean of 2.69 and a standard deviation of .64. In the state-wide study the alpha for the index of adult day care program responses was .90 based on 21 cases and 19 items reflecting a high level of internal reliability. The mean for the index was 2.78 with a standard deviation of .78. For caregivers, the alpha was .91 based on 35 cases and 19 items. The mean for the index was 1.95 with a standard deviation of .74.

TABLE 3.4
FREQUENCIES FOR ADC PROGRAM AND CAREGIVER
TASK FREQUENCY INDEX[1]

	ADC Program (N=13)		Caregivers (N=20)	
	Mean	S.D.	S.D.	Mean
Meals planning and/or preparation	2.45	1.75	1.35	.99
Serve a meal	1.08	.28	1.25	.64
Marketing or shopping	3.85	1.40	1.30	.57
Household cleaning	4.23	1.54	1.55	1.28
Laundry	4.31	1.25	1.55	1.15
Escort	3.58	1.73	1.50	.83
Companionship	2.33	1.72	1.16	.37
Personal help with bathing, eating, dressing, toileting	1.50	.67	1.75	1.29
Simple nursing tasks	1.58	.79	2.00	1.29
Budgeting assistance	4.33	1.15	1.35	.74
Teaching proper nutrition	2.46	.88	2.33	1.78
Helping with family problems	1.61	.87	2.25	1.62
Recreational activities	1.38	1.12	2.39	1.38
Minor home repairs	5.00	.00	3.15	1.56
Friendly visiting	3.69	1.65	2.38	1.71
Identifying client needs	1.23	.44	1.42	.96
Speaking on behalf of clients at community offices	2.25	.96	2.10	1.59
Providing emotional support	1.08	.28	1.35	.99
Paying bills, writing letters	4.00	1.21	1.30	.57
SUMMARY INDEX SCORE	2.69	.64	1.73	.55

[1] Range is 1 (very often performed) to 5 (never performed).

DATA COLLECTION AND SAMPLING PLAN

From the original study of 31 area agencies on aging in Pennsylvania who contracted for adult day care services, 3 area agencies were selected for this study. These are the area agencies on aging for the southeastern counties of Chester, Delaware, and Philadelphia. In the original study, a randomly drawn 25% sample of fiscal year 1986-1987 adult day care program participant records at each area agency on aging which funded adult day care during the 1986-1987 fiscal year was analyzed with special consideration given to such characteristics as age, sex, marital status, number of deficits in ADL, availability of caregivers, tasks performed by caregivers over time, and nursing home pre-admission assessment information to analyze the influence these variables may have in shaping the elder's experience of community long-term care through participation in the service of adult day care.

These 3 county agencies provided funds to 639 adult day care participants in the southeastern region of Pennsylvania during 1986-1987 through 14 programs. This represents 49% of the total ADC population (N=1306) from which the state-wide study randomly selected its study participants. In addition to the sampled client records, area agency on aging adult day care program managers (N=3) and the universe of adult day care program directors (N=14) in the 3 counties participated in this study. At a third stage of the data collection phase, a 50% sample of the original 25% sample was randomly drawn of clients (N=79) and their caregivers (N=79) who were to be directly interviewed. Sampling strategies reflected the intent of achieving comprehensiveness, representativeness, and randomness for this population in the southeastern region of the state.

The procedure used in this study is outlined in greater detail as follows:

(1) Using a structured data collection instrument, characteristics of service recipients as well as assessment data were collected from adult day care program records for fiscal year 1986-87 (N=159) randomly drawn from the participating agencies in Chester, Delaware, and Philadelphia. The number of cases sampled represented approximately 25% of the universe in these counties and was a sub-set of the

larger state-wide program study. Chester County chose to have the instrument completed by their own staff rather than by outside trained researchers. Each protocol was expected to take 30-45 minutes to complete. Standardization of the collection process was encouraged through data collection training of both project and area agency on aging staff in order to deflate error variance. Collection of agency data involved transcribing data from client file records to a numbered, no-name instrument. (Agency staff were asked to keep a record of client names and assigned numbers for six months in case it was necessary to verify particular data.) At the end of the study, all instruments were to be destroyed. Since clients were not contacted directly in this phase of the study and their names were unknown to the researcher, signed client agreements to participate in the study were not necessary (Paragraph 2380.91(2) Adult Services Manual, Pennsylvania Department of Public Welfare (88780) No 117, August 1984). Prior to use, the instrument was critiqued by two area agency on aging deputy directors, one area agency on aging director, an adult day care program director, and the advisory committee for the larger Pennsylvania Department on Aging study.

(2) A second phase of research, a sub-set of which is analyzed in this study, entailed the use of a structured mail survey instrument designed to gather administrative program details from each of the area agencies on aging for the counties of Chester, Delaware, and Philadelphia. Each county agency funded adult day care programs in fiscal year 1986-1987. The subset of characteristics regarding program routinization and technicality, and staff education and training were analyzed in this study. This instrument was expected to take agency staff between 1 and 4 hours to complete depending on the number of programs the agency funded, i.e., Delaware County and Chester County each funded 4 programs during the study year, whereas the area agency in Philadelphia funded 6 programs. This instrument, in its entirety, was also critiqued by 2 area agency on aging deputy directors, 1 area agency on aging director, an adult day care program director, and an advisory committee established for the Pennsylvania state evaluation of adult day care programs. In effect, this detailed review of all data collection instruments was considered the equivalent of a pretest allowing for the modification and ultimate refinement of instruments prior to actual administration.

(3) A third phase of the research, utilized from the state-wide study, entailed the administration of semi-structured field interviews undertaken with randomly drawn and willing primary informal caregivers (N=79) and mentally intact, physically capable, and willing clients (N=79) represented among this study's sub-set of client files selected during phase 1 (this was a 50% randomly selected sub-sample of the original 25% randomly selected clients for whom file data was collected.) The anticipated high attrition of unable or unwilling clients/caregivers was compensated for by doubling the number selected during the initial random sub-sampling of this population. An attempt was made to interview each individual separately in a face-to-face meeting. Each interview was expected to require 1 hour of time. All prospective study participants were fully informed on matters of confidentiality and the voluntary nature of their participation. Objectives of this phase included determining what service recipients and informal caregivers stated as reasons for using adult day care; what caregivers and participants indicated were their met and unmet service needs; information on the technical and routine qualities of their caregiving; the employment and health status of caregivers; and which services, over time, caregivers provided to frail elders.

(4) A fourth and final phase of the field research involved analyzing a sub-set of mailed interviews to the universe of adult day care directors whose programs received area agency on aging funding (N=14) in the counties of Chester, Delaware, and Philadelphia for fiscal year 1986-1987. This structured survey instrument required approximately 1.5 hours to complete and sought to determine patterns of participant utilization; aspects of program technicality and routinization; levels of staff education; services offered, program model indices, and the location of participants who have left the program since the study year.

The combination of research strategies as outlined above, insured the participation, in varying degrees, of agencies which fund and those which deliver adult day care services as well as consumers of this service. Table 3.5 summarizes the population category, type of data to be collected and the respondent N for each study group.

TABLE 3.5
DATA SOURCES

Population Category	Type of Data	Respondent N
Client Files (25% random sample)	Secondary (Structured data collection from AAA client files)	159
Clients (50% random sub-sample)[1]	Primary (Semi-structured field interviews)	79
Caregivers (50% random sub-sample)[1]	Primary (Semi-structured[1] field interviews)	79
ADC Directors (Universe)	Primary (Structured mail interviews)	14
AAA Program Managers (universe)	Secondary (Structured data collection from program and fiscal reports)	3

[1] Refers to sub-sample of original 25% random sample: 5 in Chester County; 23 in Delaware County; and 51 in Philadelphia County.

SAMPLE RESPONSE

The results of the sampling process are presented in Tables 3.6, 3.7, 3.8, and 3.9. By grouping the "not reached," "institutional-ized," "terminated and/or deceased," with the "unwilling," a high rate of non-response resulted for the client/caregiver interviews. Even so, the proportion of older people able and willing to be interviewed compares favorably with the experiences of other researchers (Horo-witz and Dobrof, 1982).

TABLE 3.6
AREA AGENCY AND PROGRAM RESPONSE BY COUNTY

	Frequency (N)	Percent %
Area Agencies on Aging Sampled (3)	3	100.00%
Chester County		
Delaware County		
Philadelphia County		
Adult Day Care Programs Sampled (14)	13	92.86%
In Chester County (4)	4	100.00%
Coatesville Area Senior Ctr		
Manatawny Adult Day Care		
New Beginnings		
Pat's Adult Day Care		
In Delaware County (4)	4	100.00%
Crozer Chester Medical Center		
Squire Intellectually Impaired ADC Program		
Squire Rehabilitation ADC Prog		
Watkins Avenue Senior Center		
In Philadelphia County (6)	5	83.33%
Community Senior Respite Ctr		
Interac, Inc.		
Pennsylvania Hospital Adult Day Health Center		
Philadelphia Geriatric Ctr		
Primary Comm Health Care, Inc.		
Terry Thurmond Center	*	

*Of the 14 programs sampled, only the Terry Thurmond Center in Philadelphia County did not respond.

TABLE 3.7

ADULT DAY CARE CLIENT RESPONSE BY COUNTY

	Frequency (N)	Percent %
Adult Day Care Clients Interviewed (79)	13	16.46%
In Chester County (5)		
Deceased	2	
Institutionalized[1]	1	
Unable to locate	2	
Interviewed	0	00.00%
In Delaware County (23)		
Deceased	4	
Institutionalized[1]	6	
Unable to Locate	5	
Unable to Comprehend	1	
Unwilling	1	
Interviewed	6	26.09%
In Philadelphia County (51)		
Decease	15	
Institutionalized[1]	4	
Terminated[2]	4	
Unable to Comprehend	5	
Unable to Locate[3]	3	
Unwilling	2	
Never attended ADC	3	
File Location Unknown to Agency	8	
Interviewed	7	13.73%

[1] This refers to 1986-1987 ADC participants who had since become residents of a nursing facility. Through contact with the area agency, an attempt was made to interview all clients in nursing homes; however, after placement area agencies appear to lose contact with clients and/or the very impairments that created the need for placement deter interviewing.

[2] According to this agency this term is used for several different reasons: the client withdrew; the caregiver withdrew the client; the client was no longer eligible for day care for a variety of reasons; the client was institutionalized; the client died.

[3] This term is descriptive of several different situations: the client moved without leaving a forwarding address; the agency could not find the file; or repeated attempts by researchers to locate the client failed.

TABLE 3.8
ADULT DAY CARE CAREGIVER RESPONSE BY COUNTY

	Frequency (N)	Percent %
Adult Day Care Caregivers Interviewed (79)	20	25.32%
In Chester County (5)		
Client Deceased,		
Caregiver Not Interviewed	2	
Unable to Locate	2	
Interviewed	1	20.00%
In Delaware County (24)[1]		
Client Deceased,		
Caregiver Not Interviewed	4	
Client Institutionalized,		
Caregiver Not Interviewed	5	
Unable to Locate	5	
Unwilling	2	
Interviewed	8	33.33%
In Philadelphia County (51)		
Deceased Client,		
Caregiver Not Interviewed	7	
Client Institutionalized,		
Caregiver Not Interviewed	4	
Client Unable to Comprehend,		
Caregiver Not Interviewed	2	
Unable to Locate[2]	4	
Unwilling	4	
Client Unknown	8	
Clients Terminated, Caregivers		
Not Located	4	
Clients Without Caregivers	7	
Interviewed	11	21.57%

[1] One client had two caregivers willing to be interviewed. See Table 3.9.

[2] This term may mean one of several things: the caregiver moved without leaving a forwarding address; the agency could not find the client's file; or repeated attempts by researchers to locate the caregiver failed.

TABLE 3.9
ADULT DAY CARE CLIENT FILE DATA RESPONSE BY COUNTY

	Frequency (N)	Percent %
Adult Day Care Client File Data Collected (159)	134	84.28%
In Chester County (12)		
Client Never Entered ADC Prog[1]	1	
Duplicate File	1	
Completed File Data Collection	10	83.33%
In Delaware County (46)		
File Unlocated	3	
Completed File Data Collection	43	93.48%
In Philadelphia County (101)		
Unknown Clients[2]	12	
File Unlocated	1	
Client Never Attended ADC Prog[1]	5	
Duplicate File	1	
Lost File	1	
Completed File Collection	81	80.20%

[1] This refers to clients who were assessed by service managers as appropriate for adult day care but who never actually attended the program during 1986-1987.

[2] This term can mean one of several things: the client was assessed by a service manager but had no further contact with the area agency; the agency could not find the client's file; the client was "grandfathered" into current programs from the Channeling demonstration of the early 1980's and prior to computerization so that the client name did not appear in computer print-outs used by the Agency in providing data for this study; or there was an error in the spelling of the client's name which impeded locating the client's file. In this county there were several clients with the same or similar first and last name combinations and no middle initial.

RESEARCH QUESTIONS AND HYPOTHESES

This was a descriptive study of the complementary roles performed by adult day care programs and primary groups in meeting the long-term dependency needs of the frail elderly. The theoretical framework for this analysis was Litwak's theory of shared functions detailed in the literature review section of this paper.

The present system of community care is criticized for putting too much emphasis on institutional services without concern for enhancing the quality of patients' lives (a major objective of supportive services). Most often dependent populations prefer to remain at home. For these and other reasons stated in previous sections of this analysis, long-term care has emerged as a national policy goal. Both those concerned with human and financial costs of long-term care have concluded that wholesale institutional care is no longer the solution for meeting the needs of the chronically ill. As Block and his associates (1987) demonstrated, there is a history of tension between social justice and economic efficiency with a historical tendency towards "meanness" in social welfare. However, Crystal (1982), Hardin (1987), Harlow (1987), Kane and Kane (1987), Litwak (1978), and others assert that there are present and compelling reasons for this tendency to be reconsidered.

The role of the family in long-term care has been confirmed (Brubaker, 1987; Cantor, 1980; 1985; Shanas, 1979a; 1979b). However, the stress this caregiving involves may lead to premature institutionalization for dependent elders when caregivers do not receive adequate caregiving assistance or respite (Brubaker, 1987; Callahan et al, 1981; Christianson and Stephens, 1986). Consequently, policy makers are beginning to explore strategies for bolstering and strengthening the informal support system. The avoidance of premature institutional care is seen as a way to curtail the spiraling costs of this formal service.

Studies have shed light on the nature and magnitude of the informal care system and have raised questions about the capacity of informal caregivers to continue providing the bulk of long-term care without support (Brody, 1981; 1985; 1986; Cantor, 1983; Horowitz and Dobrof, 1982; Stephens and Christianson, 1986; Stoller, 1983). Kane (1987) cautions that the challenge is to supplement and not supplant family care and/or the private purchase of assistance.

However, the financial, emotional, and physical costs of community care absorbed by family caregivers is incalculable and obscures the true cost-savings which may be possible when community care and institutional care are compared. We know clients prefer community care (Butler and Lewis, 1982). The biting question, suggested by Litwak, is how might informal care and formal support services be utilized as a cooperative continuum in humanely and cost-effectively meeting the dependency needs of the frail elderly in the community, and perhaps, delaying or avoiding institutionalization. The focus of this study, adult day care, is one of the emerging programs offering services to the frail elderly client and respite for the caregiver in a community setting.

Litwak (1985) makes the assumption that the informal system is better adapted to perform the nonuniform aspects of care; that is, those that are simple, idiosyncratic, extremely unpredictable or require contingencies. And, that the formal care system is better able to handle those aspects of care which require expert knowledge and large scale resources. This study tested the validity of those assumptions at the community level for one population. By empirically testing Litwak's theoretical assumptions, the goal is not to provide the solution but to search for common ground in serving both sides of the debate regarding the humane and cost-effective meeting of the long-term care needs of the dependent elderly. Indeed, in providing humane, efficient long-term care there most likely will be a cost to all.

The purposes of this study were:

(a)   to examine client factors associated with being at-risk of institutionalization;

(b)   to examine the caregiving tasks performed by both the formal organization and the informal system of caregiving;

(c)   to examine the total cost of publicly funded social services received by this program's population through area agencies on aging;

(d)   to examine the extent to which the formal system of care succeeds over time in working with the informal caregiving network to maintain the frail elder in the community; and particularly,

(e)   to test Litwak's theory of complementary roles at the community level.

These purposes led to the following research questions and hypotheses:

Questions regarding the bureaucratic concern of economic effectiveness included (a) Does the program reach the target group, those at-risk of institutionalization? (b) Does the program supplement rather than supplant traditional family care roles? (c) Does the program help to conserve scarce public long-term care dollars? The following research questions addressed these concerns.

(1)   Do these adult day care programs serve the people they were established to serve, the frailest, those most likely to be institutionalized?
(2)   Does the informal system reduce, over time, the amount of caregiving it gives to those frail elders who participate in adult day care?
(3)   How does the cost of all social services received by the clients in this study compare with the publicly funded Medicaid per diem nursing home rate?
(4)   Regarding the study questions, are there significant differences between Model I (medically oriented) and Model II (socially oriented) program variables?

Questions regarding the assumptions of Litwak's theory of complementary roles included: (a) To what extend do formal organizations use technical knowledge and task routinization to deliver this service? (b) To what extend do informal caregivers perform nonroutinized tasks using non-technical knowledge? The following questions addressed these assumptions.

(1)   Does the community program of adult day care perform routinized tasks using technical knowledge?
(2)   Do caregivers meet the needs of the frail elderly by performing tasks which are nonroutinized and require nontechnical knowledge?
(3)   Which functions of care are provided by informal caregivers and which by the formal system of care?

A question regarding the humanistic perspective of informal support asked:

Does sharing caregiving tasks between the informal network and the formal organization provide effective, humane care in meeting the dependency needs of the elderly (and perhaps other dependent adult populations)?

In addition to examining adult day care client characteristics for at-risk of institutionalization factors, qualities of technicality and routinization, and the complementary roles, over time, of formal and informal systems of care, Litwak's theory of shared functions was tested by means of the following five hypotheses:

(1)   Caregivers, over time, will tend to continue to provide care to the frail elderly even when the elderly for whom they care attend an adult day care program.

(2)   Caregivers of adult day care participants will tend to manage tasks which are personal, i.e., grooming and bathing.

(3)   Caregivers of adult day care participants will tend to manage tasks which are unpredictable.

(4)   Adult day care programs will tend to perform tasks which are predictable.

(5)   Adult day care programs will tend to perform tasks which are more technical.

DATA ANALYSIS

Univariate frequency distributions, and bivariate frequency distributions are provided. Cronbach's alpha was used to test internal reliability of indices. Table 3.10, Identification of Major Study Variables, indicates the study's independent and dependent variables and suggests variables which may intervene.

TABLE 3.10

IDENTIFICATION OF MAJOR STUDY VARIABLES

Independent Variables	Intervening Variables	Dependent Variables

I. ADC Participant
A. Sociodemographics
  1. Age
  2. Sex/Ethnicity
  3. Marital Status
  4. Living Arrangement
B. Impairments
  1. Health Related:
    physical/mental
  2. ADL Related
C. Length of time in AAA System
	I. Service Experience &
	  Attitudes
	A. Utilization of ADC services
	  1. Times per week
	  2. Hours per visit
	B. Use of Other Services
	C. Current Service Needs
		I. Institutional Risk
		A. Placement Consideration
		B. Perception of Possibility of
		  Eventual Placement
		C. Location of Clients Who
		  Have Left ADC

II. Caregiver/InformalSystem
A. Sociodemographics
  1. Age
  2. Sex/Ethnicity
  3. Employment
    a. Occupation
    b. Parttime/Fulltime
B. Health Status
C. Family Supports/Conflicts
  1. Marital Status
  2. Household Composition/Res-
    ponsibilities
  3. Involvement of Nuclear and
    Extended Kin in Caregiving
    Tasks
D. Caregiving Functions
  1. Tasks Performed
    a. Predictable/Routinized
    b. Technical Knowledge
    c. Frequency of performance
  2. Length of time as caregiver
		II. Complementary Functions
		A. Length of Client Time in
		  ADC
		B. Caregiver Satisfaction
		C. Client Satisfaction
		D. Change in Levels of Natural
		  Support over Time
		E. Technicality of Tasks
		  Performed by Caregiver
		F. Technicality of Tasks
		  Performed by ADC
		G. Task Predictability of
		  Caregivers
		H. Task Predictability of ADC

III. ADC Program/Formal Organi-
  zation
A. Staff
  1. Education
  2. Training
  3. Parttime/Fulltime
B. Services Provided
  1. Predictable/Routinized
  2. Technical Knowledge
		III. Cost-Effectiveness
		A. Total Cost of Services
		  Received by Client Through
		  the AAA

IV. AAA Service Management A. Services Planned B. Services Received		

STUDY LIMITATIONS

(1) In this study, analysis was performed on existing client files in 3 county agencies. As a result, these study data are accurate in describing client and caregiver characteristics to the extent that these files represented uniform definition and collection of client and caregiver characteristics. It should be noted that while an equal percent of the program population by county was randomly selected this resulted in unequal county sample totals, i.e., for client file data collection the range of cases sampled was 10 for Chester County to 81 for Philadelphia County.

(2) Variations between case managers in both assessing and recording client needs, and between researchers in gathering the adult day care file data are also sources of probable decreased reliability of the data.

(3) Variations between interviewers in collecting primary data gathered by means of caregiver and client questionnaires was another probable source of decreased data reliability.

(4) The data represent a one time survey and analysis of the population.

Limitations of sample size, data accuracy and data collector differences may have also biased the sample. Limitation of sample size restricted the use of statistical measures of association of study variables and the statistical comparison of population means. Based on these limitations, there must be caution in generalizing results. On the other hand, approaching secondary data sources and primary data sources—providers and beneficiaries—resulted in the collection of data reflective of varied perspectives and experiences.

END NOTES - CHAPTER 3

Aiken, Michael and Jerald Hage. *"Organizational Interdependence and Intra-Organizational Structure." American Sociological Review, 33, No 6 (December 1968), pp. 912-930.*

Block, Fred, Richard Cloward, Barbara Ehrenreich and Frances Fox Piven. *The Mean Season. New York: Pantheon Books, 1987.*

Brody, Elaine M. *"Parent Care as a Normative Family Stress." The Gerontologist, 25, No 1 (1985, pp. 19-29.*

Brody Elaine, m. *"Women in the Middle and Family Help to Older People." The Gerontologist, 21, No 5 (1981), pp. 471-480.*

Brody, Elaine M. and C. Schoonover. *"Patterns of Care for the Dependent Elderly When Daughters Work and When They Do Not." The Gerontologist, 26, No 4 (1986), pp. 372-381.*

Brody, Stanley. *"Strategic Planning: The Catastrophic Approach." The Gerontologist, 27, No 2 (1987), pp. 131-138.*

Brubaker, Timothy. *Aging, Health and Family: Long Term Care. Beverly Hills, CA: Sage Publications, 1987.*

Butler, Robert N., M. D. and Myrna I. Lewis. *Aging & Mental Health. St. Louis, MO: The C. V. Mosby Co., 1982.*

Cantor, Marjorie H. *"The Informal Support System, Its Relevance in the Lives of the Elderly." In Aging and Society. Eds. E. Borgatta and N. McClusky. Beverly Hills, CA: Sage Publications, 1980, pp. 111-146.*

Cantor, Marjorie H. *"Neighbors and Friends: An Overlooked Resource in the Informal Support System." Research on Aging, 1, No 30 (1979), pp. 434-463.*

Cantor, Marjorie. *"Strain Among Caregivers: A Study of Experience in the United States." The Gerontologist, 23, No 66 (1983), pp. 597-603.*

Clark, Robert F. "The Costs and Benefits of Community Care: A Perspective from the Channeling Demonstration." *Pride Institute Journal of Long Term Home Health Care*, 6, No 2 (Spring 1987), pp. 3-13.

Crystal, Stephen, *America's Old Age Crisis*. New York: Basic Books, 1982.

Dobrof, Rose and Eugene Litwak. *Maintenance of Family Ties of Long-Term Care Patients: Theory and Guide to Practice*. Rockville, MD: National Institute of Mental Health, 1977, pp. 1-79.

Dono, John, C. M. Falbe, B. L. Kail, E. Litwak et al. "Primary Groups in Old Age." *Research on Aging*, 1, No 4 (1979), pp. 403-433.

Ficke, Susan Coombs, ed. *An Orientation to the Older Americans Act*. Revised Edition. Washington, DC: National Association of State Units on Aging, July 1985.

Finestone, S. and A. J. Kahn. "The Design of Research." *Social Work Research*. Ed. M. A. Polansky. Chicago, IL: The University of Chicago Press, 1975.

Gortner, Harold F. et al. *Organization Theory: A Public Perspective*, Chicago, IL: The Dorsey Press, 1987.

Hardin, Thomas. "No Center Is An Island: Network Building in Adult Day Care." *Adult Day Care Quarterly*. Washington, DC: National Institute of Adult Day Care, a membership unit of the National Council on the Aging, 2, No 4 (1987).

Harlow, Karen S. et al. "Use of Formal and Informal Services in Community-Based Long-Term Care." *Proceedings of the 1987 Public Health Conference on Records and Statistics. Data for An Aging Population*. Washington, DC: U. S. Department of Health and Human Services, December 1987, pp. 93-98.

Horowitz, A. and Rose Dobrof. "The Role of Families in Providing Long-Term Care to the Frail and Chronically Ill Elderly Living in the Community." Final Report Submitted to the Health Care Financing Administration Grant #18-P-97541/2-02. New York: Brookdale Center on Aging of Hunter College, 1982.

Kane, Rosalie and Robert Kane. <u>Long-Term Care: Principles, Programs, and Policies</u>. *New York: Springer Publishing Co., 1987.*

Kane Rosalie. *"Long-Term Care." In* <u>Encyclopedia of Social Work</u>*, Vol 2, 18th edition. Silver Spring, MD: National Association of Social Workers, 1987, pp. 59-72.*

Kaye, Lenard W. *"Home Care Services for Older People: An Organizational Analysis of Provider Experience." Diss. Columbia University, 1982.*

Kaye, Lenard W. and Patricia M. Kirwin. <u>An Evaluation of Adult Day Care Programs in Pennsylvania</u>. *Bryn Mawr, PA: The Bryn Mawr College Graduate School of Social Work and Social Research, July 1989. Pennsylvania Department of Aging Contract No 871003.*

Kemper, Peter, Robert Applebaum et al. *"Community Care Demonstrations: What Have We Learned."* <u>Health Care Financing Review</u>*, 8, No 4 (Summer 1987), pp. 87-100.*

Kirwin, Patricia M. <u>An Evaluation of the Relationship Between Formal and Informal Systems in the Service of Adult Day Care for the Frail Elderly</u> *(Doctoral dissertation, Bryn Mawr College, 1989).* <u>Dissertation Abstracts International</u>*, 50, 2245A.*

Kirwin, Patricia M. *"You Heard What I Said, but Do You Know What I Meant?"* <u>Generations</u>*, in press.*

Litwak, Eugene. *"Agency and Family Linkages in Providing Services." In* <u>Reaching People: The Structure of Neighborhood Services</u>*, Vol 3.* <u>Social Service Delivery Systems: An International Annual</u>*. Eds. D. Thurz and J. Vigilante. Beverly Hills, CA: Sage Publications, 1978, pp. 59-95.*

Litwak, Eugene. <u>Helping the Elderly</u>. *New York: The Guilford Press, 1985.*

McKillip, Jack. <u>Need Analysis</u>. *Beverly Hills, CA: Sage Publications, 1987.*

O'Brien, Carole Lium. <u>Adult Day Care, A Practical Guide</u>. *California: Wadsworth Health Services, 1982.*

Perrow, Charles. <u>Complex Organizations: A Critical Essay</u>. *New York: Random House, 1979.*

Robinson, James C. "Philosophical Origins of the Economic Valuation of
    Life." *The Milbank Memorial Fund Quarterly*, 64, No 1 (1986), pp.
    133-155.

Rossi, Peter H. and Howard E. Freeman. *Evaluation: A Systematic Approach*. Beverly Hills, CA: Sage Publications, 1982.

Shanas, Ethel. "The Family as a Social Support System in Old Age." *The
    Gerontologist*, 19, No 2 (1979b), pp. 169-174.

Shanas, Ethel. "Social Myth as Hypothesis: The Case of the Family Relations
    of Old People." *The Gerontologist*, 19, No 1 (1979a), pp. 3-9.

Springer, Dianne and Timothy Brubaker. *Family Caregivers and Dependent
    Elderly*. Beverly Hills, CA: Sage Publications, 1984.

Stephens, Susan A. and Jan B. Christianson. *Informal Care of the Elderly*.
    Lexington, MA: D. C. Heath and Company, 1986.

Stoller, E. P. "Parental Caregiving by Adult Children." *Journal of Marriage
    and the Family*. (November 1983), pp. 851-858.

Stone, Robyn et al. *Caregivers of the Frail Elderly: A National Profile*.
    Washington, DC: U. S. Department of Health and Human Services,
    1987.

Sussman, Marvin. "Bureaucracy and the Elderly Individual: An Organizational Linkage Perspective." In *Family Bureaucracy and the Elderly*.
    Eds. E. Shanas and M. Sussman. Durham, NC: Duke University
    Press, 1977.

U. S. Senate Special Committee on Aging in conjunction with the American
    Association of Retired Persons. *Aging America: Trends and Projections*. Washington, DC, 1984.

Von Behren, Ruth. *Adult Day Care in America: Summary of a National
    Survey*. Washington, DC: National Council on Aging, National
    Institute on Adult Daycare, October 1986.

Weber, Max. *The Theory of Social Economic Organizations*. Eds. and
    translation A. M. Henderson and T. Parsons. New York: Oxford
    University Press, 1947.

Weiler, P. G. and E. Rathbone-McCuan. *Adult Day Care: Community Work with the Elderly.* New York: Springer Publishing Co., 1978.

Weissert, William. "Rationales for Public Health Insurance Coverage of Geriatric Day Care: Issues, Options and Impacts." *Journal of Health Politics, Policy and Law,* 3, No 4 (Winter 1979), pp. 555-567.

Weissert, William. "Two Models of Geriatric Day Care: Findings from a Comparative Study." *The Gerontologist,* 16, No 5 (1976), pp. 420-427.

Wilson, Albert J. *Social Services for Older Persons.* Boston, MA: Little, Brown and Company, 1984.

CHAPTER 4

STUDY FINDINGS

"What was so shocking in Galileo's
astronomical discoveries? That there
was so much going on in the sky and
the astronomical order was so much
less definite than one could happily
believe before."
Wolfgang Kohler

This chapter presents descriptive and interpretative data responsive to the study's questions as detailed in Chapter 3. The findings were derived from both original and secondary informational sources. Results which address the following study questions are included:

(1)   Client factors associated with being at-risk of institutionalization;

(2)   Caregiving tasks performed by both the formal organization, and the informal system of caregiving;

(3)   The total cost of publicly funded social services received by adult day care participants through area agencies on aging;

(4)   The extent to which the formal system of care succeeds over time in working with the informal caregiving network to maintain the frail elder in the community; and particularly,

(5)   The results of testing Litwak's theory of complementary roles at the community level.

However prior to the presentation of these findings, profiles of the different respondent groups and county demographic trends will be presented. With the exception of demographic trends, the profiles are based on responses to a series of questions included in the study instruments (N=5) used in this analysis: area agency on agency questionnaires (N=3); adult day care program director questionnaires (N=13); caregiver (N=20) and client interview protocols (N=13); and, client file data collection instruments (N=134).

RESPONDENT GROUP PROFILES

Table 4.1, County Demographic Trends, highlights the projected growth of the over 65 population for the 3 counties included in this study. In 1993, the over 65 population in the 3 counties, is projected to total 381,285. The over 65 population will comprise 15.5 percent of the population in Philadelphia County, 15.9 percent in Delaware County, and 11.3 percent in Chester County. As the table demonstrates, the segment of the population over 65 is increasing in both number and as a percent of population. It is the projected growth in this segment of the population that has engaged society's interest in developing a sound long-term care knowledge base.

Caregiver and adult day care client socio-demographic data were gathered through the interview process and through client file data collection. Table 4.2, Socio-Demographic Characteristics of Interviewed Caregivers, and Table 4.3, Socio-Demographic Characteristics of Interviewed Clients, profile the interview data results for these two respondent groups. As Table 4.2 discloses, the age for the interviewed caregivers ranged from 32-83 years with a mean of 64. Spouses accounted for 60 percent of this group while daughters comprised an additional 30 percent. Seventy percent of the interviewees had been providing care for 4 to 6 years. Forty-seven percent of these caregivers were employed. Clients, in 75 percent of the cases, lived with their caregiver and ranged in age from 63 to 88 years with a mean of 76.

TABLE 4.1
COUNTY DEMOGRAPHIC TRENDS[1]

	1980 Census		1988 Est.		1993 Proj.	
	Number	% of Total Pop.	Number	% of Total Pop.	Number	% of Total Pop.
Chester County[2]						
Age: 55-64	30,222	9.5%	30,224	8.5%	29,094	7.8%
65 +	28,686	9.1%	37,374	10.6%	42,312	11.3%
Total	58,908	18.6%	67,598	19.1%	71,406	19.1%
County Med. Age	30.5		33.0		34.7	
Delaware County[3]						
Age: 55-64	67,695	12.2%	62,161	11.2%	56,512	10.1%
65 +	71,322	12.9%	83,416	15.0%	88,543	15.9%
Total	139,017	25.1%	145,577	26.2%	145,055	26.0%
County Med. Age	32.5		34.8		36.5	
Philadelphia County[3]						
Age: 55-64	189,310	11.2%	165,020	10.0%	147,017	9.1%
65+	237,370	14.1%	249,083	15.2%	250,430	15.5%
Total	421,680	25.3%	414,103	25.2%	397,447	24.6%
County Med. Age	31.7		33.2		34.5	

[1] Source: 1980 Census, July 1, 1988 UDS Estimates (DTA) Urban Decision Systems, P.O. Box 25953, Los Angeles, CA 90025 (213) 820-8931, 01/12/89.

[2] Chester County total population in 1980 census = 316,660 (758 sq. miles).

[3] Delaware County total population in 1980 census = 555,007 (184 sq. miles).

[4] Philadelphia County total population in 1980 census = 1,688,210 (136 sq. miles).

TABLE 4.2
SOCIO-DEMOGRAPHIC CHARACTERISTICS OF
INTERVIEWED CAREGIVERS
(N=20)

Variable	N	%	Mean	Range
Age of Caregiver			63.94	32-83
Age of Client			75.68	63-88
Sex of Caregiver				
Female	13	65.00		
Male	7	35.00		
Total	20	100.00		
Sex of Client				
Female	14	70.00		
Male	6	30.00		
Total	20	100.00		
County				
Philco[1]	11	55.00		
Delco[2]	8	40.00		
Chesco[3]	1	5.00		
Total	20	100.00		
Relationship to Client				
Spouse	12	60.00		
Daughter	6	30.00		
Son-in-Law	1	5.00		
Other	1	5.00		
Total	20	100.00		
Marital Status				
Married	16	80.00		
Widowed/Single	4	20.00		
Total	20	100.00		
Years of Caregiving				
1 To 3 Years	4	20.00		
4 To 6 Years	14	70.00		
7 To 10 Years	2	10.00		
Total	20	100.00	4.55	1-10
Client Lived With Caregiver				
Yes	15	75.00		
No	5	25.00		
Total	20	100.00		

TABLE 4.2 (Continued)
SOCIO-DEMOGRAPHIC CHARACTERISTICS OF
INTERVIEWED CAREGIVERS
(N=20)

Variable	N	%	Mean	Range
Caregiver Employment				
Yes	9	47.37		
Parttime - (5)[4]				
Full Time - (4)				
No	10	52.63		
Total	19	100.00		
Caregiver Learned About ADC				
Agency Referral[5]	10	50.00		
Son/Daughter	5	25.00		
AAA	3	15.00		
Co-Workers	1	5.00		
ADRDA[6]	1	5.00		
Total	20	100.00		
Helpful Aspects of ADC				
Respite	18	75.00		
Transportation	4	16.67		
Allows Caregiver to work	2	8.33		
Total	24	100.00		
Client Still in ADC				
Yes	9	45.00		
No	11	55.00		
Total	20	100.00		
Location of Clients No Longer in ADC				
In Own Home With Other	4	36.36		
Deceased	3	27.27		
In Rehab./Nursing Home	2	18.18		
In Someone Else's Home	1	9.09		
In Own Home And Alone	1	9.09		
Total	11	99.99		

[1] Philadelphia County.
[2] Delaware County.
[3] Chester County.
[4] Two of 5 reporting parttime employment had worked fulltime before becoming caregivers.
[5] Community agencies primarily include home health care agencies, Visiting Nurse Associations, and hospitals.
[6] Alzheimers Disease and Related Disorders Association.

TABLE 4.3
SOCIO-DEMOGRAPHIC CHARACTERISTICS OF INTERVIEWED CLIENTS
(N=13)

Variable	N	%	Mean	Range
Age			76.25	67-90
Sex				
Female	8	61.54		
Male	5	38.46		
Total	13	100.00		
County				
Chesco[2]	0	.00		
Delco[3]	6	46.15		
Philco[4]	7	53.85		
Total	13	100.00		
Attendance				
Days Per Week			2.61	1-5
Client Learned of AFC From				
Daughter	5	41.67		
Agency Referral	5	41.67		
Spouse	1	8.33		
Other	1	8.33		
Total	12[1]	100.00		
Client Still Attends ADC				
Yes	8	61.54		
No	5	38.46		
Total	13	100.00		
Primary Reason for Participation				
Socialization	3	37.50		
Respite For Client	3	37.50		
Respite For Caregiver	2	25.00		
Total	8[5]	100.00		
Satisfaction with Program				
Yes	11	91.67		
No	1	8.33		
Total	12[1]	100.00		

[1] One missing response.
[2] Chester County.
[3] Delaware County.
[4] Philadelphia County.
[5] Five missing responses.

As recounted in Table 4.3, clients were predominantly female with a mean age of 76.3 years. They attended an adult day care program an average of 2.6 days per week. Their primary reasons for attending the program were socialization and respite for themselves and for their caregivers.

Data collected from AAA client files, as set forth in Table 4.4, reflect a slightly higher client mean age, 77.6, with 60 percent of the 134 clients being unmarried. Again, females outnumbered males. As cited in Chapter 2, the risk of nursing home placement is known to increase with age and is positively associated with living alone. The median income per month for this population was $600.

The poverty income level in Pennsylvania during the study period was $481; however, it is common for social service agencies to use 125 percent of the poverty level or $601 per month as an income floor. Therefore, 50 percent of this study's population was at or below the commonly defined state level of poverty in 1986-1987.

The importance of the informal network in initiating and perhaps negotiating relationships between the client and the formal system of care can be seen in Table 4.4 which indicates that, in this study, relatives were the source of client referral to the area agency on aging 50 percent of the time. The second most commonly cited source of referrals was another community agency. Specifically cited agencies included a rehabilitation center, home health care agencies, and the Visiting Nurse Association. It is interesting that adult day care programs and senior centers refer clients to the area agencies on aging. This suggests that these community programs are more visible and may act as magnets attracting vulnerable community elders and their caregivers to the less visible aging network and its array of contracted services. Table 4.4 also discloses the relatives' basis for initiating the relationship with the area agency. While more than one reason for initiating formal service may have been selected, in 42 percent of the cases relief of caregivers was a selected reason.

Adult day care program staff members were unanimous in believing that their programs delayed institutionalization and reduced caregiver stress as related in Table 4.5, Socio-Demographic Characteristics of Adult Day Care Programs Funded by Three Area Agencies on Aging. The number of clients participating in each program ranged from 6 to 150 per day at a mean cost per client per day of $25.57.

TABLE 4.4
SOCIO-DEMOGRAPHIC CHARACTERISTICS OF CLIENT FILE DATA
(N=134)

Variable	N	%	Mean	Range
Age			77.62	54-97
Sex				
Female	76	57.14		
Male	57	42.80		
Total	133	100.00		
County				
Chesco[1]	10	7.46		
Delco[2]	43	32.09		
Philco[3]	81	60.45		
Total	134	100.00		
Marital Status				
Widowed/Single	75	60.48		
Married	49	39.52		
Total	124	100.00		
Living Arrangement				
Lives with Other(s)	116	90.60		
Lives Alone	12	9.40		
Total	128	100.00		
Basis for Clients' Initial AAA Service Request[4]				
Relief of Caregivers	66	42.04		
Maintenance of Self-Care	32	20.38		
Awaiting Nurs. Home Pl.	15	9.55		
Change in Health Status	13	8.28		
Rehabilitation	12	7.64		
Socialization	9	5.73		
Other	5	3.18		
Convalescence	4	2.56		
Limited Self-Care Ability	1	.64		
Total[5]	157	100.00		
Referral Source				
Relative	41	50.00		
Community Agency[6]	12	14.63		
ADC Program	10	12.20		
Hospital	8	9.75		
Senior Center	7	8.54		
Nursing Home Pre-Adm.	4	4.88		
Total	82	100.00		

TABLE 4.4 (Continued)
SOCIO-DEMOGRAPHIC CHARACTERISTICS OF CLIENT FILE DATA
(N=134)

Variable	N	%	Mean	Range
Indicated Client Social Supports				
Daughter	94	32.08		
Son	52	17.75		
Spouse	50	17.06		
Siblings	28	9.56		
Grandchildren	17	5.80		
Neighbor/Friend	15	5.12		
Other Relative	12	4.10		
Other	9	3.07		
Son-in-Law	8	2.73		
Daughter-in-Law	4	1.37		
ADC Staff	2	.68		
Other Agency	2	.68		
Total	293	100.00	2.19	0-6
Income Per Month				
$ 0	4	3.20		
$ 200-399	31	24.80		
400-599	27	21.60		
600-799	25	20.00		
800-999	14	11.20		
1000-1999	7	5.60		
1200-1399	6	4.80		
1400-1599	2	1.60		
1600 & Over	9	7.20		
Total	125	100.00	$600.00	$0-3,000

[1] Chester County.
[2] Delaware County.
[3] Philadelphia County.
[4] More than one category was selected in some cases.
[5] The basis for initial service request was not indicated in 17 cases.
[6] E.g., home health care agencies, Visiting Nurse Associations, and hospitals.

TABLE 4.5
SOCIO-DEMOGRAPHIC CHARACTERISTICS OF ADULT DAY CARE
PROGRAMS FUNDED BY THREE AREA AGENCIES ON AGING
(N=13)

Variable	N	%	Mean	Range
Programs by County				
Chesco[1]	4	30.77		
Delco[2]	4	30.77		
Philco[3]	5	38.46		
Total	13	100.00		
Unduplicated ADC Clients by County				
Chesco	49	7.67		
Delco	183	28.64		
Philco	407	63.69		
Total	639	100.00	213.00	49-407
Unduplicated Clients by Program			61.84	6-150
Average Cost Per Day Per Client				
Chesco	$19.56			
Delco	30.53			
Philco	26.62			
Total	$76.71		$25.57	$10.25-42.88
Program Model[4]				
Social	7	58.33		
Medical	5	41.67		
Total	12[5]	100.00		
Type of Area Agency Funding				
Program Funded[6]	5	38.46		
Client Funded[7]	8	61.54		
Total	13	100.00		
Convinced ADC Delayed Institutionalization				
Yes	13	100.00		
No	0	.00		
Total	13	100.00		
Convinced ADC Reduced Caregiver Stress				
Yes	13	100.00		
No	0	.00		
Total	13	100.00		

[1] Chester County.
[2] Delaware County.
[3] Philadelphia County.
[4] As indicated by individual program's response.
[5] One missing response.
[6] Area agency funds the adult day care program.
[7] Area agency funds the adult day care client.

The program officers for area agencies on aging, which funded the programs sampled in this study, were also unanimous in their conviction that day care delayed institutionalization and reduced stress for caregivers as seen in Table 4.6, Socio-Demographic Characteristics of Area Agencies on Aging Funding Adult Day Care Programs. In addition, this table specifies the total cost of all area agency services received by adult day care participants in 1986-1987. As shown, the range of cost is $27 to $3,689 per client for Chester and Delaware Counties. When Philadelphia County is included, the range becomes stratospheric, rising to $59,750.

For a host of reasons, Philadelphia County is extraordinarily unique and cannot, without understanding this uniqueness, be compared with Chester and Delaware Counties. Chester and Delaware Counties are representative of the range of counties comprising the Commonwealth as seen in the state-wide study from which the data in this study is but a segment (Kaye and Kirwin, 1989). Philadelphia is a singular county. Indeed, the area agency for the county is larger than the Pennsylvania Department of Aging in number of staff and size of facility. Philadelphia was 1 of 10 national sites chosen for the Channeling demonstration, a rigorous nationwide test of the viability of institutional diversion for at-risk clients through the utilization of case management and enhanced community-based care. In this demonstration, Medicare dollars were available for purchasing medical services and supplies as well as food supplements. This county was also one of the first counties in the Commonwealth to be funded by the Pennsylvania Department of Aging to perform pre-admission assessments for those seeking nursing home placement. This program is known as the LAMP Program (Long-Term Care Assessment and Management Program). Both Channeling and LAMP significantly extended the array of social and medical services and supplies which the Philadelphia Corporation of Aging (PCA) was able to deliver to clients. This also increased costs making an uninformed comparison between Philadelphia and counties delivering a more commonly delivered continuum of services inappropriate.

In addition, PCA was unable to submit 1986-1987 study year service costs disaggregated from client cost incurred in previous years. As explained by an agency data analyst, at the close of each fiscal year (June 30th), the cost of services for that year is "bucketed" into the

TABLE 4.6
SOCIO-DEMOGRAPHIC CHARACTERISTICS OF AREA AGENCIES ON AGING
FUNDING ADULT DAY CARE PROGRAMS
(N=3)

Variable	Number	Total Cost	Mean	Range
Cost of All AAA Services Rec'd				
By Sampled ADC Clients in '86-'87				
Chester County	10	$14,266	$1,427	$138-3,591
Delaware County	43	73,481	1,709	27-3,689
Philadelphia County[1]	383	2,484,881	6,488	182-59,750
Total	436	$2,572,628	$5,901	
AAAs Convinced ADC Delayed Institutionalization				
Yes	3			
No	0			
Total	3			
AAAs Convinced ADC Reduced Stress for Caregivers				
Yes	3			
No	0			
Total	3			

[1] Philadelphia County's figures differ from Chester County and Delaware County in the following ways: a) Philadelphia was unable to submit 1986-87 costs disaggregated from client costs incurred in previous years; therefore, the County submitted 1987-88 costs which, generally, are no more than 3% higher than 1986-87 costs due to an agency funding cap; b) Philadelphia County provided costs for the total 1986-87 ADC population served; whereas, Chester and Delaware Counties provided costs for this study's population; and, c) Philadelphia County, as a national Channeling demonstration site and state LAMP location received funding from sources unavailable to other study counties and therefore, delivered a wider array of services than other counties.

cost of services received in previous years by client. However, the agency was able to provide the cost of services delivered during 1987-1988. These figures, generally speaking, were less than 3 percent above costs for the study year due to a funding cap reflecting the 3 percent increase in funding the agency received from the Pennsylvania Department of Aging for 1987-1988.

In addition, whereas Chester and Delaware Counties submitted, for study purposes, the cost of services received by this study's population, Philadelphia submitted costs for nearly every adult day care participant. The total program population, as indicated by PCA, was 401 while cost data for 383 clients was actually submitted for study analysis.

Still, there is another reason which makes an uninformed comparison of Philadelphia County's cost of service with Chester, Delaware, or, indeed, any other county in the Commonwealth inappropriate. In Philadelphia, transportation, an integral component of day care has been a difficult service to efficiently deliver. The problems experienced in delivering transportation led PCA to institute a new coordination system under the auspices of KETRON, Inc. in July 1988. The problems with transportation involve regulations of the 203 Shared Ride Program, the lack of a coordinated city-wide transportation system, the unique needs of the population requiring service, and the higher than average service costs existing in Philadelphia, according to PCA spokespersons and the agency's Fall/Winter 1989 quarterly newsletter Update (available through the Philadelphia Corporation of Aging).

In 1986-1987, adult day care transportation for nearly 18 percent of the population was classed as an "escort, non-ambulatory, non-independent" sector of service. This sector of the transportation service, a very costly model, was contracted for in early 1986, with the expectation that a significant percent of the day care population would use the service. When this did not happen, the total expended cost for this contract was divided among those agency clients who did use the service. The astronomical unit cost for this highly individualized service was $170.80 per unit. One client used 283 units ($48,336.40 total cost) while another required 342 units for a total cost of $58,413.60. It bears repeating: this is not a representative service cost. It reflects an aberration related to the county's long-standing transportation service delivery problems and an unfortunate contractual method of funding. According to a PCA analyst, the funding for the "escort, non-ambulatory, non-independent" contract did not depend on the number of persons who actually used the service, but on an estimated number of potential users.

To summarize, it is incongruous to directly compare Philadelphia County data with those of the other counties in this study for the following reasons: (1) Philadelphia's service costs represent a different year than used for the other counties; (2) One county model of transportation service is uncommonly costly and skews the comparison; and, (3) Philadelphia delivers an array of social and medical services not available in other counties. However, because of its national reputation, sphere of service, and leadership in the Commonwealth, an informed comparison of Philadelphia data with those of Chester and Delaware Counties is appropriate for examining the questions posed in this analysis.

FINDINGS

Questions this study addressed regarding the bureaucratic concern of economic effectiveness included the following:

(1)   Do these adult day care programs serve the people they were established to serve, the frailest, those most likely to be institutionalized?

(2)   Does the informal system reduce, over time, the amount of caregiving it gives to those frail elders who participate in adult day care?

(3)   How does the cost of all social services received by the clients in this study compare with the publicly funded Medicaid per diem county nursing home rate?

(4)   In regard to the above questions, are there significant differences between Model I (medical model) and Model II (social model) program variables?

Do these adult day care programs serve the people they were established to serve, the frailest, those most likely to be institutionalized?

Client factors associated with at-risk of institutionalization in this study were measured by the following: (A) high at-risk of institutionalization was defined as requiring assistance in 3 of 4 activities of daily living (ADL) and in at least one instrumental activity of daily living (IADL); (B) moderate at-risk of institutionalization was defined as requiring assistance in 1 to 2 activities of daily living and at least in one instrumental activity of daily living.

As Table 4.7, Client ADL and IADL Factors Associated with Being At-Risk of Institutionalization, indicates 67 percent of this population at the time of the assessment needed assistance with bathing; 55 percent with dressing; 43 percent with walking; and 16 percent with eating. A National Center for Health Statistics (NCHS) report based on a national survey of older people living in the community done in 1984, ("Aging in the Eighties: Functional Limitations of Individuals Age 65 Years and Over") found that the order of need in personal care activities and home management activities were identical to that indicated in this analysis (Fowles, 1988). That is, the tasks appear to be listed in a descending order of difficulty, i.e., bathing is the most difficult activity to perform without assistance and eating the least difficult. Clients, therefore, who have difficulty feeding themselves will most likely have difficulty in performing any other listed activity of daily living. The percent of need for each activity was, in this study, significantly higher than in the NCHS study.

Table 4.7 also discloses this population's high level of need for assistance in performing IADL. Ninety-three per cent or more of the population required assistance in performing 5 of these activities: Shopping, cooking, housekeeping, laundry, and traveling. Indeed, when the data were disaggregated, only 1 client, for whom data were

TABLE 4.7

CLIENT ADL AND IADL FACTORS ASSOCIATED WITH BEING AT-RISK OF
INSTITUTIONALIZATION[1]

	Can Handle Alone		Needs Assistance	
	N	%	N	%
ADL				
Eating (N=131)	110	83.97	21	16.03
Walking/Getting Around (N=131)	75	57.25	56	42.75
Dressing (N=132)	59	44.70	73	55.30
Bathing & Shaving (N=130)	43	33.08	87	66.92
IADL				
Telephoning (N=127)	55	43.31	72	56.69
Handling Finances (N=124)	14	11.29	110	88.71
Home Repairs (N=111)	13	11.71	98	88.29
Heavy Housekeeping (N=124)	12	9.68	112	90.32
Light Housekeeping (N=122)	9	7.38	113	92.62
Cooking (N=125)	9	7.20	116	92.80
Shopping (N=127)	9	7.09	118	92.91
Traveling (N=121)	7	5.79	114	94.21
Laundry (N=125)	7	5.60	118	94.40

[1] As indicated in client file data.

collected, did not require assistance with at least 1 IADL. It therefore appears that a person's need for assistance in performing IADL may be an even more meaningful measure of the concept "at-risk" than the need for assistance in ADL. Those who cannot shop or cook for themselves are not likely to maintain physical health without assistance and, therefore, may be at significant risk.

When disaggregated, the data revealed that 53 clients required assistance in 3 to 4 ADL and in at least 1 IADL. These clients (40 percent), by this study's definition were at high risk of institutionalization. Forty-one clients were identified as requiring assistance in 1 or 2 ADL and at least in 1 IADL. That is, an additional 30 percent of the clients were at moderate risk of institutionalization. Forty clients (30 percent) did not require assistance in any ADL and were, therefore, at low risk of institutionalization as measured in this study (See Table 4.14, p. 150).

In summary, it would appear that a total of 70 percent of this study's population were at moderate to high risk of institutional placement. The number of IADL in which a client needs assistance appears, in this study, to be a more powerful measurement of at-risk of institutionalization than deprivations in ADL.

Does the informal system reduce, over time, the amount of caregiving it gives to those frail elders who participate in adult day care?

Information available on informal caregiving in collected file data indicated, for the most part, the number of available caregivers and the activities they performed at the time of the assessment; however, at subsequent client reassessments, comments on the informal system were negligible. From the perspective of the formal organization, this represents a limitation in this study's ability to analyze the consistency of informal caregiving over time when formal services are introduced. (Note: This limitation existed across all counties in the state-wide study and, therefore, represents an area where training, technical assistance, and/or monitoring is needed). However, in Table 4.4, which reflects client file data characteristics, it was shown that for this study's population, there was an average of 2.20 social supports at the time of assessment.

From these same data records, we know that some clients and their caregivers received area agency services, including adult day care, beginning in 1980. Cases began to close in 1985 as shown in Table 4.8, Year of Case Opening and Case Closing for Study Population, which suggests that the formal system of care assisted the informal caregiving network in maintaining the frail elder in the community over that period of time between 1980-1985. Indeed as Table 4.9, Reason for Case Closing, highlights, 74 percent of case closings were due to death or entry into a nursing home.

A second indication of the sustained relationship of informal networks and the formal system is the response of caregivers to the question, "When the client had been receiving ADC services had the caregiver found that they provided care more or less often than they did before outside help was provided"? The possible responses were: more often, about the same, and less often. Of the 12 caregivers who responded to this question, 75 percent indicated they were providing about as much or more care than they provided before receiving the service of day care. This would seem to further indicate that adult day care supplements rather than supplants informal caregiving for this population. All 20 caregivers indicated that day care reduced the stress of caregiving. Sixty percent indicated that day care reduced their stress "very much so." Nine of the interviewed caregivers were employed and, in 75 percent of the cases, the client was living with the caregiver. The average number of years care had been provided was 4.6. As cited in Chapter 2, each of these variables is known to contribute to the stress of caregiving.

A third indication of the sustained relationship between the informal network and formal system emerged in the interview process. When caregivers were asked what they felt the client would do after leaving adult day care, the most frequent response was that the client would stay in their home. It appeared difficult for clients to project a future, to plan for a time after day care. Indeed, when asked how long the client would participate in adult day care, the responses ranged from "as long as the client is accepted" to "as long as I can afford it."

In summary, from the data available for analysis, it appears that the informal system does not reduce over time the amount of caregiving it provides to those frail elders who may be adult day care participants. More complete area agency on aging file documentation on the provision of care by the informal network over time might strengthen and support this finding. Significantly, 75 percent of the interviewed caregivers stated that they were still providing about as much or more care while using the service of day care as they had before using the service.

These data tend to support Cantor's theory of compensatory social supports. This theory asserts that it is only when due to physical, financial or emotional factors caregivers can no longer continue to provide care without assistance that they will accept formal support (1980; Cantor and Little, 1985).

TABLE 4.8
YEAR OF CASE OPENING AND CASE CLOSING FOR STUDY POPULATION[1]

	Year Case Opened (N=134)	Year Case Closed (N=74)
1980	1	
1981	1	
1982	1	
1983	4	
1984	8	
1985	36	3
1986	60	25
1987	23	46
Total	134	74

[1] As indicated in client file data.

TABLE 4.9
REASON FOR CASE CLOSING[1]
(N=71)

	N	%
Death of client	20	28.17
Entered nursing home	33	46.48
Moved	6	8.45
Program no longer useful	6	8.45
Using other program	1	1.41
Other	5	7.04
Total	71	100.00

[1] As indicated in client file data.

How does the cost of all social services received by the clients in this study compare with the publicly funded Medicaid per diem county nursing home rate?

The mean cost per client for all services delivered by area agencies on aging for this population was $1,427 for Chester County, $1,709 for Delaware County, and $6,488 for Philadelphia County. This is summarized in Tables 4.10, 4.11, and 4.12 which list all area agency social services adult day care participants received by county. It is surprising to note how few services, other than day care, these frail clients and their caregivers received in Chester and Delaware Counties.   As Table 4.10, Chester County AAA Program Costs, demonstrates, just 2 of the 10 Chester County day care participants sampled in this study received any additional assistance, and these were *de minimus*.

In Delaware County, additional services such as home delivered meals, respite care, homemaker, mental health counseling, and attendant care are listed under "other" in Table 4.11, Delaware County AAA Program Costs. The listed transportation and meal costs were received by the day care participants not as additional services, but as components of day care. Therefore, these costs are to be included in the cost of day care services. Consequently, the cost for additional agency services received by day care clients was small: less than $410 per year per client.

In Philadelphia, congregate meals, center services, and transportation, as in Delaware County, were received by day care participants as program components. These costs, therefore, should be included in total day care program costs. Additional agency services received by day care clients averaged $1,837 per client. The wider array of services available in Philadelphia than in other counties, some of which were extraordinarily expensive, is manifested by a comparison across these counties.

By examining Table 4.13, Comparative Cost Per Client Per Diem by County, we can compare the cost of all social services funded by area agencies received by this study's population to Medicaid per diem rates. Because Medicaid rates are set per diem, adult day care costs are also stated per diem. These costs reflect actual program

TABLE 4.10
CHESTER COUNTY AAA PROGRAM COSTS [1,2,3,4]
(N=10)

Clients		ADC	Homemaker	Respite	Total
103		$ 3,591			$ 3,591
104		1,273			1,273
105		3,000			3,000
106		970			970
107		1,177	$ 837		2,014
108		1,200			1,200
109		250			250
110		1,402			1,402
112		430			430
113		42		$ 96	138
	TOTAL	$ 13,333	$ 837	$ 96	$ 14,266
	AVERAGE	$ 1,333	$ 84	$ 10	$ 1,427

[1] Fiscal Year 1986-1987
[2] Additional cost for transportation not provided.
[3] Additional cost for service management not provided.
[4] Client contributions for service not provided.

TABLE 4.11
DELAWARE COUNTY AAA PROGRAM COSTS[1] (N=43)

		P R O G R A M S		F Y 1 9 8 6 - 8 7			
Client	Transport.	Meals	ADC	Other[2]	Total	Less Contribs.	Net Cost
1	$ 0	$ 174	$ 2,388	$ 440	$ 3,002	$ 0	$ 3,002
2	0	170	2,025		2,195	830	1,365
3	242	277	3,263	435	4,216	235	3,981
4	6	35	425		466	300	166
5	13	59	725		797	160	637
6	0	285	3,475		3,760	1,390	2,370
7	342	387	4,750		5,479	1,790	3,689
8	313	357	4,350		5,020	1,600	3,420
9	43	72	875	378	1,368		1,368
10	11	12	150		173	60	113
11	85	174	2,075		2,334	520	1,814
12	0	176	2,150	50	2,376	140	2,236
13	0	18	2,213		2,231	500	1,731
14	0	4	38		42	20	22
15	2	123	1,538		1,662	410	1,252
16	0	18	225	219	462	80	382
17	23	41	488		552	120	432
18	0	2	25		27	0	27
19	0	2	25		27	10	17
20	0	14	163		177	70	107
21	5	14	150		170	70	100
22	117	131	1,625	465	2,338	640	1,698
23	4	4	50		58	0	58
24	0	105	1,288		1,392	270	1,122
25	0	21	250	270	541	100	441
26	31	35	425	19	509	0	509
27	108	121	1,500	152	1,881	270	1,611
28	230	80	3,238	2,175	5,722	1,100	4,622
29	7	35	400		442	40	402
30	189	209	2,625		3,023	830	2,193
31	9	10	250		269	50	219
32	50	51	700	399	1,200	220	980
33	12	180	2,250		2,442	900	1,542
34	79	86	1,088	255	1,507	0	1,507
35	2	16	225		243	60	183
36	63	72	875		1,010	450	560
37	85	96	925	39	1,145	260	885
38	7	8	100		115	20	95
39	103	117	1,425		1,644	168	1,476
40	7	8	50		65	15	50
41	209	236	2,888		3,332	1,140	2,192
42	272	308	3,763		4,342	1,500	2,842
43	232	264	3,225		3,722	475	3,247
TOTAL	$ 2,900	$ 4,610	$ 60,675	$ 5,295	$ 73,481	$ 16,813	$ 56,668
AVG	$ 67	$ 107	$ 1,411	$ 407	$ 1,709	$ 400	$ 1,318

[1] As indicated in AAA questionnaire. A random sample of the 181 clients who received day care in 1986-87 was selected for this Table.

[2] Includes home-delivered meals, respite care, homemaker, mental health counseling and attendant care.

TABLE 4.12
PHILADELPHIA CORPORATION FOR AGING[1,2]
DAY CARE CLIENT ANALYSIS (FISCAL YEAR 87-88)

Description	Actual Cost	Units	Average Cost	Units
Administration	$00.00		$00.00	
Home Delivered Meals	37,322.56	10,059	97.44	26
Congregate Meals	98,037.28	23,122	255.97	60
Center Services	4,104.84	948	10.71	2
Employment Services	00.00		00.00	
Volunteer Services	00.00		00.00	
Transportation	1,098,359.89	41,231	2,867.78	107
Outreach	00.00		00.00	
Information and Referral	00.00		00.00	
Service Management	115,595.51	2,189	301.81	5
Counseling	19,191.90	74	50.10	
Protective Services	6,196.68	83	16.17	
Homemaker	310,399.99	36,544	810.44	95
Home Health	71,624.94	6,041	187.01	15
Home Support - Chck	2,512.32	356	6.55	
Day Care	580,833.16	21,423	1,516.53	55
Placement Services	1,681.74	1	4.39	
Legal Services	00.00		00.00	
Ombudsman	00.00		00.00	
Attendant Care	28,704.54	3,095	74.94	8
Medical Equipment and Supply	00.00		00.00	
Additional Cost - Home	00.00		00.00	
Additional Cost - Cong	00.00		00.00	
Hi Pro Meal Supplement	2,282.31	2,839	5.95	7

TABLE 4.12 (Continued)
PHILADELPHIA CORPORATION FOR AGING[1,2]
DAY CARE CLIENT ANALYSIS (FISCAL YEAR '87-'88)

Description	Actual Cost	Units	Actual Cost	Units
Other Services (28-33)	00.00		00.00	
In-Kind Services, Volunteers	$00.00		$00.00	
Total	00.00		00.00	
Housing	00.00	1	00.00	
OCO Case Management	102,528.86	1,481	267.69	3
Preadmission Assessment	00.00		00.00	
Dementia Services	00.00		00.00	
Care Giver Support	13.18	32	00.03	
Health Promotion	00.00		00.00	
** Unknown **	5,490.80	746	14.33	1
Day Care Totals	2,484,880.52	50,315	6,487.93	131
Total Clients		383		

	ADC COST	OTHER SERVICES	ALL SERVICES
PROGRAM	$ 580,833		
CONGREGATE MEALS	98,037		
CENTER SERVICES	4,105		
TRANSPORTATION	1,098,360		
TOTAL	$ 1,781,335	$ 703,545	$ 2,484,880
AVERAGE	$ 4,651	$ 1,837	$ 6,488

[1] This analysis was submitted as shown by the Philadelphia Corporation for Aging. Actual Cost and Actual Units data are provided on Program Funding Reports (PFR).
Actual cost divided by 383 = average cost.
Actual units divided by 383 = average units.

[2] Client contributions for service were not provided.

TABLE 4.13
COMPARATIVE COST PER CLIENT PER DIEM BY COUNTY

	AAA Serv[1]	ADC Prog[2]	General Nursing Facility[3]	
	(N=3)	(N=13)	SNC[4]	IC[5]
Chester County	$ 3.91	$ 3.65	$54.79	$45.89
Delaware County	4.68[6]	4.34	54.79	45.89
Philadelphia County	17.78	12.74	54.79	45.89

[1] The per diem is the average cost to the area agency on aging for services for an adult day care client for study year 1986-1987 by county divided by 365 days and does not reflect possible client contributions.

[2] The per diem is the average cost to the AAA for adult day care service per client for each county for study year 1986-1987 divided by 365 using AAA provided figures.

[3] Net operating ceiling effective for Level A counties for July 1, 1986 through June 30, 1987 (Pennsylvania Bulletin, 16, No 42 [Saturday, October 18, 1986], p. 3997).

[4] SNC = skilled nursing care.

[5] IC = intermediate care.

[6] Delaware County uses a sliding fee code for most services. If the cost of AAA services is offset by these collected fees, which average $400 per client per year, the average per client per diem cost of all agency services is $3.61.

costs divided by a 365 day period (as opposed to program days) to reflect the comparison with full time nursing home costs.

The per diem Medicaid rates, of $54.79 for skilled nursing and $45.89 for intermediate care, were a cost base and not a cost total. Added to these rates set by the Pennsylvania Department of Welfare, Office of Medical Assistance, were certain incurred medical and drug expenses. In addition, personal items were purchased by the resident from small monthly allowances provided by Medicaid. The Medicaid per diem is, therefore, not all inclusive. Nor are the public costs for area agency on aging services all inclusive. Clients were, in fact, receiving Social Security (N=92), Medicare (N=113), SSI (N=1), and Medicaid (N=14) benefits. And, clients receiving community social services must also be sheltered, fed, clothed, and medically cared for. In addition, caregivers incur unmeasurable costs related to stress, loss of privacy, and lost opportunities.

In sum, on the face of it, the public cost for institutional care, as measured in this analysis, emerges as significantly more costly than the total public cost of all area agency on aging social services received by the population in this study.

In regard to the study questions, are there significant differences between Model I and Model II program variables?

As noted, only 2 of the 10 sampled program clients in Chester County received any service other than day care. Of these 10 clients, 5 were considered at high risk of institutionalization as shown in Table 4.14 which portrays programs by county, program model, funding type and number of clients at-risk. In Delaware County, the total day care program population included a smaller percent of high at-risk clients than did either Chester or Philadelphia County.

Nevertheless, as reflected in the table, Delaware County averaged the highest per diem cost. The County funded 4 programs, 3 in senior centers and 1 located on a hospital campus. On the other hand, Chester County funded a client's attendance in a day care program situated in a senior center for a significantly lower per diem cost than Delaware County. Still, cost is only one program descriptive. This study was not attempting to measure program effectiveness, nor does it consider program contributions or fees which might offset program cost.

Table 4.15, Program Model by Clients At-Risk of Institutionalization, indicates the number of clients at various levels of risk for institutional placement, as defined in this study, for each day care program sampled. For social models, 31 percent were at high risk of placement, and another 31 percent were at moderate risk. For medical models 62 percent were at high risk and 24 percent were at moderate risk of placement. This pattern appears to indicate a significant difference between the frailty of clients who attend social model programs and those who attend medical model programs as defined in this study. However, this is not wholly consistent with recent findings published by the National Institute of Adult Daycare (NIAD) that indicate that most of the early model theory has been discarded. Over the years, the lines of demarcation between early model types have blurred (Von Behren, 1988). It may be true that more medically oriented programs do serve a more frail population. It is also possible that the lack of a universally accepted indicator for "at-risk" has led to variant interpretations of this term. In addition, it is also possible that these programs perceived greater frailty among their clients than did more socially oriented day care staff. That is, program staff, who had a wider range of available resources, may have perceived that those they served required those resources. This is a question deserving further research.

As revealed in an analysis of service use over time as shown in Table 4.16, Use of AAA Services Over Time for ADC Participants, the activities categorizing a program as Model I, or a medical model, were not used by study participants. These activities were provided through contracted services as opposed to staff provided services. Therefore, program participants appear not to have required the contracted services which distinguish a day care program as "medical" as compared to "social."

The range of program cost by day was $10.25-$42.88, as reflected in Table 4.14, ADC Programs by County, Model, Funding Type, Cost, Nursing Home Rate and Clients At-Risk.

There appears to be a small difference in cost per day between the social ($25.97) and medical ($24.94) models of day care as defined in this study and indicated in Table 4.17, Cost of Adult Day

TABLE 4.14
ADULT DAY CARE PROGRAMS BY COUNTY, MODEL, FUNDING TYPE,
COST, NURSING HOME RATES AND CLIENTS AT-RISK

Program	Model[1]	Type Funding	ADC Cost /Day[2]	Nursing Home SNC	IC	Clients at Risk[3] Hi	Mod	Low
CHESTER COUNTY[4]								
Coatesville Area Senior Ctr	Social	Client	$10.25	$54.79	$45.89	2		2
Manatawny ADC	Social	Client	21.00			none sampled		
New Beginnings	Social	Client	25.00					2
Pat's ADC	Medical	Client	22.00			3		1
Average Cost Per Day			$19.56					
DELAWARE COUNTY[5]								
Crozer Chester Medical Ctr	Social	Program	$24.02			1	2	2
Squire Intell. Impr'd ADC	Social	Program	34.48			2	3	7
Squire Rehabilitation ADC	Social	Program	20.75			2	7	4
Watkins Avenue Senior Ctr	Social	Program	42.88			2	5	6
Average Cost Per Day			$30.53					
PHILADELPHIA COUNTY[6]								
Community Senior Respite Ctr	Social	Client	$27.74			11	6	6
Interac, Inc.	Social	Program	27.60			8	5	5
Pennsylvania Hospital ADC	Medical	Client	28.75			none sampled		
Philadelphia Geriatric Ctr	Medical	Client	25.00			8	4	2
Prim. Comm. Health Care, Inc.	Medical	Client	24.00			7	3	1
Terry Thurmond						7	6	2
Average Cost Per Day			$26.62					
		Total (134)				53	41	40
						40%	30%	30%

[1] As defined in Chapter 3. See Table 3.1.
[2] Data provided by Adult Day Care questionnaires.
[3] As defined in Chapter 3. (High at risk of institutionalization = need for assistance in 3 of 4 ADL + 1 IADL; moderate at risk of institutionalization = need for assistance in 1 to 2 ADL + 1 IADL). See Table 4.7, p. 154.
[4] N = 10
[5] N = 43
[6] N = 81

TABLE 4.15

PROGRAM MODEL BY CLIENTS AT-RISK OF INSTITUTIONALIZATION

Program[1]	Model		Clients At-Risk		
	Medical (N=29)/Social (N=90)		Hi	Mod	Lo
Coatesville Senior Center		X	2		2
New Beginnings		X			2
Crozer Chester Med. Center		X	1	2	2
Squire Intel. Impr'd		X	2	3	7
Squire Rehabilitation		X	2	7	4
Watkins Avenue Sr. Center		X	2	5	6
Community Senior Respite		X	11	6	6
Interac, Inc.		X	8	5	5
Total		8	28	28	34
Percentage			31.1	31.1	37.8
Pat's ADC	X		3		1
Phila. Geriat. Ctr	X		8	4	2
Prim. Commu. Health	X		7	3	1
Total	3		18	7	4
Percentage			62.1	24.3	13.8

[1] No participants from Manatawny or PA Hospital were included in this sample. The Terry Thurmond Center did not return a completed questionnaire and therefore their program model is not known. Participants from that Center, therefore, are not included in this portion of the analysis.

TABLE 4.16

USE OF AAA SERVICES OVER TIME BY ADC STUDY PARTICIPANTS[1]

Services	T1	(N=99)[2]	T2	(N)=96	T3	(N=75)	T4	(N=46)	T5	(N=28)
	#	%	#	%	#	%	#	%	#	%
Attendant Care	3	3.03	2	2.08					1	3.57
Heavy Housecleaning	xxxxxxxxxxxxxxxxxxxxxxxxxxxxxxxxxxxxxxxxxxxxxxxxxxxxxxxxxxxxxxxxxxxxxxxxxxxxx									
Phone Reassurance	1	1.01	1	1.04	1	1.33				
In-Home Meals	7	7.07	6	6.25	5	6.67	5	10.87	2	7.14
In-Home Respite	1	1.01			1	1.33	1	2.17	1	3.57
In-Home Personal Care	10	10.10	8	8.33	6	8.00	1	2.17	1	3.57
In-Home Care to Prepare for ADC	1	1.01	9	9.37	1	1.33	1	2.17	1	3.57
Laundry/Light Housekeeping	9	9.06	6	6.25	6	8.00	3	6.52	1	3.57
Med-Alert Devices	xxxxxxxxxxxxxxxxxxxxxxxxxxxxxxxxxxxxxxxxxxxxxxxxxxxxxxxxxxxxxxxxxxxxxxxxxxxxx									
Escort Shopping	xxxxxxxxxxxxxxxxxxxxxxxxxxxxxxxxxxxxxxxxxxxxxxxxxxxxxxxxxxxxxxxxxxxxxxxxxxxxx									
Protective Services										
Home Repair/Chore	xxxxxxxxxxxxxxxxxxxxxxxxxxxxxxxxxxxxxxxxxxxxxxxxxxxxxxxxxxxxxxxxxxxxxxxxxxxxx									
Friendly Visitor	1	1.01	2	2.08	1	1.33	1	2.17	1	3.57
Counseling	1	1.01	1	1.04	2	2.67	2	4.35		
Transportation	10	10.10	12	12.50	13	17.34	9	19.56	7	25.00
Homemaker	32	32.32	35	36.46	30	40.00	21	45.65	17	60.71
Other			1	1.04						

[1] As indicated in client file data.

[2] N at T1-T5 indicates number of clients receiving adult day care service at each time of assessment, reassessment.

TABLE 4.17
COST OF ADULT DAY CARE PER DAY BY PROGRAM MODEL

Medical Model	Cost Per Day	Social Model	Cost Per Day
Pat's ADC	$22.00	Coatesville Senior Center	$10.25
PA Hospital ADC	28.75	Manatawny ADC	21.00
Phila. Geriatric Center	25.00	New Beginnings	25.00
Prim. Comm. Health Care	24.00	Crozer Chester ADC	24.02
Total	$24.99	Squire Intell. Impr'd	34.48
Average Cost=$24.94		Squire Rehabilitation	20.75
		Watkins Avenue Sr Ctr	42.88
		Community Sr Respite	27.74
		Interac	27.60
		Total	$233.72
		Average Cost=$25.97	

Note: The Terry Thurmond Center is not included in this portion of the analysis. Program staff did not return a completed study questionnaire; therefore, neither program cost nor model information were available.

Care Per Day by Program Model. More importantly, however, area agencies on aging that **funded clients' participation** in day care, spent fewer service dollars than agencies which **contracted for program service** and, therefore, funded the program and not the individual client attending the program. This is shown in Table 4.18, Cost of Adult Day Care Per Day by Funding Type.

Finally by comparing program cost by model and funding type as shown in Table 4.19, Comparison of ADC Cost by Program Model and Funding Type, it appears that in this study, area agencies which **funded clients attending a social model** of adult day care spent, on average, $21 per day in 1986-1987 as compared to area agencies which **program-funded a social model** of day care which, in this study, on average, cost the area agency $30 per day in 1986-1987. There were no program-funded medical models of day care included in this study.

Area agencies which funded clients attending a medical model of day care, on average, spent $24.94 per client per day in 1986-1987. That is to say, the major cost differential is not the program model but the method of funding the delivery of service.

In summary, it appears in this study, that client-funded participation in a social adult day care program is less costly to the AAA than either client-funded participation in a medical model of adult day care, or a program-funded day care center. Overall, the models appear more similar than dissimilar by cost. This finding is consistent with a recent NIAD report which indicates that the lines of distinction between model types have blurred. However, the program may differ in the percent of at-risk clients served. It was suggested that the difference in frailty of the clients served may be a matter of perception, or variant definitions for at-risk, rather than an empirically measurable difference. This is supported by the lack of use of services associated with medical model programs by the study population. It is interesting to note that Model I, or medical program models, identified in this study were privately operated and client-funded. By comparison Model II programs, or social models, were **either** client-funded or program-funded in this study.

TABLE 4.18
COST OF ADULT DAY CARE PER DAY BY FUNDING TYPE

Program Funded ADC		Client Funded ADC	
Program	Cost	Program	Cost
Crozer Chester	$24.02	Coatesville SeniorCenter	$10.25
Squire Intel. Imprd.	34.48	Manatawny ADC	21.00
Squire Rehab. ADC	20.75	New Beginnings ADC	25.00
Watkins Avenue Center	42.88	Pat's ADC	22.00
Interac	27.60	Community Sr Respite	27.74
Total	$149.73	PA Hospital ADC	28.75
Average=$29.95		Philadelphia Geriatric Ctr	25.00
		Prim. Comm. Health	24.00
		Total	$183.74
		Average=$22.97	

Note: The Terry Thurmond Center is not included in this portion of the analysis. Program staff did not return a completed study questionnaire; therefore, neither program cost nor model information were available.

TABLE 4.19

COMPARISON OF ADC COST BY PROGRAM MODEL AND FUNDING TYPE

Medical Program Model Client-Funded	Cost	Social Program Model Client-Funded	Cost	Program Funded	Cost
Pat's ADC	$22.00	Coatesville	$10.25	Crozer Chester	$24.02
PA Hospital	28.75	Manatawny	21.00	Squire Intel.	34.48
Phila. Geri. Ctr	25.00	New Beginnings	25.00	Squire Rehab.	20.75
Prim. Comm. Health	24.00	Comm. Sr. Respite	27.74	Watkins Ave.	42.88
Total	$99.94	Total	$83.99	Interac, Inc.	27.60
				Total $149.73	
Average=$24.94		Average= $21.00		Average=30.00	

Note: The Terry Thurmond Center is not included in this portion of the analysis. Program staff did not return a completed study questionnaire; therefore, neither program cost nor model information were available.

Do caregivers and adult day care program staff perform routinized tasks using technical knowledge?

The results of the ranking of technical knowledge administered to adult day care program directors and caregivers is shown in Table 3.2 (p. 96). The range for the index is 1 to 3, where 1=the most important way of learning about caregiving, and 3=the third most important way of learning about caregiving. Caregivers most frequently reported that they learned how to perform their caregiving roles through non-technical means (93.8 percent). And, adult day care staff also indicated that they most frequently learned their role through non-technical means (78.9 percent). However, 21 percent of day care staff, as opposed to 6 percent of caregivers received some technical job training.

The results of the Routinization of Technology Scale, as shown in Table 3.3 (p. 99) indicate that the mean response for adult day care staff, where 1=highly non-routine and 4=highly routine, was 2.11 and 2.70 for caregivers. It would appear that caregivers find their jobs more routine than day care staff. This difference was not expected.

It may be that caregivers, after a sustained period of caregiving, experience the possible non-routineness of his/her role as, indeed, routine. The average caregiver in this study provided care for 4.6 years. On the other hand, responding staff members were not asked how long they had been performing their function. Also to be considered is the fact that caregivers were caring for 1 person while staff members had a range of 6-150 clients for whom they were providing program services. Considering this difference, it is not surprising, perhaps, that caregivers considered their jobs to be more routine than did program staff. Additionally, the comments of 1 program staff person may help to clarify the context for routinization: "There is a routine way in which one handles problems and things that are done to provide a structure every day but within the routine one never knows what will happen and flexibility also abounds. Must [sic] go with the flow."

In sum, it appears as though adult day care program staff received some technical training which was augmented by on-the-job experience. Additionally, adult day care staff found their functions more unpredictable than did caregivers. These findings are counter-intuitive considering the formal organization's theoretical division of tasks based on technical knowledge and task simplification. Further, it appears that caregivers do learn their caregiving roles by non-technical means. However, without controlling for intervening variables such as length of caregiving time, number of dependent people being cared for, etc. it appears that caregivers find their roles slightly more routine than program staff. This is counter to Litwak's theory of shared functions, or complementary roles.

Which functions of care are provided by informal caregivers and which by the formal system of care?

The similarities and differences in tasks performed by formal and informal networks in this study are revealed in Table 3.4 (p. 102) which depicts the results of the Task Frequency Index measurement. The range for this 19-item index was 1 (very often performed) to 5 (never performed). Using 2.5 as the midpoint of the index, only 1 item was infrequently performed by the informal network: minor home repairs (mean 3.15). At the same time the formal network **never** performed this task (mean 5.0).

However, there were several other instrumental activities of daily living that were infrequently performed by the formal network as the following list indicates:

	Mean	S.D.
Marketing or shopping	3.85	1.40
Household cleaning	4.23	1.54
Laundry	4.31	1.25
Escort service	3.58	1.73
Budgeting assistance	4.33	1.15
Friendly visiting	3.69	1.65
Paying bills/writing letters	4.00	1.21

Of the nineteen tasks listed in the table several tasks appear to be more frequently performed by the formal network than the informal system for this group of adult day care program participants as the following list indicates:

Task	ADC Program		Caregiver	
	Mean	S.D.	Mean	S.D.
Serve a meal	1.08	.28	1.25	.64
Personal help with bathing, eating, dressing, toileting	1.50	.67	1.75	1.29
Helping with family problems	1.61	.87	2.25	1.62
Recreational activities	1.38	1.12	2.39	1.38
Identifying client needs	1.23	.44	1.42	.96
Providing emotional support	1.08	.28	1.35	.99

In each case, however, the standard deviation from the mean for caregivers was higher than for adult day care program staff perhaps indicating small differences in actual task frequency performance between these two networks. A limiting factor in the task analysis was a lack of task definition. For instance, how do these networks define "companionship," "friendly visiting," and "providing emotional support"? How would these networks distinguish between these tasks? Would their task distinctions overlap? Another limitation of definition is in interpreting the networks' response. For instance, for the task "helping with family problems" or "minor home repairs" a low frequency response may indicate that there is a low frequency of family problems or low need for home repairs and not that a client's needs are not being met. Because day care is a non-residential community program, variables such as shelter, week-end or 24-hour care, and personal tasks such as haircuts or attendance at religious activities were not included.

In summary, it appears from Table 4.3, that caregivers performed a wider range of caregiving activities than was performed by adult day care program staff. Shopping, cleaning, laundry, and financial assistance were primarily provided by the informal network. Both systems provided personal care as well as emotional support. Little assistance with home repairs was provided by either system of support.

This study also addressed the humanistic perspective of informal support: *Does sharing caregiving tasks between the informal*

network and the formal organization provide effective humane care in
meeting the dependency needs of the elderly?

Older adults, as documented in Chapter 2, have voiced their desire to remain in the community as long as possible. Ninety-one percent of the clients whose file data were analyzed lived with another person who provided care. These caregivers often made the difference between remaining in the community and institutionalization for these frail clients. Indeed, 70 percent of these clients were at moderate to high risk of institutionalization. And, caregivers who were interviewed in this study had been providing care for 4.6 years for a frail elder who, in 75 percent of the cases, lived in their home. Nearly 50 percent of these caregivers were employed. Unanimously, caregivers reported that adult day care provided respite which reduced their stress by allowing them to work and/or have personal time. Both caregiver and client satisfaction with the program was also unanimous. While the definition for the concept "humaneness" remains elusive, the unanimity of consumer satisfaction and reduced caregiver stress lends credence to defining the community care analyzed in this study as humane. As is seen in Table 4.14 (p. 150), adult day care and total area agency on aging public social service cost was considerably less per day than the public nursing home per diem in these counties. Private costs were not measured.

In sum, as Aldridge et al. (1982) have written, "We are [also] faced with the mandate to be cost-effective, but we have not yet found a way to measure the quality of serving people that makes cost/benefits analysis reflective of the social work value system" (p. 19). Nevertheless, clients and caregivers were unanimous in their satisfaction with this program. From this perspective, perhaps, the sharing of client care by formal systems and informal networks is effective and humane.

HYPOTHESIS TESTING

In addition to examining adult day care program and client characteristics for at-risk of institutionalization factors; qualities of technicality and routinization; and the complementary roles, over time, of formal and informal systems of care, a further purpose of this study was to test Litwak's theory of shared functions. The results of testing Litwak's theory are   presented below and the following research hypotheses are then accepted or rejected:

(1)   Caregivers, over time will tend to continue to provide care to the frail elderly even when the elderly for whom they care attend an adult day care program.

(2)   Caregivers of adult day care participants will tend to manage tasks which are personal.

(3)   Caregivers of adult day care participants will tend to manage tasks which are unpredictable.

(4)   Adult day care programs will tend to perform tasks which are predictable.

(5)   Adult day care programs will tend to perform tasks which are more technical.

In this analysis there has been a strong mutual dependence of data and theory: Litwak's theory determining which of the multitudinous facts provided by adult day care programs, participants, caregivers, and public funding sources would be selected for investigation, and the data lending support to the theory. The hypotheses tested in this analysis have been drawn from Litwak's theoretical construct of shared functions between formal organizations and informal networks. Potentially, these hypotheses are supported by the data, the data can not prove the theory; they may only support it (Rosenberg, 1968). On the other hand, data may disprove a hypothesis.

Briefly summarized, Litwak's theory, as discussed in Chapter 2, asserts that formal organizations and primary groups generally manage complementary aspects of the same goal, so that each is essential to the other's goal attainment (1985; Litwak and Falbe, 1982). Since formal organizations normally achieve efficiency of scale through the employed benefits of technology and the routinization of task performance, then formal organizations should handle uniform, i.e., predictable events which require technical knowledge, and primary groups should handle non-uniform, i.e., unpredictable events which require everyday knowledge if effectiveness is the desired goal (1985; 1978). However, Litwak has acknowledged, that motivated by societal values, the formal organization may take on activities for which there is little knowledge (or where the tasks are simple enough for primary group performance using everyday knowledge) or where tasks are non-uniform. Then, according to Litwak and Figueira (1970), the formal organization tends to more nearly resemble the family creating a closer working relationship than is usually common between these two systems.

Hypothesis **1:** Caregivers, over time, will tend to continue to provide care to the frail elderly even when the elderly for whom they care attend an adult day care program.

     The collected and analyzed data noted the extent of involvement of informal supports, for most clients, at the time of the initial assessment; however, file data noting involvement of the informal system over time was weak. Nevertheless, 75 percent of the interviewed caregivers in this study indicated that they were providing about as much or more care than they provided before receiving day care.

     In 1980, Congress posed a similar question: "Does the availability of community based long-term care to frail older people at-risk of institutionalization serve to reduce consumption of nursing home care, and thereby reduce public expenditures?" (Eisenberg and Amerman, 1988, p. 22). The findings showed that Channeling services did not reduce informal caregiving. In fact, Eisenberg and Amerman "suspect that the prudent prescribing of formal community care actually enhances informal caregivers' ability to function and to sustain caregiving over time" (p. 25).

     These data which tend to support the stated hypothesis may alleviate the bureaucratic concern for economic effectiveness.

Hypothesis **2:** Caregivers of adult day care participants will tend to manage tasks which are personal.

     From the analyzed data, this hypothesis is supported; however, as indicated in Table 3.4 (p. 102), Frequencies for ADC Program and Caregiver Task Frequency Index, caregivers tend to perform both physical and instrumental activities. The range for this index was 1 to 5, where 1=very often performed and 5=never performed. The mean for caregiver performance of personal help with bathing, eating, dressing, and toileting was 1.75. Indeed, as shown in this table caregivers performed a wide range of caregiving activities including personal care. Eighty percent of the assistance received by day care participants was provided by informal supports. It should be noted that adult day care programs also manage personal tasks (Mean=1.50, S.D.=.67).

Hypothesis 3: Caregivers of adult day care participants will tend to manage tasks which are unpredictable.

The Scale of Routinization, previously used by Aiken and Hage (1968) and Kaye (1982), was the indicator used in this study to measure the concept of predictability. The results of this scale may be seen in Table 3.3 (p. 99). Where the potential score range was from 1 (highly non-routine) to 4 (highly routine), the mean score for caregivers was 2.7. This suggests that caregivers found caregiving somewhat non-routine to somewhat predictable. While this tends to support the hypothesis, and Litwak's theory, the support is weak. It was suggested that differences in task predictability may be influenced by the number of people a caregiver is caring for and the length of caregiving time.

Hypothesis 4: Adult day care programs will tend to perform tasks which are predictable.

The mean score response for program staff to the Scale of Routinization shown in Table 3.3 (p. 99) was 2.11 indicating that staff experienced their program tasks as somewhat unpredictable. This does not support the hypothesis. It may be that the scale failed to measure the concept of predictability. Content validity may have been undermined by a lack of definition of scale terminology. That is, there may be insufficient information to state definitively whether these data do or do not support Litwak's tenet asserting that formal organizations perform tasks which are predictable. From program staff responses we do know that program hours and staff numbers are predictable, that meals and transportation are group activities presumably occurring at more or less predictable hours.

Hypothesis 5: Adult day care programs will tend to perform tasks which are more technical.

Technical knowledge was measured in this study by a 7-item ranking probe first used by Kaye (1982). The results of the probe indicated that 15 percent of adult day care staff learned how to perform their tasks through more technical learning experiences than did caregivers. This weakly supports the hypothesis and, therefore, one aspect of Litwak's theory which indicates that formal organizations will perform more technical tasks than will the informal system. The assumption was made, for purposes of measuring this concept, that performing more technical tasks would usually require more technical education than the performance of non-technical tasks. Litwak asserted that the informal system commonly required less technical knowledge in the performance of its role. The results of Kaye's probe supports this: caregivers reported learning caregiving skills by non-technical means 94 percent of the time.

Results of Hypotheses Testing:

(1)   Caregivers, over time will tend to continue to provide care to the frail elderly even when the elderly for whom they care attend an adult day care program. *Supported with qualification.*

(2)   Caregivers of adult day care participants will tend to manage tasks which are personal. *Supported.*

(3)   Caregivers of adult day care participants will tend to manage tasks which are unpredictable. *Supported with qualification.*

(4)   Adult day care programs will tend to perform tasks which are predictable. *Rejected with comment.*

(5)   Adult day care programs will tend to perform tasks which are more technical. *Supported with qualification.*

In summary, the systems analyzed in this study, emerge more
parallel than complementary in that both systems of care provided
help in virtually the same areas. However, caregivers provided help
24-hours a day, 7 days a week, throughout the year, whereas, clients
attended day care an average of 2-3 days per week for 4-8 hours per
day. Adult day care's primary service appears to be respite: primarily
respite for caregivers but also respite for clients from their diminish-
ing outlets for social contact, stimulation, and interrelationship with
peers. Even in the most compatible of relationships, time apart may
both renew, and stimulate self-image, confidence, knowledge and
perceptions.

In this study, adult day care programs did not generally
perform care which was significantly more technical or predictable
than the care provided by the informal system. This was so even
though 5 programs were defined in this study as medically oriented
programs providing medical assessment and treatment as well as
psychiatry, podiatry, physical therapy, and occupational and speech
therapy. These program characteristics in the aggregate, may have
skewed program staff responses towards greater technicality and
predictably than might otherwise have been indicated. On the other
hand, many of the services included in a medically oriented program
were not generally provided by program staff. They were contracted
for externally and were not received by the study population.

Overall, there was generally more predictability and task
simplification in adult day care routines than the analyzed indices
revealed. For instance, adult day care programs have clearly defined
program hours; but, informal caregiving is idiosyncratic and provided
on a 24-hour basis. Meals for program participants are, for the most
part, prepared by one contracted provider rather than individually
prepared as is the case in the informal network. Some program
participants may, however, elect to bring a brown bag lunch from
home to meet their individual food preferences. Meals are served at
a scheduled time in the program day. At home, meal service times are

more dependent on the individual vagaries of family routines. Transportation is similarly more scheduled by formal systems than by informal networks.

Indeed, it may be the very predictability of adult day care and its dependable quality of service delivery at low cost which fosters a respite partnership between the formal system and the informal network. The formal system is able, perhaps, to assist the informal network through the provision of parallel care. Licensure of day care centers assures a level of professional care which is not assured, in Pennsylvania at this time, by paid in-home respite workers. All of the programs analyzed in this study were licensed by the Department of Public Welfare. Maintenance of this licensure requires yearly inspection.

This parallel relationship is not precisely what Litwak contended in his theory of shared functions. Litwak maintained that tasks comprised of a more technical component were best performed by the formal system; whereas, tasks comprised of a less technical component were best performed by the informal network. Since day care programs perform many of the same family-like tasks as caregivers, and, therefore, are not a highly technical service, Litwak's theory is, on the surface, not wholly supported by this study. However, Litwak and Figueria (1970) also maintained that a parallel working relationship between these 2 systems would occur if motivated by societal values.

Day care for the frail elderly emerges in this study as a mild intervention offering modest respite services through a parallel supporting relationship with caregivers. Many questions remain to be answered by future research including: (1) Are perceptions of routineness influenced by the length of time spent in caregiving and/or the number of frail elders being cared for?; (2) Does the use of common operational definitions across different populations alter response selection?; (3) Is shared caring for dependent elders in the community humane and efficient?; and (4) Is the concept of humane and efficient care a shared community value?

END NOTES - CHAPTER 4

Aiken, Michael and Jerald Age. *"Organizational Interdependence and Intra-Organizational Structure." American Sociological Review*, 33, No 6 (December 1968), pp. 912-930.

Aldridge, Martha, Harry Macy and Thomas Walz. *Beyond Management: Humanizing the Administrative Process. Iowa: University of Iowa School of Social Work, 1982.*

Cantor, Marjorie. *"The Informal Support System, Its Relevance in the Lives of the Elderly." In Aging and Society. Eds. E. Borgatta and N. McClusky. Beverly Hills, CA: Sage Publications, 1980, pp. 111- 146.*

Cantor, Marjorie and Virginia Little. *"Aging and Social Care." In Handbook of Aging and the Social Sciences. Eds. Robert Binstock and Ethel Shanas. New York: Van Nostrand Reinhold Co., 1985, pp. 745-781.*

Eisenberg, David and Emily Amerman. *"A New Look at the Channeling Demonstration," Part II. Perspective on Aging, XVII, No 1 (1988), pp. 20-23.*

Fowles, Donald G. *"Functional Disability," Aging, No 357 (1988), pp. 39-41.*

Kaye, Lenard W. *"Home Care Services for Older People: An Organizational Analysis of Provider Experience." Diss. Columbia University, 1982.*

Kaye, Lenard, W. and Patricia M. Kirwin. *An Evaluation of Adult Day Care Programs in Pennsylvania. Bryn Mawr, PA: The Bryn Mawr College Graduate School of Social Work and Social Research, July 1989. Pennsylvania Department of Aging Contract No 871003.*

Litwak, Eugene. *"Agency and Family Linkages in Providing Services." In Reaching People: The Structure of Neighborhood Services, Vol 3. Social Service Delivery Systems: An International Annual. Eds. D. Thursz and J. Vigilante. Beverly Hills, CA: Sage Publications, 1978, pp. 59-95.*

Litwak, Eugene. *Helping the Elderly. New York: The Guilford Press, 1985.*

Litwak, Eugene and Cecilia Falbe. *"Formal Organizations and Community Primary Groups: Theory and Policy of Shared Functions as Applied to the Aged." Conference on Organizational Theory and Public Policy, State University of New York at Albany, April 1-2, 1982.*

Litwak, E. and J. Figueira. *"Technical Innovation and Ideal Forms of Family Structure in an Industrial Society." In Families in East and West: Socialization Process and Kinship Ties. Eds. R. Hill and R. Konig. Paris: Mouton, 1970, pp. 348-396.*

Rosenberg, Morris. *The Logic of Survey Analysis. New York: Basic Books, Inc., 1968.*

Von Behren, Ruth. *Adult Day Care: A Program of Services of the Functionally Impaired. Washington, DC: The National Council on the Aging Inc., National Institute on Adult Daycare, July 1988.*

CHAPTER 5

SUMMARY, CONCLUSIONS,
AND FUTURE RESEARCH QUESTIONS

*"An old Man in a House is a good
Sign."*
Benjamin Franklin

This final chapter is divided into three sections. The first
summarizes the study purpose and major findings derived from the
data analysis. The second section briefly discusses conclusions and
recommendations based on study findings. The final section will
present questions for future research.

The primary purpose of this study was to test Litwak's theory
of complementary roles as performed by adult day care programs and
primary groups in meeting the long-term care dependency needs of
the frail elderly in three southeastern Pennsylvania counties. As
conceptualized, the results were expected to reveal how tasks were
divided between the informal caregiving network and the formally
organized service of adult day care. By doing so, this study attempted
to contribute to the expansion of the present embryonic knowledge
base from which community service delivery might be conceptualized.
It was expected that these results also might be generalized to other
populations requiring long-term community care.

The questions addressed in this study required that the
complementary nature of the caregiving relationship be examined from
both the formal and the informal caregivers' points of view. Consequently, the populations of interest consisted of caregivers of adult day
care participants, program participants, center directors, and, area
agency on aging program managers. To further triangulate the
measurement, data from program participant assessment and care plan
records collected from area agency on agency files were also analyzed.
These five data sources comprised a subset of a larger statewide study
of adult day care programs funded by the Pennsylvania Department of
Aging (Kaye and Kirwin, 1989).

The answers to the questions posed in this study are important if Daniels' (1988) assertion is valid: The number of elderly, the fact that they are living much longer than they used to, and the sometimes high cost of sustaining their lives has outdated the once traditional concept that the young had a special obligation to take care of the old. To stay in the community, however, most individuals do receive the assistance they require from their spouse or other family members or friends. It is believed that less than one-half of the community long-term care population receives assistance from providers of formal community-based services. It has been asserted, therefore, that the provision of social care by social agencies may underpin and sustain a high level of family care and, lacking such a system, family capacity for sustained care may rapidly erode leading to a situation in which institutional care is completely substituted for informal care.

In Helping the Elderly (1985), Litwak most comprehensively set forth his theory of shared functions, a theory he began articulating in 1960. Simply stated, Litwak's theory asserts that tasks that require technical knowledge, and are more routine and predictable than not, are best accomplished by formal organizations. Informal networks are best at performing tasks that require non-technical knowledge, and are idiosyncratic or highly non-routine. That is, uniform events, e.g., those of moderate complexity, which can be mastered through disciplined study and occur with some regularity, can best be managed by formal organizations. (Litwak's theory was amplified in Chapter 2.) The theory of shared functions—also referred to as complementary roles, claims that many tasks have both technical and non-technical aspects and are, in part, predictable and also unpredictable. By leaving non-technical, unpredictable aspects of care to informal networks and having formal systems perform the predictable technical functions of care, Litwak argued the frail elderly could remain in the community even as their ability to meet their personal and self-management care needs continued to decline.

This theory was tested in this analysis as described in Chapter 4. Questions specific to testing the theory of shared functions included the following:

Wisdom To Live By . . .

ON NEGOTIATING
When a concession is made voluntarily, it provides the greatest incentive for reciprocity.

Henry Kissinger,
former secretary of state

ON POSITIVE THOUGHT
One of the things I learned the hard way was it does not pay to get discouraged. Keeping busy and making optimism a way of life can restore your faith in yourself.

Lucille Ball, actress

ON PLANNING
We can't cross a bridge until we come to it; but I always like to lay down a pontoon ahead of time.

Bernard Baruch, financier

ON LEADERSHIP
The final test of a leader is that he leaves behind him in other men the conviction and the will to carry on.

Walter Lippmann, journalist

Leadership is action, not position.

Donald McGannon,
broadcasting executive

ON WORDS AND ACTIONS
What you do speaks so loudly that I cannot hear what you say.

Ralph Waldo Emerson, poet

ON TAKING ACTION
There isn't a plant or a business on Earth that couldn't stand a few improvements — and be better for them. Someone is going to think of them. Why not beat the other fellow to it?

Roger Babson, economist

While markets may fluctu

a long line of proven perf

opportunity to be the one v

(1)   Which functions of care are provided by informal caregivers and which by the formal system of care?
(2)   Do caregivers meet the needs of the frail elderly by performing tasks that are non-routinized and require non-technical knowledge?
(3)   Does the adult day care program perform routinized tasks using technical knowledge?

SUMMARY OF FINDINGS

The typical adult day care program participant in this study, as seen in file data, was a widowed or single 78 year old female, having a median income of $600 per month living with another, usually a daughter. Typically, it was the relative's contact with the area agency that led to the client's participation in adult day care. Seventy percent of the program participants were at moderate to high risk of institutional placement when caregivers contacted area agencies seeking assistance in their caregiving roles. By definition, in this study, at-risk was primarily a measure of the need for assistance in performing activities of daily living such as bathing, walking, dressing, and eating. The results of the analysis, however, tend to support recently emerging empirical evidence that the need for assistance in accomplishing the instrumental activities of daily living, such as cooking, shopping, and financial tasks, are more indicative of being at-risk than are the physical activities of daily living. If this finding is replicated in further studies, we may be approaching a more reliable index of at-riskness than has previously existed. Attendance in adult day care programs for the participants in this study was, therefore, the result of social work case assessment after the caregiver initiated contact with the area agency on aging and the case management process. Participants attended day care, on average, 2.6 days per week. Nearly one-half of the participating caregivers were employed and ranged in age from 32-83 years.

Analysis of the data revealed that for this population a wide range of tasks was provided by both the informal and formal systems of care. The formal system, however, seldom shopped, did household cleaning, laundry, minor home repairs, personal finances, friendly visiting, or provided escort services. The informal system seldom performed home repairs but often performed all other personal and self-management tasks of daily living. Seventy percent of the caregivers had been providing care for 4-6 years.

Program officers were unanimous in their conviction that adult day care delayed institutionalization and reduced caregiver stress. The cost for a program day ranged from $10.25-$42.88. Except for day care, study participants received surprisingly few additional social services. Participants in Philadelphia County received considerably more services than participants in either Chester or Delaware Counties. A preliminary analysis of the data suggested that clients at high risk of institutionalization were more frequently in a medical program model and, although it is counter-intuitive, this model was less costly per day than the social model of programming. But, elaboration of this empirical relationship revealed that program cost was strongly dependent on the program's funding arrangement with area agencies on aging rather than the "at-riskness" of the sample population. Agencies that funded individual client program days paid less per client per program day than did agencies that contracted for adult day care service and, therefore, funded the program. The previous theory-driven differences between program models appear to have blurred.

In testing the premises of Litwak's theory of complementary roles, the analysis revealed that caregivers learned how to perform their caregiving functions through non-technical means 94 percent of the time whereas adult day care program staff learned their skills through technical means 21 percent of the time. This percent was unexpectedly small.

Testing for task routinization also provided less than clear, emphatic results. It appears that caregivers found their jobs more routine than program staff; yet both systems found their functions generally non-routine.

That is, on close inspection of the data, it appeared that formal and informal help were more parallel than complementary in that both networks provided help with virtually the same aspects of personal care and management tasks, both found their functions non-routine, and both learned much about their role performance on-the-job, i.e., each learned by doing.

Approaching primary and secondary data sources provided for the collection of data reflective of varied perspectives and experiences. By comparing indices across the study's different populations, it is probable that some terms connoted different meanings to different segments of the sampled populations.

Litwak maintained that both informal primary groups and larger formal organizations were needed to provide adequate care for the elderly because each would manage complementary aspects of the same goal. The results of this study have shown that there is much diversity among the dependent aged and their caregiving systems. Although not explicitly stated in his work, Litwak's typology focused on a kinship structure most reflective of the middle class socio-economic segment of society. Yet, 50 percent of this study's population had monthly incomes below 125 percent of the state poverty level. That is, 50 percent of the study sample was generally not reflective of the socioeconomic middle class. Distinctive values that may be held by individuals in our society are, for the most part, undifferentiated in Litwak's theory. Because values inform our decision-making, this could be considered a weakness in Litwak's conceptual model.

Parsons, on the other hand, in Toward A Grand Theory of Action (1951), as well as in other works, may have supplied insight into the role differing values may play in society, particularly in families. He clearly insisted in "The Social Structure of the Family" (1949), that no aspect of our social life is more deeply embedded in "layers of sentiment and of motivation of which we are normally scarcely even aware" than our individual values (p. 173).

To determine "which primary group best provides which services with each change in the health status of the older person" after the loss of a spouse, for instance, Litwak matches groups with services on the dimensions of whether several caregivers, similar life-styles, continued proximity and long-term commitment are required (1985, p. 74). That primary groups will naturally select and maintain functions that differentially assist the frail elderly is assumed without furnishing theoretical insights for the myriad values and motivations that might be expected to be found in these primary groups. Nor does Litwak appear to consider the extent of agreement on values that may exist between formal and informal organizations.

He does, however, assume than an agreement on the goal of meeting the dependency needs of the frail elderly exists between these helping networks.

Values and the roles they play in decision-making have been detailed by Parsons, particularly in his theoretical pattern variables constructed to examine the psychological continuum of social system needs and individual needs. Pattern variables are a conceptualization of role patterns ascribed by the social system and pursued by the individual. Parsons' five pattern variables are paired and suggest the direction of orientation: (1) difficulty-neutrality; (2) self-orientation; (3) particularism-universalism; (4) quality-performance; and (5) specificity-diffuseness.

The first two alternate pairs are concerned with the express-ive-discipline problem of roles that confronts all action systems, e.g., subordination to versus freedom from certain value standards. The first three alternative pairs are defined in reference to the ego as actor. Parsons asserted that they were exhaustive on the same level of generality. The remaining alternative pairs reference the *character-istics* of the social objects themselves, that is, from the ego's point-of-view of the *alter* in the complementary role orientation structure or to ego himself as an object and with reference to the *scope* of relevance of alter as object.

These five alternate pairs of value-laden role possibilities constitute a system (1951, 1960). Their permutations and combina-tions yield a system of types of possible role-expectation patterns on the relational level—namely defining the pattern of orientation to the actors in the role relationship. This system would consist of 32 types. ". . . the actor must make 5 specific dichotomous choices before any situation will have a determinate meaning" (1951, p. 76). Pattern variables "are inherently patterns of cultural value-orientation, but they become integrated both in personalities and in social systems" (Parsons and Shils, 1951, p. 79).

Parson's theoretical construct suggests the complexity and potential futility of attempting to order individual values and societal role expectations. Paired pattern variables, in particular, help explain how values and differing role-expectations among socioeconomic groups, the sexes, different generations, etc., can cause tension.

Human affairs are too vagarious, disordered, unstructured, uncertain and diverse to permit facile generalizations. Simplifying assumptions setting ideal type molar provisions allow us to make sense of diverse data. Parsons' pattern variables, making no simplifying assumptions, remain a theoretical construct difficult to test empirically. On the other hand, Litwak provides a theory that is testable. Nevertheless, it is important to remember that the simplifying assumptions necessary for theory to be testable discount the myriad vagaries of the population. Knowledge of Parsons' theoretical pattern variables provides a valuable analytic perspective to the empirical results of testing sociological theories, in this case Litwak's conceptual model, by helping to categorize dichotomies of decisions, normative demands, and value orientations.

Concepts are ideas. They are useful intellectually in analyzing the processes of an organization or program. Still, concepts don't live—people do. We must never forget that a program or organization is formed by live people, not by a collection of intellectual concepts. By this is meant that the feelings and the sense of humanity of family and organizational members must always be considered, no matter which concept is being used for program or organizational analysis. What is proposed by Litwak is that there is a continuum of organizational structures as well as one of tasks (1985). "Primary groups can handle the most extreme nonuniform tasks, human relations structures can manage moderately nonuniform tasks, and rationalistic structures can manage nonuniform tasks least of all" (Litwak, 1985, p. 14). In this study, day care programs are moderately nonuniform. That is, they have a routine, but within the context of that routine, events may prove to be non-routine. Day care programs perform family-like activities. Further, perceptions of routineness may be influenced by the number of frail persons one is responsible for and the length of time one has been active in the caregiving role.

In sum, Litwak maintains that both informal primary groups and larger formal organizations are needed to provide adequate care for the elderly because each will manage complementary aspects of the same goal. Generally, he does not explicate the presence of differing values, or attempt to account for the extent to which informal and formal groups may agree on the goals and values of the service. Such agreement appears to be assumed.

Durkheim's theoretical reasoning in The Division of Labor in Society (1933) may provide the explanatory link between Parsons and Litwak. Durkheim's argument was, generally, that population density increased moral density (i.e., rates of contact and interaction); moral density lead to competition, which threatened the social order; in turn, competition for resources resulted in the specialization of tasks; and specialization created pressures for mutual interdependence and an increased willingness to accept the morality of mutual obligation (Durkheim, 1933; Turner, 1986). That is, Durkheim reasoned as society expanded, specialization would increase. Interdependence would flow from specialization and increase society's willingness to accept the morality (humaneness?) of a mutual obligation among its members.

As our society has technologically expanded, families have, in many cases, expanded their societal roles. These role changes have led to variant forms of specialization requiring interdependence. For instance, once upon a time, each family planted, harvested, raised animals and slaughtered to feed itself. Soon one family harvested and another slaughtered. The family that slaughtered was dependent on the other for bread. This interdependence led to mutual obligation. Likewise, in the less distant past, families became interdependent with the school system for the education of their children. The division of education by specialization increased society's general willingness to accept—to varying degrees—a mutual obligation to cooperate in educating children.

In this study, through the "mild intervention with modest effects" of the community day care program, interdependence in the maintenance of dependent elders is coordinated between two systems of care (Lawton et al., 1989).

Social systems, Durkheim argued, have equilibrium points around which normal functioning occurs. Litwak refers to this as the Balance Theory of Coordination. This theory is beyond the scope of the present analysis.

The results of this study have shown that there is significant diversity among the dependent aged and their caregiving systems in age, living arrangements, income level, and need for assistance. Yet, neither Durkheim, Parsons, nor Litwak provides a model for resolving the conflicts in goals and values that inevitably will occur where there is diversity.

Seventy-five percent of the interviewed caregivers cited respite as a program benefit. It is this aspect of the informal/formal system relationship that emerges as the most significant benefit of a linkage that is manifestly more parallel than complementary. This aspect also reflects the Durkheimian pressure for mutual interdependence in using scarce resources—public dollars and private caregiving costs—and an increased societal willingness to accept the mutual obligation of caring for one another. The transition to a new social order is not made consciously, according to Durkheim, but rather evolves through the division of labor, unbridled competition and the resulting need for a new social order.

CONCLUSIONS AND RECOMMENDATIONS

Respite may be the crux of the theme "Sharing the Caring" a day long conference sponsored by the National Council on the Aging's National Institute of Adult Daycare during the 1989 Annual Confer-, ence and Exhibition. As promoted in the First Invitation (1988) "'Sharing the Caring' expressed the cooperative relationship between adult day care staff, participants, families, and the community."

Family caregiving is a stressful omnipresent responsibility sometimes requiring a "36 hour day." Caregivers often conduct their various responsibilities without adequate "time out" for themselves, because temporary care alternatives are largely unavailable or prohibitively expensive. In a few cases the "role overload" may result in elder abuse. As underscored buy Strang and Neufeld (1990) respite care tends to support family caregiving by allowing needed personal time for the caregiver on a temporary, predictable, reliable, and trustworthy basis.

If a primary value of adult day care is respite, then the program may be an efficient model of service delivery. The alternative is often one-on-one, in-home respite care with its risks of unreliable, unqualified workers at a higher dollar cost per hour.

In this way, perhaps, help provided by the more predictable service relationship of the formal system can be interwoven with help provided by members of the ongoing informal social network to produce a respite partnership capable of reducing reliance on professional care while enhancing and sustaining the interpersonal quality of the helping relationship.

Viewed from this lens, the results of this study are not a surprise. One might expect adult day care to perform similar tasks as the informal caregivers. And, if this is so, the level of technical knowledge acquired by the workers in the formal system might be expected to parallel the level of technical knowledge acquired by caregivers.

While the recent public debate on financing community long-term care services, such as adult day care, has tended to focus on cost savings, there may exist independent and valid reasons for a public investment in community care. Probably the most important reason is that the elderly strongly prefer to reside in their homes rather than in nursing homes. Fully 95 percent of the chronically disabled elderly in the community in 1982 said they would prefer to stay out of a nursing home as long as possible (U. S. Department of Health and Human Services, 1982). Community-based long-term care preserves the elderly's independence, autonomy, and choice.

Recipients of adult day care, in particular, tend to report higher morale, well-being, and life satisfaction than non-recipients in demonstration projects (Stassen & Holahan, 1981). There are limits, of course, to what adult day care can accomplish. There is only weak evidence that the program lowers mortality rates. Nor does it significantly improve physical and mental functioning, although several studies suggest that adult day care prevents or postpones further deterioration of a person's functional abilities (Stassen and Holahan, 1981).

Another reason for expanding community-based services such as adult day care is to reduce unmet demands for care among the dependent aged in the community. The dependent aged often report that they need assistance with their daily activities (Fowles, 1988). Approximately 70 percent of dependent aged in the community in 1982 were receiving help solely from their family and friends, often at great personal sacrifice in terms of time, effort, emotional strain, and sometimes financial expense (Stephens and Christianson, 1986). While there may be consumers of community care who are not be at high risk of institutionalization, they still require daily assistance. Too, adult day care programs appear to reduce the burden on caregivers by offering scheduled, dependable respite from daily responsibilities, and this access to the aging network's continuum of services may supply other services that the dependent aged reportedly desire.

Unpaid caregivers prefer wider access to community services rather than tax deductions or cash payments (Huttman, 1985). Although the Channeling demonstration did not find that expanded community services reduced emotional, physical, or financial strain among unpaid providers, it did find significant short-term (six-month) improvement in their ratings of overall life satisfaction (Kemper et al., 1987). A final reason to expand community-based services such as adult day care is to reduce financial burden on the elderly and their families by spreading the cost more evenly over the population rather than on the small percent of the elderly and their caregivers who may require such high levels of community care in order to avoid institutional placement. Case estimates from the Brookings-ICF Long-Term Care Financing Model for 1986-90 suggest that almost 20 percent of the $8.7 billion spent annually on community-based care will be financed by out-of-pocket expenditures (Rivlin and Weiner, 1988).

In conclusion, fears of uncontrolled public costs have blocked past initiatives to expand community-based services. Yet, for the population in this study, services besides day care were surprisingly meager. Too, since clients attended day care less than 3 days a week, the cost of service was small. By averaging the study participants' program days over the year. The cost for day care ranged from $3.65 to $12.74 per day (Table 13-4, p. 165). A key policy issue is whether use and expenditures can be controlled. There are several ways that have been suggested by Kemper and his associates (1988).

Cost-sharing and case management may help to avoid excessive use and to coordinate services (including those of unpaid helpers). Restricting community-based service, limiting the type of services offered, and regulating the total number or frequency of attendance also may help to control use. Other alternatives include financing expanded community-based services as an indemnity benefit (as do most private insurance policies) or as a benefit limited to an annual dollar maximum (as does the social/health maintenance organization demonstrations).

Nonetheless, and while by no means trivial, expanded community-based service costs are unlikely to be large compared with nursing home expenditures even assuming a large increase in use. Today, nursing facilities are operating at capacity. Any expansion of their population will involve construction costs as well as operating expenses.

From the income side of the debate, community care for frail elders acknowledges the societal shift of women into the work force. This expansion is a necessity for many today. In many cases, it takes two incomes to support the family. And from the institutional perspective, two employed persons in a household will fill a critical need in the future when the population of workers (age 16-65) is projected to shrink. Employed persons increase our national productivity, contribute to the general tax base, and pay into the Social Security Trust Fund. These factors need to be weighted against the cost of community care.

Although expansion of community-based services such as adult day care is likely to increase public costs, they are also likely to increase the quality of life for program participants. Moreover, expanded community services are not likely to lead to a wholesale substitution of paid services for unpaid care. Nevertheless, the policy issue should not be whether expanded public financing for adult day care will reduce costs. The real issues are how much community care society is willing to pay for, who should receive it, and how it can be efficiently delivered (Kemper et al., 1987).

As a national community, we lack an adequate understanding of the meaning and ethical implications of long-term care for the aged and other dependent populations in the lives of individuals, families, and the broader society; we lack as well a serviceable vocabulary of concepts and categories with which to address its meaning and implications. Above all, as Jennings and his associates (1988) have reminded us, we lack a guiding vision of how a just and good society should accommodate the special needs of its long-term care members, care for them, and support them and their caregivers in their quest to live meaningful, satisfying lives with—and in spite of—their growing dependencies. This is equally true for any age segment of the population with long-term care needs. It is not the program solution of the day that matters long term but rather the principles it reflects and the direction of its development.

In addition, the prospects for competition among age groups for limited public benefits and scarce economic resources are sobering. When as individuals we express our preference for community care or institutional care for the impaired elderly or for another dependent segment of the population, we lack the information necessary to calculate the societal cost for all populations across the generations that result if our preference is granted.

FUTURE RESEARCH RECOMMENDATIONS

(1) For future empirically-based research on social service use, caregiving functions over time, and client factors associated with being at-risk of institutionalization, improved client file documentation is necessary. This documentation would, in addition, more precisely inform case management supervisors and new case workers of a client's available resources, personal desires, and history when a new case worker becomes responsible for an existing caseload. Turnover of case management workers is an issue of social work concern. The most frequently cited reason for this turnover is low pay. A third reason for agencies to insist on complete documentation over time for professional case management has to do with the increasingly litigious nature of our society.

(2) There is a need for uniform definitions of terms such as "at-risk of institutionalization," "client requires assistance," (How much assistance is needed? Is this hands-on or verbal coaxing?), "friendly visiting," (Is a visit to cook or to write a letter a friendly visit?)

(3) Additional questions deserving further research include:

(A) Are there empirically measurable differences between the clients served at medical and social programs of day care?

(B) Are there measurable programmatic differences between these models?

(C) Do perceptions of task routineness change over time? What variables affect this perception?

(D) Do program staff experience burden or stress in patterns similar to caregivers?

(E) Is the idea of humane and efficient care for dependent populations a shared community value?

(F) Is shared caring for dependent populations through the use of family-like community services, such as day care, a humane and efficient use of societal resources?

Continuing research that includes both client and agency perspectives is needed. As Cole (1988) has suggested, there is also a need for a greater infusion of the humanities and arts into gerontological research to overcome the epistemological, historical, moral, existential, and aesthetic blind spots that have accompanied the growth of scientific knowledge about aging (p. 7). Indeed, research informed by the conceptual knowledge bases of divergent disciplines including sociology and psychology is needed to enrich the philosophical grounding and historical context for the theory of shared functions between formal organizations and primary groups. There is a continuing need to clarify our values and question our assumptions. If we, as a society, cherish the ethic of humanistic care for all people, we must cultivate a tolerance for intractable ambiguities, an appreciation for experience that eludes quantification, and a habit of self-examination.

END NOTES - CHAPTER 5

Cole, Thomas. "The Role of the Humanities in Aging." *The Aging Connection*, IX, No 6 (December 1988/January 1989), p. 7.

Daniels, Norman. *Am I My Parent's Keeper?* New York: Oxford University Press, 1988.

Durkheim, Emile. *The Division of Labor in Society.* New York: Macmillan, 1933.

Kaye, Lenard W. and Patricia M. Kirwin. *An Evaluation of Adult Day Care Programs in Pennsylvania.* Bryn Mawr, PA: The Bryn Mawr College Graduate School of Social Work and Social Research, July 1989. Pennsylvania Department of Aging Contract No 871003.

Kemper, Peter, Robert Applebaum et al. "Community Care Demonstrations: What Have We Learned." *Health Care Financing Review,* 8, No 4 (Summer 1987), pp. 87-100.

Lawton, Powell M., Elaine M. Brody and Avalie R. Saperstein. "A Controlled Study of Respite Service for Caregivers of Alzheimer's Patients." *The Gerontologist,* 29, No 1 (1989), pp. 8-16.

Litwak, Eugene. *Helping the Elderly.* New York: The Guilford Press, 1985.

Parsons, Talcott. "Pattern Variables Revisited: A Response to Robert Dubin." *American Sociological Review,* 25 (1960), pp. 467-482.

Parsons, Talcott. "The Social Structure of the Family." In *The Family: Its Function and Destiny.* Ed. R. Anshen. New York: Harper and Brothers, 1949, pp. 173-201.

Parsons, Talcott. *The Social System*. Glencoe, IL: *The Free Press*, 1951.

Parsons, Talcott and Edward Shils. *Toward a General Theory of Action*. New York: Harper and Row, 1951.

Rivlin, Alice M. and Joshua M. Weiner. *Caring For The Disabled Elderly: Who Will Pay?* Washington, DC: The Brookings Institution, 1988.

Stassen, Margaret and John Holahan. *Long-Term Care Demonstration Projects: A Review of Recent Evaluations*. Washington, DC: The Urban Institute, February 1981.

Strang, Vicki and Anne Neufeld. "Adult Day Care Programs A Source for Respite." *Journal of Gerontological Nursing*, 16, No 11 (November 1990), pp. 16-20.

Stephens, Susan A. and Jan B. Christianson. *Informal Care of the Elderly*. Lexington, MA: D. C. Health and Company, 1986.

Turner, Jonathan H. *The Structure of Sociological Theory*. Chicago, IL: The Dorsey Press, 1986.

U. S. Department of Health and Human Services. *1982 National Long-Term Care Survey and Informal Caregivers Survey*. Washington, DC: Government Printing Office, 1982.

BIBLIOGRAPHY

"A Few Key Facts." Perspective On Aging, XVI, No 6 (November/-December 1987), p. 5.

Aaronson, Linda. "Adult Day Care: A Developing Concept." Journal of Gerontological Social Work, 5, No 3 (Spring 1983), pp. 35-47.

Achenbaum, W. Andrew. "Historical Perspectives on Public Policy & Aging." Generations, XII, No 3 (Spring 1988), pp. 27-29.

Achenbaum, W. Andrew. Old Age in the New Land. Baltimore, MD: Johns Hopkins University Press, 1978.

Achenbaum, W. Andrew. Social Security: Visions and Revisions. New York: Cambridge University Press, 1986.

Adult Day Care: A Community-Based Long-Term Option. Harrisburg, PA: Pennsylvania Council on Aging, 1983.

"Adult Day Care Program: Watkins House Senior Center" Final Report to the Commonwealth of Pennsylvania Department of Aging in Response to R.F.P. #84-2 Category E.1, July 1984.

Adult Day Programs for the Elderly Proceedings. Published with the cooperation of the Publications and Advertising Office, Utica College of Syracuse University, January 1982.

Aging Action Alert. Silver Spring, MD: CD Publications No 2, February 14, 1986.

Aging America: Trends and Projections, 1985-86 Edition. Washington, DC: U. S. Department of Health and Human Services. PF3377 (1985).

Aging America: Trends and Projection, 1987-88 Edition. Washington, DC: U. S. Senate Special Committee on Aging in conjunction with AARP, FCOA, and AoA, 1988.

Aldrich, E. Funding and Spending for Human and Non-Human Resources in 100 Adult Day Care Centers Across the U. S. A. Available from the Executive Director, Central Geriatric Day Care Center, Warwick, RI, April 1978.

Aldridge, Martha, Harry Macy and Thomas Walz. Beyond Management: Humanizing the Administrative Process. Iowa: University of Iowa School of Social Work, 1982.

Amann, Anton. Open Care for the Elderly in Seven European Countries. New York: Pergamon, 1980.

Anderson, M. "The Impact on the Family Relationships of the Elderly of Changes Since Victorian Times in Governmental Income-Maintenance Provision." In Family, Bureaucracy, and the Elderly. Ed. E. Shanas and M. B. Sussman, Durham, NC: Duke University Press, 1977, pp. 36-59.

Ansak, Marie-Louise. Adult Day Care Programs: Hearings before the Subcommittee on Health and Long Term Care of the Select Committee on Aging. House of Representatives. Washington, DC: Government Printing Office, April 23, 1980, pp. 43-45.

Ansbacher, H. L. and R. Rowena, eds. The Individual Psychology of Alfred Adler. New York: Basic Books, 1956.

Antonucci, Toni and Hiroko Akiyana. "Social Networks in Adult Life and A Preliminary Examination of the Convoy Model." The Gerontologist, 42, No 5 (1987), pp. 519-527.

Arling, Greg, Elizabeth B. Harkins and Michael Romaniuk. "Adult Day Care and the Nursing Home: The Appropriateness of

Care in Alternative Settings." Research on Aging, 6, No 2 (June 1984), pp. 225-242.

Arling, Greg, Elizabeth Harkins, and Michael Romaniuk. Adult Daycare in Perspective: A Comparison of the Adult Daycare Study and the Study of the Virginia Nursing Home Pre-Admission Screening Program. Richmond, VA: Virginia Center on Aging, 1982.

Arling, Greg and W. J. McAuley. "The Feasibility of Public Payments for Family Caregiving." The Gerontologist, 23, No 3 (1983), pp. 300-306.

Armstrong, Edward. "Executive Class Should Address the Reality of Aging." Philadelphia Business Journal, January 7-13, 1985, p. 7.

Aronna, Beatrix. Health Aging: A Community Responsibility. Canada: Council on Aging of Ottawa-Carleton, 1983.

Asbury, C. and J. Merrill. "Dementia Long Term Care Services: The Emerging Role of Adult Day Centers." Pride Institute Journal of Long Term Home Health Care, 8, No 4 (Fall 1989), pp. 28-34.

Assessment and Evaluation Strategies In Aging: People, Populations and Programs. Proceedings of a National Conference and Related Workshops. Conference Chairperson, George Maddox. Asheville, NC: May 19-21, 1977.

Austin, Michael J. "A Network of Help for England's Elderly." Social Work, 21 (March 1976), pp. 114-119.

Banks, David R., et al. "Extending Long-Term Care Services into the Community." Nursing Homes, 32, No 5 (Sept/Oct 1983), pp. 26-31.

Barnard, Chester I. The Functions of the Executive, MA: Harvard University Press, 1962.

Beattie, W. M., Jr. "Aging and the Social Sciences." In Handbook of Aging and the Social Sciences. Eds. R. H. Binstock and E. Shanas. New York: Van Nostrand Reinhold Co., 1976, pp. 619-642.

Beauchamp, Dan. "Community: The Neglected Tradition of Public Health." Hastings Center Report (December 1985), pp.28-36.

Bellin, C. "Relocating Adult Day Care: It's Impact on Persons with Dementia." Journal of Gerontological Nursing, 16, No 3 (March 1990), pp. 11-14.

Benjamin, A. E., et al. "Shifting Commitments to Long-Term Care: The Role of Coordination." The Gerontologist, 24, No 6 (1984), pp. 598-603.

Berkman, L. J. and L. S. Syme. "Social Networks, Host Resistance, and Mortality: A Nine-Year Follow-Up Study of Alameda County Residents." American Journal of Epidemiology, 190, No 4 (1979), pp. 186-204.

Berman, Stephen, et al. "Respite Care: A Partnership Between a Veterans Administration Nursing Home and Families to Care for Frail Elders at Home." The Gerontologist, 27, No 5 (1987), pp. 581-584.

Bilitski, Joan Scialli. "Assessment of Adult Day Care Program and Client Health Characteristics in U. S. Region III." Diss. West Virginia University, 1985.

Billingsly, Andrew. "Family: Contemporary Patterns." Encyclopedia of Social Work, Vol I, 18th edition. Silver Spring, MD: N.A.S.W., 1987, pp. 520-528.

Blaser, Peg R. "Illinois Adult Day Care Parallels National Trend." Perspective on Aging, XII, No 3 (May/June, 1983), pp. 20-23.

Blau, P. The Dynamics of Bureaucracy. Chicago, IL: University of Chicago Press, 1955.

Blau, Z. S. Black Children/White Children: Competence, Socialization, and Social Structure. New York: The Free Press, 1981.

Blieszner, Rosemary, et. al. "Rural-Urban Differences in Service Use by Older Adults." In Aging, Health, and Family, Ed. Timothy Brubaker. Beverly Hills, CA: Sage Publishing Co., 1987, pp. 162-174.

Block, Fred, Richard Cloward, Barbara Ehrenreich, and Francis Fox Piven. The Mean Season. New York: Pantheon Books, 1987.

Borgatta, Edgar F. and Christopher Hertzog, eds. "Methodology and Aging Research." Research on Aging. 7, No 1 (1985), entire issue, p. 152.

Brannon, M. R. "Staffing Considerations." In Planning and Managing Adult Day Care: Pathways to Success. Ed. L. C. Webb. Maryland: National Health Publishing, 1989, pp. 73-83.

Brody, Elaine. Long-Term Care of Older People: A Practical Guide. New York: Human Sciences Press, 1977.

Brody, Elaine M. "Parent Care as a Normative Family Stress." The Gerontologist, 25, No 1 (1985), pp. 19-29.

Brody, Elaine, M. "Women in the Middle and Family Help to Older People." The Gerontologist, 21, No 5 (1981), pp. 471-480.

Brody, Elaine M. and C. Schoonover. "Patterns of Care for the Dependent Elderly When Daughters Work and When They Do Not." The Gerontologist, 26, No 4 (1986), pp. 372-381.

Brody, Elaine and Stanley Brody. "Aged: Services." In Encyclopedia of Social Work, Vol 1, 18th edition. Silver Spring, MD: National Association of Social Workers, 1987, pp. 106-127.

Brody, Stanley. "Continuity of Care." Newsletter. Research and Training Center for Rehabilitation, University of Pennsylvania, 3, No 2 (Spring 1987a), p. 5.

Brody, Stanley. "Strategic Planning: The Catastrophic Approach." The Gerontologist, 27, No 2 (1987b), pp. 131-138.

Brody, S. J., S. W. Poulshock and C. F. Masciocchi. "The Family Caring Unit: A Major Consideration in the Long Term Support System." The Gerontologist, 18, No 6 (1978), pp. 556-561.

Brown, Charlane and Mary O'Day. "Services to the Elderly." In Handbook of the Social Services. Eds. Neil Gilbert and Harry Specht. Englewood Cliffs, NJ: Prentice-Hall, Inc., 1981.

Browne, William P. and Laura Katz Olson. Aging and Public Policy: The Politics of Growing Old in America. Westport, CT: Greenwood Press, 1983.

Brubaker, Timothy. Aging, Health and Family: Long Term Care. Beverly Hills, CA: Sage Publications, 1987.

Burke, M., T. Hudson, and P. Eubanks. "Number of Adult Day Care Centers Increasing, But Payment Is Slow." Hospitals, 64, No 21 (November 5, 1990), pp. 34,36,38.

Burris, K. "Recommending Adult Day Care Centers." Nursing and Health Care, 2, No 8 (1981), pp. 437-441.

Burt, Martha, et al. Services to Disabled Adults: Community Living Arrangements and Day Programming. St. Paul, MN: Department of Public Welfare of Minnesota, 1983.

Busse, Ewald W. and George Maddox. The Duke Longitudinal Studies of Normal Aging, 1955-1980. New York: Springer Publishing Co., 1985.

Butrin, JoAnn. "Day Care: A New Idea?" Journal of Gerontological Nursing, 11, No 4 (1985), pp. 19-22.

Butler, Robert N. "An Overview of Research on Aging and the Status of Gerontology Today." The Milbank Memorial Fund Quarterly Health and Society, 61 (1983), pp. 351-396.

Butler, Robert. Why Survive Being Old in America. New York: Harper & Row, 1975.

Butler, Robert N., M. D. and Myrna I. Lewis. Aging & Mental Health. St. Louis, MO: The C. V. Mosby Co., 1982.

Butler, Robert N. and Herbert P. Gleason, eds. Productive Aging: Enhancing Vitality in Later Life. New York: Springer Publishing Co., 1985.

Callahan, J., et al. "Responsibility of Families for Their Severely Disabled Elders." Health Care Financing Review, (Winter 1980), pp. 29-48.

Callahan, James J. and Stanley S. Wallack, eds. Reforming the Long-Term Care System. Lexington, MA: D. C. Heath & Company, 1981.

Cantor, Marjorie. "The Informal Support System, Its Relevance in the Lives of the Elderly." In Aging and Society. Eds. E. Borgatta and N. McClusky. Beverly Hills, CA: Sage Publications, 1980, pp. 111-146.

Cantor, Marjorie H. "Neighbors and Friends: An Overlooked Resource in the Informal Support System." Research on Aging, 1, No 4 (1979), pp. 434-463.

Cantor, Marjorie. "Strain Among Caregivers: A Study of Experience in the United States." The Gerontologist, 23, No 6 (1983), pp. 597-603.

Cantor, Marjorie and Virginia Little. "Aging and Social Care." In Handbook of Aging and the Social Sciences. Eds. Robert Binstock and Ethel Shanas. New York: Van Nostrand Reinhold Co., 1985, pp. 745-781.

Cantor, M. H., and M. J. Mayer. "Factors In Differential Utilization of Services By Urban Elderly." Journal of Gerontological Social Work, 1, No 1 (1978), pp. 47-61.

Capitman, John. "Community-Based Long-Term Care Models, Target Groups, and Impacts on Service." The Gerontologist, 26, No 4 (1986), pp. 389-397.

Capitman, John A. Evaluation of Adult Day Health Care Programs in California Pursuant to Assembly Bill 1611, Chapter 1066, Statutes of 1977. Sacramento, CA: Office of Long Term Care and Aging, Department of Health Services, May 1982.

Capitman, John, et al. "Public and Private Costs of Long-Term Care for Nursing Home Pre-Admission Screening Program Participants." The Gerontologist, 27, No 6 (1987), pp. 780-787.

Carrilio, Terry and David Eisenberg. "Informal Resources for the Elderly: Panacea or Empty Promises." Journal of Gerontological Social Work, 6, No 1 (September 1983), pp. 39-47.

Chappell, Neena. "Social Supports and the Receipt of Home Care Services." The Gerontologist, 25, No 1 (1985), pp. 47-54.

Chappell, Neena and Margaret J. Penning. "The Trend Away From Institutionalization." Research on Aging, 1, No 30 (September 1979), pp. 361-387.

Chappell, Neena, et al. "Adult Day Care and Medical and Hospital Claims." The Gerontologist, 27, No 6 (1987), pp. 773-779.

Christianson, Jon and Susan Stephens. Informal Care to the Impaired Elderly: Report of the National Long Term Care Demonstration Survey of Informal Caregivers. Channeling Evaluation Technical Report Number 3. Princeton, NJ: Mathematica Policy Research, Inc., revised February 1986.

Clark, Robert F. "The Costs and Benefits of Community Care: A Perspective from the Channeling Demonstration." Pride Institute Journal of Long Term Home Health Care, 6, No 2 (Spring 1987), pp. 3-13.

Cobb, S. "Social Support as a Moderator of Life Stress." Psychosomatic Medicine, 38 (1976), pp. 300-314.

Cole, Thomas. "Aging & Meaning." Generations, X, No 2 (Winter 1985), pp. 49-52.

Cole, Thomas. "The Role of the Humanities in Aging." The Aging Connection, IX, No 6 (December 1988/January 1989), p. 7.

"Comments on the Weissert Report." Home Health Care Services Quarterly, 1, No 3 (Fall 1980), pp. 97-121.

"Community Care." In Dictionary of Social Welfare. Eds. Noel and Rita Timms. London: Routledge & Kegan Parul, 1982, pp. 36-37.

Community Research Applications, Inc. Evaluation, Report of the Mosholu-Montefiore Day Care Center for the Elderly in the Northwest Bronx. New York, NY: September 1975.

Conrad, Kendon. "Shedding New Light On Adult Day Care." Perspective on Aging, XVI, No 6 (November/December 1987), pp. 18-21.

Conrad, Kendon, et al. Assessing the Structure, Population, and Process of Adult Day Care Programs: Report to the AARP Andrus Foundation. Evanston, Ill: Center for Health Services and Policy Research, Northwestern University, January 1, 1986 to December 31, 1986.

Conrad, K. J., P. Hanrahan, and S. L. Hughes. "Survey of Adult Day Care in the United States: National and Regional Findings." Research on Aging, 12, No 1 (March 1990), pp. 36-56.

Cooley, Charles Horton. Social Organization. New York: Charles Scribner's Sons, 1909, pp. 23-28.

Coser, Lewis A. and Bernard Rosenberg, eds. Sociological Theory: A Book of Readings. New York: The MacMillan Company, 1957.

Creedon, Michael A., ed. Issues for an Aging American: Employees and Eldercare: A Briefing Book. Bridgeport, CT: University of Bridgeport, Center for the Study of Aging, 1987.

Crossman, Linda. "Adult Day Care: Coming of Age." The Aging Connection, 8, No 4 (August/September 1987), pp. 1,3.

Crystal, Stephen. America's Old Age Crisis. New York: Basic Books, 1982.

Curtis, Michael, ed. The Great Political Theories. New York: Avon Books, 1962.

Daniels, Norman. Am I My Parent's Keeper? New York: Oxford University Press, 1988.

Dawson, Deborah, et al. "Aging in the Eighties: Functional Limitations of Individuals Age 65 Years and Over." Advancedata, 133 (June 10, 1987).

"Day Care Center Brings New Perspective to Mt. Vernon Elderly." Aging, No 337 (March/April 1983), pp. 32-33.

"Day Care Center Delivers Several Types of Services." Aging, Nos 277-278 (November/December 1977), pp. 26-27.

de Schweinitz, Karl. England's Road to Social Security. Philadelphia, PA: University of Pennsylvania Press, 1943.

Dilworth-Anderson, Peggye. "Supporting Family Caregiving Through Adult Day-Care Services." Aging, Health, and Family. Ed. Timothy Brubaker, Beverly Hills, CA: Sage Publications, 1987, pp. 129-142.

Dobelstein, Andrew. Politics, Economics, and the Public Welfare. New Jersey: Prentice-Hall, 1986.

Dobrof, Rose and Eugene Litwak. Maintenance of Family Ties of Long-Term Care Patients: Theory and Guide to Practice. Rockville, MD: National Institute of Mental Health, 1977, pp. 1-79.

Doherty, Neville and Barbara Hicks. "The Use of Cost-Effectiveness Analysis in Geriatric Day Care." The Gerontologist, 15, No 5 (1975), pp. 412-417.

Dono, John, C. M. Falbe, B. L. Kail, E. Litwak, et al. "Primary Groups in Old Age." Research on Aging, 1, No 4 (1979), pp. 403-433.

Doty, Pamela. "Family Care of the Elderly: The Role of Public Policy." The Milbank Quarterly, 64, No 1 (1986), pp. 34-75.

Dukakis, Michael and Richard Rowlan. Creating Opportunities for Elder Independence in a Long Term Care System, Executive Office of Elder Affairs, Boston, MA, 1985.

Durkheim, Emile. The Division of Labor in Society. New York: Macmillan, 1933.

Eggert, G., et al. "Caring for the Patient with Long-Term Disability." Geriatrics, 32 (1977), pp. 102-114.

Ehrlich, Phyllis and Tena Frank. "Family Lifeline: Bridging the Miles," The Gerontologist, 28, No 1 (1988), pp. 108-111.

Eisenberg, David and Emily Amerman. "A New Look at the Channeling Demonstration," Part II. Perspective on Aging, XVII, No 1 (1988), pp. 20-23.

Eisenstadt, S. N. "Bureaucracy, Bureaucratization, and Debureaucratization." In Complex Organizations: A Sociological Reader. Ed. Amitai Etzioni. New York: Holt, Rinehart, and Winston, Inc., 1961, pp. 268-276.

English, David and Celia M. Berdes. Program Evaluation and Evaluation Research: Theory, Issues and Applications Useful in Long-Term Care Gerontology Centers. Washington, DC: Elm Services, Inc. Developed under AOA Contract #HEW 105-79-3008, September 1980.

Estes, C. C. and Howard E. Freeman. "Strategies of Design and Research for Intervention." In Handbook of Aging and the Social Sciences. Eds. Robert Binstock and Ethel Shanas, New York: Van Nostrand Reinhold Co., 1976, pp. 536-560.

Estes, C L., R. J. Newcomer and Associates. Fiscal Austerity and Aging: Shifting Government Responsibility for the Elderly. Beverly Hills, CA: Sage Publications, 1983.

Estes, Carroll. The Aging Enterprise. San Francisco, CA: Jossey-Bass, 1979.

Estes, Carroll L. and Charles A. Harrington. "Fiscal Crisis, Deinstitutionalization, and the Elderly." American Behavioral
Scientist, 24, No 6 (1981), pp. 811-826.

Etzioni, Amitai. Complex Organizations. New York: Holt, Rinehart
and Winston, Inc., 1961.

Etzioni, Amitai. "Industrial Sociology: The Study of Economic
Organizations." Social Research, 25, No 3 (1958), pp. 303-
324.

Eustis, Nancy N., Jay N. Greenberg, and Sharon K. Patten. Long-
Term Care for Older Persons: A Policy Perspective. Monterey, CA: Brooks/Cole Publishing Company, 1984.

"Factors Correlated With Entering Long-Term Care Institutions."
NIAD News, 3, No 1 (1983), p. 5.

FallCreek, Stephanie and Neil Gilbert. "Aging Network in Transition:
Problems and Prospects." Social Work, 26, No 3 (1981),
pp. 210-216.

Faris, Ellsworth. The Nature of Human Nature. New York: Mc-
Graw-Hill Book Company, Inc., 1937.

Federal Register, Part II. Department of Health and Human Services.
Washington, DC: Office Human Development Services 52,
No 250 (Wednesday, December 30, 1987), pp. 49252-49319.

Felder, Leonard. "Caregiver Support Programs Spreading Nationwide."
The Aging Connection, IX, No 2 (April/May 1988), p. 7.

Fengler, Alfred P. and Nancy Goodrich. "Wives of Elderly Disabled
Men: The Hidden Patients." The Gerontologist, 19, No 2
(1979), p. 175.

Ferguson, Kathleen, Ronald Lucchino and Trudy White. An Adult
Day Care Program for the Elderly: An Operational Manual.

Utica, New York: Institute of Gerontology, Utica College, revised 1982.

Ficke, Susan Coombs, ed. An Orientation to the Older Americans Act. Revised Edition. Washington, DC: National Association of State Units on Aging, July 1985.

Field Reports on Day Care. Physical & Occupational Therapy In Geriatrics, 3, No 4 (1984), pp. 61-74.

Finestone, S. and A. J. Kahn. "The Design of Research." Social Work Research. Ed. M. A. Polansky. Chicago, IL: The University of Chicago Press, 1975.

Fischer, C. S., R. M. Jackson, et al., ed. Networks and Places: Social Relations in the Urban Setting. New York: The Free Press, 1977.

Fischer, David Hackett. Growing Old In America. New York: Oxford University Press, 1978.

Fowles, Donald G. "Functional Disability," Aging, No 357 (1988), p. 39-41.

Frankena, William L. Ethics. New Jersey: Prentice-Hall, Inc., 1973.

Frankfather, D. L., et al. Family Care of the Elderly. Lexington, MA: Lexington Books, 1981.

Friedan, Betty. "The Mystique of Age." In Productive Aging. Ed. Robert Butler and Herbert Gleason. New York: Springer Publishing Co., pp. 37-46.

Friedman, Milton. Capitalism and Freedom. Chicago, IL: The University of Chicago Press, 1962.

From Max Weber. Essays in Sociology. H. H. Gerth and C. Wright Mills, trans. and ed. New York: A Galaxy Book, 1958.

Fuchs, Victor R. Who Shall Live? New York: Basic Books, 1974.

Gelfand, Donald and Jody K. Olsen. The Aging Network: Programs and Services. New York: Springer Publishing Co., 1980.

George, Linda K. "The Burden of Caregiving: How Much? What Kinds? For Whom? Advances in Research. Durham, NC: Duke University Medical Center, 8, No 2 (1984) pp. 1-7.

Gerth, H. H., and C. Wright Mills. From Max Weber: Essays in Sociology. New York: Oxford University Press, 1946.

Gilbert, Neil and Harry Specht. Dimensions of Social Welfare Policy. Englewood Cliffs, NJ: Prentice-Hall, 1974.

Giddens, Anthony. Capitalism and Modern Social Theory. London: Cambridge University Press, 1971.

Glasse, Lou. "Public Policy, Personal Caregiving arc Closely Tied to Each Other." Perspectives on Aging, XVI, No 2 (March/ April 1987), pp. 14-15.

Gleason, Herbert. "Financing Medical and Health Care for Older Americans." In Productive Aging. Ed. Robert Butler and Herbert Gleason. New York: Springer Publishing Co., 1985, pp. 105-112.

Glenner, Joy and George G. Glenner. "The Crucible—Family Dilemmas in Alzheimer's Disease: Day Care—An Alternative." Activities, Adaptations & Aging, 13, No 1/2 (1988/89), pp. 1-23.

Goldstein, Francis M. and Stephanie R. Egly. "Adult Day Care: An Extension of the Family." Aging, No 348 (1985), pp. 19-21.

Goldstein, R. "Adult Day Care: Expanding Options for Service." Journal of Gerontological Social Work, 5, Nos 1-2 (Fall/ Winter 1983), pp. 157-168.

Goldstein, S. M. Adult Day Care: A Basic Guide. Owings Mills, MD: National Health Publishing, 1989.

Gortner, Harold F., et. al. Organization Theory: A Public Perspective. Chicago, IL: The Dorsey Press, 1987.

Gottesman, Leonard, Barbara Ishizaki, and Stacey MacBride. "Service Management—Plan and Conception in Pennsylvania." The Gerontologist, 19 (1979), pp. 379-385.

Gottesman, Leonard E., David Eisenberg and Barbara Ishizaki. Day Care Services for Old, Disabled People. Philadelphia, PA: Philadelphia Geriatric Center, 1975.

Greene, V. Strengthening Informal Caregiver Effectiveness through Stress Reduction Counseling: Training and Policy Implications. Tucson, AZ: University of Arizona, 1985.

Greenberg, Jay N. "Evaluating the Cost of Services." In Research Instruments in Social Gerontology: Vol 3, Health, Program Evaluation and Demography. Eds. David J. Mangen and Warren A Peterson. Minneapolis, MN: University of Minn. Press, 1984, pp. 317-347.

Grimaldi, P. L. "The Costs of Adult Day Care and Nursing Home Care: A Dissenting View" [Commentary]. Inquiry, 16, No 2 (Summer 1979), pp. 162-166.

Grosser, Charles. "Community Organization," Chapter 1. New Directions In Community Organization: From Enabling to Advocacy. New York: Praeger, 1973, pp. 3-20.

Gruenberg, E. M. "The Failures of Success." The Milbank Memorial Fund Quarterly, Health and Society, 55 (1977), pp. 3-24.

Guillemard, Anne-Marie, ed. Old Age and the Welfare State. Beverly Hills, CA: Sage Publications, 1983.

Gurewitsch, Eleanor. "Geriatric Day Care. The Options Reconsidered." Aging, Nos 329-330 (July/August, 1982), pp. 21-26.

Gurland, Barry, Ruth Bennett and David Wilder. "Reevaluating the Place of Evaluation in Planning for Alternatives to Institutional Care for the Elderly." Journal of Social Issues, 37, No 3 (1981), pp. 51-70.

Gustafson, Elizabeth. "Day Care for the Elderly." The Gerontologist, 14 (February 1974), pp. 46-49.

Gustafson, James M. "Professions as 'Callings.'" Social Service Review, 56 (December 1982), pp. 503-515.

Gutowski, Michael. The Graying of Suburbia. Washington, DC: Urban Institute, 1979.

Haber, C. Beyond Sixty-Five: The Dilemma of Old Age in America's Past. Cambridge, MA: Cambridge University Press, 1983.

Habermas, Jurgen. "The Hermeneutic Claim to Universality." In Contemporary Hermeneutics. Hermeneutics as Method, Philosophy and Critique. Ed. J. Bleicher. London, England: Boston and Henley, 1980.

Hall, E. "Acting One's Age: New Rules for Old." Psychology Today, 13 (1980), pp. 66-80.

Ham, R. "Alternatives to Institutionalization." American Family, 21, No 71 (1980), pp. 95-100.

Hammerman, Jerome. "The Role of the Institution and the Concept of Parallel Services." The Gerontologist, 14, No 1 (February 1974), pp. 11-14.

Harahan, Mary. "National Long-Term Care Channeling Demonstration Program. Proceedings of the 1987 Public Health Conference on Records and Statistics. Washington, DC:

National Center for Health Statistics, July 13-15, 1987. In Data for an Aging Population, Dec. 1987, pp. 89-91.

Harder, W. Paul, Janet C. Gornick and Martha R. Burt. Adult Day Care: Supplement or Substitute? Draft Report. Washington, DC: The Urban Institute, 1983.

Harder, W. Paul, Janet Gornick and Martha Burt. "Adult Day Care: Substitute or Supplement?" The Milbank Quarterly, 64, No 3 (1986), pp. 414-441.

Hardin, Thomas. "No Center Is An Island: Network Building in Adult Day Care." Adult Day Care Quarterly. Washington, DC: National Institute of Adult Day Care, A membership unit of the National Council on the Aging, 2, No 4 (1987).

Harkins, Elizabeth and Cynthia Bowling. Study of the Virginia Nursing Home Pre-Admission Screening Program. Richmond, VA: Virginia Center on Aging, March 31, 1982.

Harkins, E. Social and Health Factors in Long-Term Care: Findings from the Statewide Survey of Older Virginians. Richmond, VA: Virginia Office on Aging, 1981.

Harel, Zev, Linda Noelker, and Brian Blake. "Comprehensive Services for the Aged: Theoretical and Empirical Perspectives." The Gerontologist, 25, No 6 (1985), pp. 644-649.

Harlow, Karen S, et al. "Use of Formal and Informal Services in Community-Based Long-Term Care." Proceedings of the 1987 Public Health Conference on Records and Statistics. Data for An Aging Population. Washington, DC: U. S. Department of Health and Human Services, December 1987, pp. 93-98.

Harrington, Charlene. "Alternatives." Generations, IX, No 4 (Summer 1985), pp. 43-46.

Harrington, Michael. The New American Poverty. New York: Penquin Books, 1984.

Harrington, Michael. The Next Left. New York: Henry Holt and Company, 1986.

Health Care Financing Administration. Long-Term Care: Background and Future Directions. Discussion Paper, Office of Policy Analysis, HCFA, 81-20047, Washington, DC, 1981, p. 15.

Health Care Financing Administration. Data on the Medicaid Program: Eligibility, Services, Expenditures. Baltimore, MD: Medicaid/Medicare Management Institute, 1979.

Hedenstrom, Joyce and Sharon Osterwald. "Adult Day Care Programs: Maintaining A Therapeutic Triad." Home Care Services Quarterly, 9, No 1 (1988), pp. 85-102.

Heydebrand, Wolf V. Comparative Organizations: The Results of Empirical Research. Englewood Cliffs, NJ: Prentice-Hall, Inc., 1973.

Hoch, C. and G.C. Hemmens. "Linking Informal and Formal Help: Conflict Along the Continuum of Care." Social Service Review, 61 (1987), pp. 432-446.

Hochschild, Arlie Russell. The Unexpected Community. Berkeley, CA: University of California Press, 1973.

Hodgson, Jr., Joseph H. and Joan L. Quinn. "The Impact of the Triage Health Care Delivery System Upon Client Morale, Independent Living and the Cost of Care." The Gerontologist, 20, No 3 (1980), pp. 364-371.

Holland, Thomas and Mareia Petchers. "Organizations: Context for Social Service Delivery." In Encyclopedia of Social Work, Vol 2, 18th edition. Silver Spring, MD: National Association of Social Workers, 1987, pp. 204-217.

Homans, George C. The Human Group. New York: Harcourt, Brace and Company, 1950.

Hooyman, Nancy and Wendy Lustbader. Taking Care. New York: The Free Press, 1986.

Horowitz, A. "Family Caregiving to the Frail Elderly." In Annual Review of Gerontology and Geriatrics, Vol 5. Eds. C. Eisdorfer, M. P. Lawton, and G. L. Maddox. New York: Springer Publishing Co., 1985, pp. 194-246.

Horowitz, A. and Rose Dobrof. "The Role of Families in Providing Long-Term Care to the Frail and Chronically Ill Elderly Living in the Community." Final Report Submitted to the Health Care Financing Administration Grant #18-P-97541/-2-02. New York: Brookdale Center on Aging, Hunter College, 1982.

"How America Treats Its Elderly." Newsweek, (November 1, 1982), pp. 60-65.

Hudson, Robert B., ed. "The Politics of Aging." Generations, IX, No 1 (1984), entire issue, pp. 51.

Hudson, Robert B. "Renewing the Federal Role." Generations, XII, No 3 (Spring 1988), pp. 23-26.

Huttman, Elizabeth. Social Services for the Elderly. New York: The Free Press, 1985.

Jacobs, B. and William Weissert. "Financing Long-Term Care." Journal of Health, Politics, Policy and Law, 12, No 1 (Spring, 1987), pp. 77-95.

Jennings, Bruce, Daniel Callahan and Arthur Caplan. "Ethical Challenges of Chronic Illness." Hastings Center Report, Special Supplement, (February/March 1988), pp. 1-16.

Joffe, Carole. "Daycare Services." In Handbook of the Social Services. Eds. Neil Gilbert and Harry Specht. Englewood Cliffs, NJ: Prentice-Hall, Inc., 1981.

Johnson, C. L. "Dyadic Family Relations and Social Support." The Gerontologist, 23, No 4 (1983), pp. 377-383.

Johnson, C. and D. J. Catalano. "A Longitudinal Study of Family Supports to Impaired Elderly." The Gerontologist, 23, No 6 (1983), pp. 612-618.

Jung, C. G. "Two Essays on Analytical Psychology." Collected Works. Volume 7. New York: Pantheon Press, 1954.

Kahana, E. and R. M. Coe. "Alternatives in Long Term Care." In Handbook for Researchers, Planners, and Providers. Ed. Sylvia Sherwood. New York: Spectrum Publications, 1975.

Kahn, Alfred J. Social Policy and Social Services. New York: Random House, 1973.

Kahn, Alfred J. "Social Services in Relation to Income Security: Introductory Notes." The Social Service Review, XXXIX, No 4 (December 1965), pp. 381-89.

Kahn, Alfred and Sheila Kamerman. "Options for Delivery of Social Services at the Local Level: A Cross-National Report." In Reaching People: The Structure of Neighborhood Services, Volume 3. Social Service Delivery Systems: An International Annual. Eds. Daniel Thursz and Joseph Vigilante. Beverly Hills, CA: Sage Publications, 1978.

Kalish, R.A. An Essay, in Adult Day Care Services: An Introduction to the Literature. Washington, DC: Elm Associates, 1980.

Kalish, Richard, Elinore Luri, Richard Wexler and Rick Zawadski. On Lok Health Services: Evaluation of a Success. San

Francisco, CA: On Lok Senior Health Services, November 1975.

Kane, Robert L. and Rosalie A. Kane. A Will and a Way: What the United States Can Learn from Canada. NY: Columbia University Press, 1985.

Kane, Rosalie and Robert Kane. Assessing the Elderly. Lexington, MA: Lexington Books, 1981.

Kane, Rosalie and Robert Kane. Long-Term Care: Principles, Programs, and Policies. New York: Springer Publishing Co., 1987.

Kane, Rosalie. "Long-Term Care." In Encyclopedia of Social Work, Vol 2, 18th edition. Silver Spring, MD: National Association of Social Workers, 1987, pp. 59-72.

Kaplan, J. "Goals of Day Care." In Day Care for Older Adults. Ed. E. Pfeiffer. Durham, NC: Duke University Press, 1976.

Katz, E. and P. F. Lazarsfeld. Personal Influence. Glencoe, IL: The Free Press, 1955.

Katz, Rosalyn. A Study of Adult Day Care Need and Demand in Allegheny County, Pennsylvania. Pittsburgh, PA: Health and Welfare Planning Association, November 1981.

Katz, S., et al. "Progress in the Development of the Index of ADL." The Gerontologist, 10 (1970), pp. 20-30.

Katz, Sidney, Amasa Ford, et al. "Studies of Illness in the Aged." Journal of the American Medical Association, 185 (1963), pp. 914-919.

Kaufman, M. "Social Policy and Long Term Care for the Aged." Social Work, 25 (1980), pp. 133-137.

Kaye, Lenard W. "Assessing the Community Care Needs of the Functionally Impaired Elderly: The Gerontological Worker's Perspective." Home Health Care Services Quarterly, 8, No 4 (1988), pp. 89-101.

Kaye, Lenard W. "Home Care for the Aged: A Fragile Partnership. "Social Work, 30, No 4 (1985), pp. 312-317.

Kaye, Lenard W. "Home Care Services for Older People: An Organizational Analysis of Provider Experience." Diss. Columbia University, 1982.

Kaye, Lenard W. and Patricia M. Kirwin. "Adult Day Care Services for the Elderly and Their Families: Lessons from the Pennsylvania Experience." Journal of Gerontological Social Work, 15, No 3/4 (1990), pp. 167-183.

Kaye, Lenard W. and Patricia M. Kirwin. "An Evaluation of Adult Day Care Programs in Pennsylvania." Bryn Mawr, PA: Bryn Mawr College Graduate School of Social Work and Social Research, 1989. Pennsylvania Department of Aging Contract No. 871003.

Kemper, Peter, Robert Applebaum, et al. "Community Care Demonstrations: What Have We Learned." Health Care Financing Review, 8, No 4 (Summer 1987), pp. 87-100.

Kermis, Marguerite, et al. "Our Parents' Keepers: An Analysis of Values and Dilemmas in Home Care of the Frail Elderly." The Journal of Applied Gerontology, 5, No 2 (December 1986) pp. 126-138.

Kerschner, Paul A. "The $3.75 an Hour Factor." Perspective On Aging, XVI, No 6 (November/December 1987), pp. 15-17.

Kerson, Toba S. and Lawrence A. Kerson. Understanding Chronic Illness, New York: The Free Press, 1985.

Kingston, Eric R., et al. The Common Stake: The Interdependence of Generations (A Policy Framework for an Aging Society). Washington, DC: The Gerontological Society of America, 1986.

Kirwin, Patricia M. "Adult Day Care: An Integrated Model." In Social Work and Alzheimer's Disease. Ed. Rose Dobrof. New York: Haworth Press, 1986, pp. 59-71.

Kirwin, Patricia M. An Evaluation of the Relationship Between Formal and Informal Systems in the Service of Adult Day Care for the Frail Elderly (Doctoral dissertation, Bryn Mawr College, 1989). Dissertation Abstracts International, 50, 2245A. Order No DA8924650.

Kirwin, Patricia M. "The Challenge of Community Long-Term Care: The Dependent Aged." Journal of Aging Studies, 2, No 3 (1988), pp. 255-266.

Kirwin, Patricia M. "Correlates of Service Utilization Among Adult Day Care Clients," Home Health Care Services Quarterly, 9, No 1 (1988), pp. 103-115.

Kirwin, Patricia M. "Extending the Inter-Generational Celebration Through the Service of Adult Day Care." Presentation at National Association of Social Workers, New Orleans, LA, September, 1987.

Kirwin, Patricia M. "Intergenerational Continuity & Reciprocity Through the Use of Community Based Services." Home Health Care Services Quarterly, 12, No 2 (Spring/Summer, 1991).

Kirwin, Patricia M. "You Heard What I Said, but Do You Know What I Meant?" Generations, in press.

Kistin, H. and R. Morris. "Alternatives to Institutional Care for the Elderly." The Gerontologist, 12, No 2 (Summer 1972, Part 1), pp. 139-142.

Klapfish, Anne. Adult Day Care Programs: Hearings Before the Subcommittee on Health and Long Term Care of the Select Committee on Aging. House of Representatives. Washington, DC: Government Printing Office, April 23, 1980, pp. 21.

Knight, Bob and Deborah Lower Walker. "Toward A Definition of Alternatives to Institutionalization for the Frail Elderly." The Gerontologist, 25, No 4 (August 1985), pp. 358-363.

Knox, Rita and Lester Marks. "Program Report: Day Center for the Elderly. Mosholu-Montefiore Community Center, Bronx, NY, No Date.

Koenen, Robert E. "Adult Day Care: A Northwest Perspective." Journal of Gerontological Nursing, 6, No 4 (1980), pp. 218-221.

Koff, Theodore H. Long-Term Care, an Approach to Serving the Frail Elderly. Boston, MA: Little Brown, 1982.

Koff, Theodore H. "Rationale for Services: Day Care, Allied Care and Coordination." The Gerontologist, 14, No 1 (February 1974), pp. 26-29.

Kostick, Abraham. "A Day Care Program for the Physically and Emotionally Disabled." The Gerontologist, 12, No 2 (Summer 1972, Part 1), pp. 134-137.

Kotz, Arnold and Julia Graham Lear, eds. The Policy Analysis Source Book for Social Problems. Washington, DC: The National Planning Association, 1975.

Kreiger, Martha, William Weissert and Joel Cohen. Characteristics of Medicaid Home and Community-Based Waiver Program

Applications Volume L. Background and Summary. Washington, DC: The Urban Institute, 1982.

Kutza, Elizabeth. The Benefits of Old Age: Social Welfare Policy for the Elderly. Chicago, IL: University Press, 1981.

Lampert, D. J. et al. "Planning for Contact Between the Generations: An Effective Approach." The Gerontologist, 30, No 4 (August 1990), pp. 553-116.

Larmer, Kay. Memorandum. National Council on the Aging, Washington, DC, March 29, 1988.

La Rocco, J., J. S. House and J. R. French, Jr. "Social Support, Occupational Stress, and Health." Journal of Health and Social Behavior, 21, No 3 (September 1980), pp. 202-218.

Laurie, W. Employing the Duke OARS "Methodology in Cost Comparisons: Home Services and Institutionalization." Center Reports on Advance in Research. Durham, NC: Duke University Center for the Study of Aging and Human Development, 2, 1978.

Lavine, Eileen Martinson. Learning to Work with the Aged. New York: Wm. Hodson Community Center for Older Persons, 1960.

La Vor, Judith and Marie Callender. "Home Health Cost Effectiveness: What Are We Missing." Medical Care, 14, No 10 (1976), pp. 866-872.

Lawton, M. Powell and Elaine Brody. "Assessment of Older People: Self-Maintaining and Instrumental Activities of Daily Living." The Gerontologist, 9, No 3 (Autumn 1969), pp. 179-186.

Lawton, Powell M., Elaine M. Brody, and Avalie R. Saperstein. "A Controlled Study of Respite Service for Caregivers of

Alzheimer's Patients." The Gerontologist, 29, No 1 (1989), pp. 8-16.

Leary, Florence. "Overcoming a Client's Resistance to Day Care." National Institute on Adult Daycare News, 2, No 3 (1982), pp. 3-4.

Lebowitz, B. "Old Age and Family Functioning." Journal of Gerontological Social Work. 2 (1978), pp. 111-118.

Lee, Philip and A. E. Benjamin. "Intergovernmental Relations: Historical and Contemporary Perspectives." In Fiscal Austerity and Aging. Eds. Carroll L. Estes, Robert J. Newcomer and Associates. Beverly Hills, CA: Sage Publications, 1983, pp. 59-81.

Leiby, James. A History of Social Welfare and Social Work in the United States. New York: Columbia University, 1978.

Lind, S. Donna and John E. O'Brien. "The General Problem of Program Evaluation: The Researcher's Perspective." The Gerontologist, 11, No 4 (Winter 1971, Part II), pp. 43-50.

Litwak, Eugene. "Agency and Family Linkages in Providing Services." In Reaching People: The Structure of Neighborhood Services, Vol 3. Social Service Delivery Systems: An International Annual. Eds. D. Thursz and J. Vigilante. Beverly Hills, CA: Sage Publications, 1978, pp. 59-95.

Litwak, Eugene. Helping the Elderly. New York: The Guilford Press, 1985.

Litwak, Eugene. "Models of Bureaucracy which Permit Conflict." In Human Service Organizations. Eds. Yeheskel Hasenfeld and Richard English. Ann Arbor, MI: University of Michigan Press, 1977a.

Litwak, Eugene. "Part II-Theoretical Bases for Practice." In <u>Mainte-nance of Family Ties of Long-Term Care Patients: Theory and Guide to Practice</u>. Rose Dobrof and Eugene Litwak. Rockville, MD: National Institute of Mental Health, 1977b, pp. 80-116.

Litwak, Eugene. "Reference Group Theory, Bureaucratic Career, and Neighborhood Primary Group Cohesion." <u>Sociometry</u>, 23 (1960), pp. 72-84.

Litwak, Eugene and Cecilia Falbe. "Formal Organizations and Community Primary Groups: Theory and Policy of Shared Functions as Applied to the Aged." Conference on Organizational Theory and Public Policy, State University of New York at Albany, April 1-2, 1982.

Litwak, E. and J. Figueira. "Technical Innovation and Ideal Forms of Family Structure in an Industrial Society." In <u>Families in East and West: Socialization Process and Kinship Ties</u>. Eds. R. Hill and R. Konig. Paris: Mouton, 1970, pp. 348-396.

Litwak, Eugene and Lydia Hylton. "Interorganizational Analysis: A Hypothesis on Co-ordinating Agencies. In <u>A Sociological Reader on Complex Organizations</u>, Second Edition. Ed. Amitai Etzioni. New York: Holt Reinhart and Winston, Inc. 1969, pp. 339-356.

Litwak, E. and S. Kulis. <u>Networks, Primary Groups, and Formal Organizations: Alternative Principles for Matching Group Structures with Tasks Among the Aged</u>. New York: Columbia University Center for the Social Sciences (Preprint Series No 88), 1982.

Litwak, E. and S. Kulis. <u>The Dynamics of Network Change for Older People: Social Policy and Social Theory</u>. New York: Center for the Social Sciences At Columbia University (pre-print series 74), 1981.

Litwak, Eugene and Charles Longino. "Migration Patterns Among the Elderly: A Developmental Perspective." The Gerontologist, 27, No 3 (June 1987), pp. 259-265.

Litwak, E. and H. Meyer. "A Balance Theory of Coordination Between Bureaucratic Organizations and Community Primary Groups." Administrative Science Quarterly, 11 (1966), pp. 31-58.

Litwak, Eugene and H. Meyer. School, Family, and Community: The Theory and Practice of School-Community Relations. New York: Columbia University Press, 1974.

Litwak, E., H. Meyer, and C. D. Hollister. "The Role of Linkage Mechanisms between Bureaucracies and Families: Education and Health as Empirical Cases in Point". In Power Paradigms and Community Research. Ed. R. J. Liebert and A. W. Imershine. Beverly Hills, CA: Sage Publications, 1977, pp. 121-152.

Litwak, Eugene and Ivan Szelenyi. "Primary Group Structures and Their Functions: Kin, Neighbors, Friends." American Sociological Review, 34, No 4 (1969), pp. 465-481.

Liu, Karbin, Pamela Doty and Kenneth Manton. "Medicaid Spend-down in Nursing Homes and the Community." Washington, DC: U. S. Department of Health and Human Services, through HCFA Cooperative Agreement No 18-C-98641/4-02, March 1989.

Liu, K., K. G. Manton, and B. M. Liu. "Home Care Expenses for the Disabled Elderly." Health Care Financing Review, 7 No 2 (1985) pp. 51-58.

Lloyd, Susan and Nancy Greenspan. "Nursing Homes, Home Health Services, and Adult Day Care." In Long Term Care: Perspectives from Research and Demonstrations. Eds. Ronald Vogel and Hans Palmer. Washington, DC: Health Care Financing

Administration, U.S. Department of Health and Human Services, 1982, pp. 133-166.

Locker, Rose and Anna Rublin. "The Roles of the Geriatric Day Program in the Spectrum of Services for Older Adults." Paper Presented at the Northeastern Gerontological Society, April 1984, Philadelphia, PA.

Long Term Care Population: Definition and Measurement. Project to Analyze Existing Long Term Care Data, Vol II. Washington, DC: Urban Institute, Office of the Assistant Secretary for Planning Evaluation, Administration on Aging, 1981.

Lorenze, Edward J., et al. "The Geriatric Day Hospital." Report presented at the 26th Annual Meeting of the Gerontological Society, Miami Beach, FL, Nov. 7, 1973.

Louis Harris and Associates, Inc. Priorities and Expectations for Health and Living Circumstances: A Survey of the Elderly in Five English-Speaking Countries. A study for the Commonwealth Fund. New York: Harris and Associates, 1982.

Lowy, Louis. Social Policies and Programs on Aging. Lexington, MA: Lexington Books, 1980.

Lyman, K. A. "Day Care for Persons with Dementia: The Impact of the Physical Environment on Staff Stress and Quality of Care." The Gerontologist, 2, No 4 (August 1989), pp. 557-560.

Mace, Nancy L. and Peter V. Rabins. The 36-Hour Day: A Family Guide to Caring for Persons with Alzheimer's Disease, Related Dementing Illness and Memory Loss in Later Life. Baltimore, MD: Johns Hopkins University Press, 1982.

Mace, Nancy L. and Peter V. Rabins. A Survey of Day Care for the Demented Adult in the United States. Washington, DC, National Council on the Aging, 1984.

Mace, Nancy L. "Report of a Survey of Day Care Centers." Pride Institute Journal of Long Term Health Care, 3, No 4 (Fall 1984), pp. 38-43.

Maldonado, Jr., David. "Aged." The Encyclopedia of Social Work, Vol I, 18th edition. Silver Spring, MD: National Association of Social Workers, 1987, pp. 95-106.

Mankoff, S. Lawrence. "Adult Day Care: A Promoter of Independent Living." Journal of the America Health Care Association, 10, No 1 (January 1984), pp. 19-21.

Manuel, Ron C., and Marc I. Berk. "A Look at Similarities and Differences in Older Minority Populations." Aging (May/June 1983), pp. 21-29.

"Marketing for Long Term Care." American Health Care Association Journal, 11, No 2 (1985), entire issue, pp. 59.

Marks, Ronald. "The Family Dimension in Long Term Care: An Assessment of Stress and Intervention. Pride Institute Journal of Long Term Home Health Care, 6, No 2 (Spring 1987), pp. 18-26.

Martico, Theresa. "Day Care for Patients with Alzheimer's Disease and Related Disorders: Description and Evaluation." Paper Presented at the SAGE Annual Meeting, October 9-11, 1985, Grossinger's, New York.

Maslow, A. H. Toward a Psychology of Being, 2nd. edition. Princeton, NJ: Van Nostrand, Reinhold, 1968.

McClure, Ethel E. More Than a Roof. St. Paul: MN Historical Society, 1968.

McCuan, Eloise and M. Elliott. "Geriatric Day Care in Theory and Practice." Social Work in Health Care, 2 (1977), pp. 153-170.

McKillip, Jack. Need Analysis. Beverly Hills, CA: Sage Publications, 1987.

Mechanic, David. Mental Health and Social Policy. Englewood Cliffs, NJ: Prentice-Hall, 1969.

Meeker, Suzanne and Nancy Duff Campbell. "Providing for Dependent Care." Business and Health, June 1986, pp. 18-22.

Mehta, N. and C. Mack. "Day Care Services: An Alternative to Institutional Care." Journal of the American Geriatric Society, 23, No 6 (1975), pp. 280-283.

Melcher, John. "Melcher Applauds Passage of Older Americans Act." Senate Special Committee on Aging. News Release, Nov. 12, 1987.

Melcher, John. "Melcher Bill Would Extend Day Care Services." Senate Special Committee on Aging. News Release, Nov. 3, 1987.

Melcher, John. "Toward Expanded Adult Day Care." Senate Special Committee on Aging. News Release, April 18, 1988.

Melemed, B. "Formulating a Public Policy for Long-Term Care: A Different View." Perspectives on Aging, 12, No 3 (1983), pp. 4, 5, 30.

Meltzer, Judith W. Respite Care: An Emerging Family Support Service. Center for the Study of Social Policy: Washington, DC: Administration on Aging. National Conference on Social Welfare, June, 1982.

Merton, Thomas. No Man is An Island. New York: Harcourt Brace and Company, 1955.

Mills, C. Wright. The Sociological Imagination. New York: Oxford University Press, 1959.

Mintzberg, Henry. The Structuring of Organizations. Englewood Cliffs, NJ: Prentice-Hall, Inc., 1979.

Montagna, Paul D. "Professionalization and Bureaucratization in Large Professional Organizations." In Comparative Organizations: The Results of Empirical Research. Ed. Wolf V. Heydebrand. Englewood-Cliffs, NJ: Prentice-Hall, Inc., 1973, pp. 534-542.

Montgomery, Rhonda. "Services for the Families of the Aged: Which Ones Will Work Best." Aging, No 347 (1984), pp. 16-21.

Morris, R. "The Development of Parallel Services For the Elderly and Disabled: Some Financial Dimensions." The Gerontologist, 14 (1974), pp. 14-19.

Morris, Robert and Delwin Anderson. "Personal Care Services: An Identity for Social Work." Social Service Review, 49, No 2 (1975), pp. 157-174.

Morris, Robert. Social Policy of the American Welfare State. New York: Harper & Row, 1979.

Murray, Charles. Losing Ground: American Social Policy 1950-1980. New York: Basic Books, 1984.

Nassif, Janet Zhur. "There's Still No Place Like Home." Generations, XI, No 2 (Winter 1986-87), pp. 5-8.

National Institute on Adult Daycare. Adult Day Care Survey Results. Unpublished Report of the National Institute on Adult Daycare, a Unit of the National Council on the Aging. Washington, DC, March 1985.

Noelker, Linda and Alven Townsend. "Perceived Caregiving Effectiveness." In Aging, Health, and Family: Long-Term Care. Beverly Hills, CA: Sage Publications, 1987, pp. 58-79.

Norman, J. William. "The Older Americans Act: Meeting the
    Changing Needs of the Elderly." Aging, (January/February
    1982), pp. 2-9.

Nowak, Carol. "Familial Caregiving to the Elderly." Business and
    Health, June 1, 1986, pp. 23-25.

O'Brien, Carole Lium. Adult Day Care, A Practical Guide. Califor-
    nia: Wadsworth Health Services, 1982.

O'Brien, Carole Lium. "Exploring Geriatric Day Care: An Alternative
    to Institutionalization," Journal of Gerontological Nursing,
    3, No 5 (September/October 1977), pp. 26-28.

O'Brien, John and Donna L. Wagner. "Help Seeking by the Frail
    Elderly: Problems in Network Analysis." The Gerontologist,
    20, No 1 (1980), pp. 78-83.

Ohnsorg, Dorothy W. "The Role of Therapy in Adult Day Care."
    National Institute of Adult Day Care News, 3, No 2 (Spring
    1983).

Ohnsorg, Dorothy W. "Burgeoning Day Care Movement Prolongs
    Independent Living." Perspective On Aging. 10, No 1
    (January/February 1981), pp. 18-20.

On Lok Senior Health Services Manual. 2nd ed. San Francisco, CA,
    1981.

Our Future Selves: A Research Plan Toward Understanding Aging.
    Report of the Panel on Research on Human Services and
    Delivery Systems. Washington, DC: National Advisory
    Council on Aging, January, 1980.

Padula, Helen. Developing Adult Day Care: An Approach to
    Maintaining Independence for Impaired Older Persons.
    Washington, DC: National Council on the Aging, 1983.

Padula, Helen. "Toward a Useful Definition of Adult Day Care." Hospital Progress, (March 1981), pp. 42-45.

Palmer, Hans C. "Adult Day Care." In Long-Term Care: Perspectives from Research and Demonstrations. Health Care Financing Administration, U. S. Dept. of Health and Human Services, 2 (1983), pp. 415-436.

Palmer, Hans C. "The Alternatives Question." In Long Term Care Perspectives from Research and Demonstrations. Eds. Ronald Vogel and Hans Palmer. Washington, DC: HCFA, 1982.

Palmer, Hans. "The System of Provision." In Long Term Care: Perspectives from Research and Demonstrations. Rockville, MD: Aspen Systems Corporation, 1985, pp. 1-63.

Palmore, Erdman, John Nowlin, and Hsioh Wang. "Predictors of Function Among the Old-Old: A 10-Year Follow-Up." Journal of Gerontology, 40, No 2 (1985), pp. 244-250.

Panella, John and Fletcher McDowell. Day Care for Dementia: A Manual of Instruction for Developing a Program. White Plains, NY: The Burke Rehabilitation Program, 1984.

Paringer, Lynn. "Forgotten Costs," Generations, IX, No 4 (Summer 1985), pp. 55-59.

Parsons, Talcott. "Pattern Variables Revisited: A Response to Robert Dubin." American Sociological Review, 25 (1960), pp. 467-482.

Parsons, Talcott. "The Social Structure of the Family." In The Family: Its Function and Destiny. Ed. R. Anshen. New York: Harper and Brothers, 1949, pp. 173-201.

Parsons, Talcott. The Social System. Glencoe, IL: The Free Press, 1951.

Parsons, Talcott. "Suggestions for a Sociological Approach to the Theory of Organizations-I." Administrative Science Quarterly (June 1956), pp. 63-85.

Parsons, Talcott and Robert Bales. Family Socialization and Interaction Process. Glencoe, IL: The Free Press, 1955.

Parsons, Talcott and Edward Shils. Toward a General Theory of Action. New York: Harper and Row, 1951.

PA Department of Aging. "Adult Day Care." Aging Information Memorandum #83-33, October 17, 1983.

Pennings, J. "The Relevance of the Structural-Contingency Model for Organizational Effectiveness." Administrative Science Quarterly, 20, No 3 (1975), pp. 393-410.

Perrow, Charles. "A Framework for the Comparative Analysis of Organizations." American Sociological Review, 32, No 3 (April 1967), pp. 194-208.

Perrow, Charles. Complex Organizations: A Critical Essay. New York: Random House, 1979.

Pfeiffer, Eric. "A Short Portable Mental Status Questionnaire for the Assessment of Organic Brain Deficit in Elderly Patients." Journal of the American Geriatrics Society, 23, No 10 (1975), pp. 433-441.

Pfeiffer, Eric, ed. National Conference on Alternatives to Institutional Care for Older Americans. Durham, NC: Center for the Study of Aging and Human Development, Duke University 1973.

Pifer, Alan and Lydia Bronte, eds. Our Aging Society. New York: W. W. Norton and Company, 1986.

Pollack, William. "Benefit Cost Analysis in Evaluative Research and Programs for the Elderly." In Evaluative Research on Social Programs for the Elderly. Gorden Streib, Chairman. Washington, DC: U. S. Dept. of HEW, Meeting held in Portland, Oregon in June 1973.

Pomeranz, William and Steven Rosenberg. "Developing An Adult DayCare Center." Journal of Long-Term Care Administration. 13, No 1 (1985), pp. 11-22.

Poplin, Dennis. Communities: A Survey of Theories and Methods of Research, 2nd. edition. New York: Macmillan Publishing Co., 1979.

"Program Evaluation Alternatives" in Long-Term Care-Alternative Modes of Day Care. By TransCentury Corporation. Washington, DC: Public Health Service Office of the Assistant Secretary for Health, National Center for Health Services Research. Start/End dates: June '74 through April '75.

P.L. 95-478. Comprehensive Older Americans Act of 1978, 92 Stat 1, October 18, 1978.

"Public Policy Agenda: Long-Term Care." Perspective on Aging, XVII, No 2 (March/April 1988), pp. 6-10.

"Public Policy Agenda 1988-1989 of the National Council on the Aging, Inc." Perspective on Aging, XVII, No 2 (March/April 1988), entire issue, 40 pp.

Raber, Patricia E. "Day Care: An Alternative to Premature Institutionalization." Today's Nursing Home, July/August 1980.

Rathbone-McCuan, et al. Cost Effectiveness Evaluation of the Levindale Adult Day Treatment Center. Baltimore, MD, Levindale Research Center, 1975.

Rathbone-McCuan, Eloise. "Geriatric Day Care: A Family Perspective." The Gerontologist, 16 (1976), pp. 517-521.

Rathbone-McCuan, and Martha Elliott. "Geriatric Day Care in Theory and Practice." Social Work in Health Care, 2, No 2 (Winter 1976-77), pp. 153-170.

Rathbone-McCuan, E. and Raymond T. Coward. "Respite and Adult Day Care Services." In Handbook of Gerontological Services. Ed. Abraham Monk. New York: Van Nostrand Reinhold, 1985, pp. 457-482.

Rawls, John. A Theory of Justice. Cambridge, MA: Harvard Press, 1971.

Reed, Charles. Adult Day Care Programs: Hearings Before the Subcommittee on Health and Long Term Care of the Select Committee on Aging. House of Representatives. Washington, DC: Government Printing Office, April 23, 1980, p. 24.

Respite Care for the Frail Elderly. A Summary Report on Institutional Respite Research and Operations Manual. Albany, NY: The Center for the Study of Aging, Inc., 1983.

Returning the Mentally Disabled to the Community: Government Needs to Do More. Washington, DC: General Accounting Office, January 1977.

Rhodes, Linda M. A Weissert Profile and Functional Task Analysis of Vintage, Inc. Adult Day Care (Pittsburgh, PA). Washington, DC: TransCentury Corporation, January 1982.

Rich, Bennett M. and Martha Baum. The Aging: Guide to Public Policy. Pittsburgh, PA: University of Pittsburgh Press, 1984.

Rivlin, Alice M. and Joshua M. Weiner. Caring For The Disabled Elderly: Who Will Pay? Washington, DC: The Brookings Institution, 1988.

Robins, Edith. "Adult Day Care: Growing Fast But Still for Lucky Few." Generations (Spring 1981), pp. 22-23.

Robins, Edith. Directory of Adult Day Care Centers. Washington, DC: U. S. Department of Health and Human Services, Health Care Financing Administration, 1980.

Robinson, James C. "Philosophical Origins of the Economic Valuation of Life." The Milbank Memorial Fund Quarterly, 64, No 1 (1986), pp. 133-155.

Rose, S. M. "Deciphering Deinstitutional Complexities in Policy and Program Analysis." Health & Society 57, (1979), pp. 429-460.

Rosenberg, Morris. The Logic of Survey Analysis. New York: Basic Books, Inc., 1968.

Rossi, Peter H. and Howard E. Freeman. Evaluation: A Systematic Approach. Beverly Hills, CA: Sage Publications, 1982.

Rossman, I., and I. M. Burnside. "The United States of America," In Geriatric Care In Advanced Societies. Ed. J. C. Brocklehurst. Baltimore, MD: University Park Press, 1975.

Roethlisberger, F. J. and William J. Dickson. Management and the Worker. Cambridge, MA: Harvard University Press, 1947.

Rothman, David and Sheila Rothman, eds. On Their Own: The Poor in Modern America. Reading, MA: Addison-Wesley, 1972.

Rothschild-Whitt, Joyce. "Conditions for Democracy: Making Participatory Organizations Work." In Co-Ops, Communes and Collectives in Social Change in the 1960s and 1970s. Ed. J. Case and R. C. R. Taylor. NY: Pantheon Books, 1979.

RTZ Associates. Day Health Services: Its Impacts on the Frail Elderly and the Quality and Cost of Long-Term Care:

Overview of the Study and Four Interim Reports. Sacramento, CA: California State Department of Health, May 1977.

Sager, A. Learning the Home Care Needs of the Elderly: Patient, Family, and Professional Views of an Alternative to Institutionalization. Final Report to the Administration on Aging, Grant No 90-A-1026. Washington, DC: Government Printing Office, 1978.

Saltz, Constance Corley, et al. "Alternatives to Institutionalization: Estimates of Need and Feasibility." Journal of Applied Gerontology, 3, No 2 (1984), pp. 137-149.

Sands, D. and T. Suzuki. "Adult Day Care for Alzheimer's Patients and Their Families." The Gerontologist, 23, No 1 (1983), pp. 21-23.

Saperstein, A. R. and E. Brody. "What Types of Respite Services Do Family Caregivers of Alzheimer's Patients Want," Revised version of paper presented at the Annual Meeting of the Gerontological Society of America. Washington, DC, November 1987.

Scanlon, William. Project to Analyze Existing Long-Term Care Data, Vol I. Summary and Conclusions. Washington, DC: Urban Institute, Office of the Assistant Secretary for Planning and Evaluation, Administration on Aging, 1981.

Schorr, Alvin L. Common Decency. New Haven, CT: Yale University Press, 1986.

Scull, Andrew S. Decarceration: Community Treatment and the Deviant. Englewood Cliffs, NJ: Prentice-Hall Inc., 1977.

Selznick, Philip. "Foundations of the Theory of Organization." American Sociological Review, 13, No 1 (1948), pp. 25-35.

Shanas, Ethel. "The Family as a Social Support System in Old Age." The Gerontologist, 19, No 2 (1979b), pp. 169-174.

Shanas, Ethel. "Social Myth as Hypothesis: The Case of the Family Relations of Old People." The Gerontologist, 19, No 1 (1979a), pp. 3-9.

Shanas, E. and M. B. Sussman, eds. Family, Bureaucracy and the Elderly. Durham, NC: Duke University Press, 1977.

Shanas, E., P. Townsend, D. Wedderburn, H. Friis, P. Milhaj and J. Stehouwer, eds. Old People in Three Industrial Societies. New York: Atherton Press, 1968.

Sherwood, Sylvia, John Morris and Hirsch Ruchlin. "Alternative Paths to Long-term Care: Nursing Home Geriatric Day Hospital, Senior Center, and Domiciliary Care Options." American Journal of Public Health, 76, No 1 (January 1986), pp. 38-44.

Shils, E. A. and M. Janowitz. "Cohesion and Disintegration in the Wehrmacht in World War II." Public Opinion Quarterly, 12, No 2 (Summer 1948), pp. 280-315.

Shore, Herbert. "What's New About Alternatives." The Gerontologist, 14, No 1 (February 1974), pp. 6-11.

Shore, Herbert. "Alternatives to Long Term Care: Fact or Fancy?" Journal of Long Term Care Administration, 2, No 1 (Winter 1973), pp. 23-35.

Siegel, Albert R., Marshall Williams and Elaine Carpenter. Adult Restorative Services: Evaluation of Adult Day Treatment in Kansas Rural Nursing Homes. Wichita, Kansas: E. S. Edgerton Medical Research Foundation, 1982.

Siegel, Jacob S. and Cynthia M. Taeuber. "Demographic Dimensions of an Aging Population." In Our Aging Society. Eds. Alan

Pifer and Lydia Bronte. New York: W. W. Norton & Co., 1986, pp. 79-110.

Sigler, Jack and Maurice Jackson. "Social Service Evaluation: A Research Problem or Problematic Research?" The Gerontologist, 11, No 4 (Winter 1971, Part II), pp. 38-42.

Silverstone, B. and A. B. Weiss. Social Work Practice with the Frail Elderly and Their Families. Springfield, IL: Charles C. Thomas, 1983.

Simmel, Georg. Conflict and the Web of Group Affiliation. Trans. K. H. Wolff. Glencoe, IL: Free Press, 1956.

Sjoberg, Gideon. "Politics, Ethics, and Evaluation Research." In Handbook of Evaluation Research. Vol II. Eds. Elmer Struening and Marcia Guttentag. Beverly Hills, CA: Sage Publications, 1975, pp. 29-51.

Skellie, F. Albert, Melton Mobley and Ruth Coan. "Cost-Effectiveness of Community-Based Long Term Care: Current Findings of Georgia's Alternative Health Services Project." American Journal of Public Health, 72, No 4 (1982), pp. 353-358.

Smallegan, M. "There Was Nothing Else to Do: Needs for Care Before Nursing Home Admission." The Gerontologist, 25, No 4 (1985), pp. 364-369.

Smyer, Michael A. "The Differential Usage of Services by Impaired Elderly." Journal of Gerontology, 35, No 2 (1980), pp. 249-255.

Snyder, Barbara and Kathy Keefe. "The Unmet Needs of Family Caregivers for Frail and Disabled Adults." Social Work In Health Care, 10, No 3 (1985), pp. 1-14.

Social Planning." In Encyclopedia of Social Work, Vol 2, 18th edition. Silver Spring, MD: National Association of Social Workers, 1987, pp. 593-602.

Soldo, B. "Supply of Informal Care Services: Variations and Effects on Service Utilization Patterns". In Project to Analyze Existing Long-Term Care Data, Volume III. Ed. W. Scanlon. Washington, DC: The Urban Institute, 1984, pp. 56-97.

Soldo, B. J. and K. G. Manton. "Health Services Needs of the Oldest Old." The Milbank Memorial Fund Quarterly, 63 (1985), pp. 286-319.

Soldo, B. J. and J. Myllyluoma. "Caregivers Who Live with Dependent Elderly." The Gerontologist, 23, No 6 (1983), pp. 605-611.

Springer, Dianne and Timothy Brubaker. Family Caregivers and Dependent Elderly. Beverly Hills, CA: Sage Publications, 1984.

Stabler, Nora. "The Use of Groups in Day Centers for Older Adults." Social Work with Groups. 4, No 3/4 (Fall/Winter 1981), pp. 49-58.

Standards for Adult Day Care. Washington, DC: National Institute on Adult Daycare, National Council on the Aging, 1984.

Stassen, Margaret and John Holahan. Long-Term Care Demonstration Projects: A Review of Recent Evaluations. Washington, DC: The Urban Institute, February 1981.

Steinberg, Raymond. "Social Program Tracking and Evaluation." In Research Instruments in Social Gerontology: Volume 3, Health, Program Evaluation and Demography. Eds. David J. Mangen and Warren A. Peterson. Minneapolis, MN: University of Minnesota Press, 1984, pp. 175-215.

Stephens, Susan A. and Jan B. Christianson. Informal Care of the Elderly. Lexington, MA: D. C. Health and Company, 1986.

Stoller, E. P. "Parental Caregiving by Adult Children." Journal of Marriage and the Family, (November 1983), pp. 851-858.

Stone, Robyn. "Aging In the Eighties, Age 65 Years and Over--Use of Community Services," Preliminary Data from the Supplement on Aging to the National Health Interview: United States, January-June 1985. Advancedata. U. S. Dept. of Health and Human Services, No 124 (September 30, 1986).

Stone, Robyn, et al. Caregivers of the Frail Elderly: A National Profile. Washington, DC: U. S. Department of Health and Human Services, 1987.

Stone, Robyn, et al. "Caregivers of the Frail Elderly: A National Profile. The Gerontologist, Vol 27, No 5 (1987), pp. 616-626.

Strang, V. and A. Neufeld. "Adult Day Care Programs: A Source for Respite." Journal of Gerontological Nursing, 16, No 11 (November 1990), pp. 16-20.

Streib, Gordon. "Bureaucracies and Families: Common Themes and Directions for Further Study." In Family Bureaucracy and the Elderly. Eds. Ethel Shanas and Marvin Sussman. Durham, NC: Duke University Press, 1977, pp. 204-214.

Streib, Gordon, F. Programs for Older Americans: Evaluations by Academic Gerontologists. Gainesville, FL: Center of Gerontological Studies and Programs by University Presses of Florida, 1981.

Struening, Elmer R. "Social Area Analysis As A Method of Evaluation." In Handbook of Evaluation Research, Vol I. Eds. Elmer Struening and Marcia Guttentag. Beverly Hills, CA: Sage Publications, 1975, pp. 519-536.

Suchman, Edward. Evaluation Research. New York: Russell Sage Foundation, 1967.

Supplement to the Encyclopedia of Social Work, 17th edition, 1983-1984. Silver Spring, MD: National Association of Social Workers, 1983, pp. 19-24.

Sussman, M. "Bureaucracy and the Elderly Individual: An Organizational Linkage Perspective." In Family Bureaucracy and the Elderly. Eds. E. Shanas and M. Sussman. Durham, NC: Duke University Press, 1977.

Sussman, Marvin. "The Family Life of Old People." In Handbook of Aging and the Social Sciences. Eds. Robert Binstock and Ethel Shanas. New York: Van Nostrand Reinhold Co., 1976.

Symonds, P. C. "Social Services and Day Care." Gerontologia Clinica, 16 (1974), pp 148-150.

Tate, Lenore A. "Adult Day Care: A Practical Guidebook and Manual." Activities, Adaptations & Aging, 11, No 2 (1988). Entire issue, 144 pp.

Taylor, John R. "Adult Day-Care Centers in Virginia." Virginia Medical, 3 (March 1984), pp. 148-150.

Technology and Aging in America. A Summary, Congress of the United States, Office of Technology Assessment, OTA-BB-265, October 1984.

Tedesco, Janet and DeWayne L. Oberlander. Adult Day Care: A Diversification Option for Hospitals. Chicago, IL: Hospital Research and Educational Trust, 1983.

Titmuss, Richard M. Commitment to Welfare. Boston, MA: George Allen and Unwin, 1968.

Tobin, Sheldon. "Evaluating Program Benefit." The Gerontologist, 11, No 4 (Winter 1971, Part II), pp. 55-58.

Tobin, Sheldon. "A Structural Approach to Families." In Aging, Health, and Family: Long-Term Care. Ed. Timothy Brubaker, Beverly Hills, CA: Sage Publications, 1987, pp. 42-55.

Tobin, Sheldon S., Stephen H. Davidson and Ann Sack. Effective Social Services for Older Americans. Michigan: University of Michigan, Institute of Gerontology, 1980.

Tobin, Sheldon, Jerome Hammerman and Vicki Rector. "Preferred Disposition of Institutionalized Aged." The Gerontologist, 12, No 2 (Summer 1972, Part I), pp. 129-133.

Tomorrow's Elderly. A report prepared by the Congressional Clearinghouse on the future for the Select Committee on Aging, House of Representatives, Ninety-Eighth Congress, Second Session, October 1984, Comm. Pub. No 98-457.

Tonti, Mario and Barbara Silverstone. "Services to Families of the Elderly." In Handbook of Gerontological Services. Ed. Abraham Monk, New York: Van Nostrand ReiNhold Company, 1985, pp. 211-239.

Toren, Nina. "Semi-Professionalism and Social Work: A Theoretical Perspective." In The Semi Professions and Their Organization. Ed. Amitai Etizioni. New York: The Free Press, 1969, pp. 142-195.

Torres-Gil, Fernando M. "Process, Politics, & Policy." Generations, XII, No 3 (Spring 1988), pp. 4-9.

Trager, Brahna. Home Health Care and National Health Policy. New York: Haworth Press, 1980.

Trager, B. and L. Reif, eds. Supplementary Discussion of Weissert Report. Home Health Care Services Quarterly, 1 Supplement, (October 1980), pp. 97-121.

Trattner, Walter I. From Poor Law to Welfare State, fourth edition. New York: The Free Press, 1989.

Tripodi, Tony. "Program Evaluation." In Encyclopedia of Social Work, Vol 2, 18th edition. Silver Spring, MD: National Association of Social Workers, 1987, pp. 366-379.

Trupiano, Florence, Mc. Initial Planning Considerations for Developing an Adult Day Care Center. North Texas State University, TX: Center for Studies in Aging, May 1978.

Turner, Jonathan H. The Structure of Sociological Theory. Chicago, IL: The Dorsey Press, 1986.

Unger, Alan and William Weissert. Data for Long-Term Care Planning: Application of a Synthetic Estimation Technique. Working Paper. Washington, DC: The Urban Institute, May 1983.

U. S. Bureau of the Census. "America in Transition: An Aging Society." Current Population Reports, special studies, series P-23, No 128. Washington, DC: Government Printing Office, 1983.

U. S. Congress. "Adult Day Care Programs: Hearings Before the Subcommittee on Health and Long Term Care of the Select Committee on Aging." House of Representatives. Washington, DC: Government Printing Office, April 23, 1980.

U. S. Congress. "Exploding the Myths." A Study by the Subcommittee on Aging, House of Representatives. One Hundredth Congress. First Session. Washington, DC: Government Printing Office, January 1987. Comm. Pub. No 99-611.

U. S. Department of Commerce, Bureau of the Census, "Population Projections of the Population of the United States by Age, Sex, and Race: 1983-2080." Current Population Reports. Washington, DC: Government Printing Office, 1984. P-25, No 952.

U. S. Department of Health and Human Services. 1979 Health Interview Survey. Washington, DC: Government Printing Office, 1979.

U. S. Department of Health and Human Services. 1982 National Long-Term Care Survey and Informal Caregivers Survey: Washington, DC: Government Printing Office, 1982.

U. S. Department of Health and Human Services. Assistant Secretary for Planning and Evaluation. Working Papers on Long-Term Care Prepared for the 1980 Under-Secretary's Task Force on Long-Term Care. Washington, DC, 1981.

U. S. General Accounting Office. The Well-Being of Older People In Cleveland, Ohio: Report to Congress. Washington, DC, 1977.

U. S. National Committee on Vital and Health Statistics. Long Term Health Care: Minimum Data Set. Preliminary Report of the Technical Consultant Panel on the Long Term Health Care Data Set. Washington, DC: U. S. Public Health Service, September 1978.

U. S. Senate, Special Committee on Aging. Adult Day Facilities for Treatment Health Care and Related Services. Washington, DC: Government Printing Office, 1976.

U. S. Senate Special Committee on Aging. Nursing Home Care in the United States: Failure in Public Policy, Introductory Report. Washington, DC: Government Printing Office, 1974, pp. 20-21.

U. S. Senate Special Committee on Aging in conjunction with the American Association of Retired Persons. Aging America: Trends and Projections. Washington, DC, 1984.

U. S. Social Security Board. Social Security in America. Washington, DC: Government Printing Office, 1937.

Van Wylen, M. D. and J. Dykema-Lamse. "Feelings Group for Adult Day Care." The Gerontologist, 30, No 4 (August 1990), pp. 557-559.

Vesperi, Maria D. City of Green Benches: Growing Old in a New Downtown, Ithaca, NY: Cornell University Press, 1985.

Virginia Department of Aging. "Study of the Public and Private Cost of Institutional and Community-Based Long-Term Care." Richmond, VA, 1983.

Vogel, Ronald and Hans C. Palmer, eds. Long-Term Care: Perspectives from Research and Demonstrations. Rockville, MD:, Aspen Systems Corporation, 1983.

Von Behren, Ruth. Adult Day Care: A Program of Services of the Functionally Impaired. Washington, DC: The National Council on the Aging Inc., National Institute on Adult Daycare, July 1988.

Von Behren, Ruth. Adult Day Care in America: Summary of a National Survey. Washington, DC: National Council on Aging, National Institute on Adult Daycare, October 1986.

Von Behren, Ruth. On Lok Health Services Adult Day Health Care: From Pilot Project to Permanent Program. Final Report, December 1974-June 30, 1978. Sacramento, CA: State Department of Health Services, July 1979.

Warren, Carol A. B. "New Forms of Social Control: The Myth of Deinstitutionalization." American Behavioral Scientist, 24, No 6 (1981), pp. 724-740.

Weber, Max. Economy and Society, 4th ed. Eds. G. Roth and C. Wittich, Vol 1 and 3. New York: Irvington Publications, 1968.

Weber, Max. The Theory of Social Economic Organizations. Eds. and translation A. M. Henderson and T. Parsons. New York: Oxford University Press, 1947.

Webster's New Universal Unabridged Dictionary, deluxe 2nd edition. New York: Simon and Schuster, 1983.

Weiler, Kim P. and L. Pickard. "Health Care for Elderly Americans: Evaluation of an Adult Day Health Care Model." Medical Care, 14, No 8 (1976), pp. 700-708.

Weiler, Philip. "Response to the Study, 'Effects and Costs of Day Care and Homemakers Services for the Chronically Ill: A Randomized Experiment.'" Home Health Care Services Quarterly, 1, No 3 (Fall 1980). Entire supplement.

Weiler, P. G. and E. Rathbone-McCuan. Adult Day Care: Community Work with the Elderly. New York: Springer Publishing Co., 1978.

Weiner, Joshua. "A Look at Policy Choices." Perspective on Aging, XVI, No 6 (November/December, 1987), pp. 10-11.

Weissert, William. Adult Day Care in the United States: A Comparative Study: Final Report, Washington, DC: TransCentury, 1975.

Weissert, William G. "Adult Day Care Programs in the United States: Current Research Projects and a Survey of 10 Centers." Public Health Reports, 92 (January/February 1977), pp. 49-56.

Weissert, William. "The Cost-Effectiveness Trap." Generations, IX, No 4 (Summer 1985a), pp. 47-50.

Weissert, William G. "Costs of Adult Day Care: A Comparison to Nursing Homes." Inquiry, 15, No 1 (1978), pp. 10-19.

Weissert, William G. "Hard Choices: Targeting Long-Term Care to the 'At Risk' Aged." Journal of Health Politics, Policy and Law, 11, No 3 (1986), pp. 463-481.

Weissert, William. "Rationales for Public Health Insurance Coverage of Geriatric Day Care: Issues, Options and Impacts." Journal of Health Politics, Policy and Law, 3, No 4 (Winter 1979), pp. 555-567.

Weissert, W. G. "Seven Reasons Why It Is so Difficult to Make Community Based Long-Term Care Cost Effective." Health Services Research, 20, No 4 (1985b), pp. 423-433.

Weissert, William. "Toward a Continuum of Care for the Elderly: A Note of Caution." Public Policy, 29 No 3 (Summer 1981), pp. 331-340.

Weissert, William. "Two Models of Geriatric Day Care: Findings from a Comparative Study." The Gerontologist, 16, No 5 (1976), pp. 420-427.

Weissert, William; Jennifer Elston, Elise Bolda, et al. "Models of Adult Day Care: Findings from a National Survey. The Gerontologist, 29, No 5 (1989), pp. 640-649.

Weissert, William; Cynthia Cready and James Pawelak. "The Past and Future of Home- and Community-Based Long-Term Care." The Milbank Quarterly, 66, No 2 (1988), pp. 309-388.

Weissert, W. G. et al. Adult Day Care: Findings from a National Survey. The Johns Hopkins Series in Contemporary Medicine and Public Health. Baltimore, MD: Johns Hopkins University Press, 1990.

Weissert, William, et al. "Effects and Costs of Day Care Services for the Chronically Ill -- A Randomized Experiment." Medical Care, 18, No 6 (1980), pp. 567-584.

Weissert, W. and W. Scanlon. Determinants of Institutionalization of the Aged. Working Paper No 1466-20. Washington, DC: The Urban Institute, 1983.

Weissert, William, Thomas Wan, and Barbara Livieratos. Effects and Costs of Day Care and Homemaker Services for the Chronically Ill: A Randomized Experiment: Executive Summary. Washington, DC: National Center for Health Services, U. S. Dept. of Health, Education and Welfare, January 19, 1979.

Wetle, Terrie. "Long-Term Care: A Taxonomy of Issues". Generations, X, No 2 (1985), pp. 30-34.

White, T. B. "Community-Based Adult Day Care Programs in Florida. In Adult Day Care: A Practical Guide. Ed. C. L. O'Brien, Monterey, CA: Wadsworth Health Sciences Division, 1982.

White House Conference on Aging, "Adult Day Care - Related Recommendations." NIAD NEWS, 2, No 1 (1982), pp. 6-7.

Whyte, W. H. The Organization Man. New York: Simon and Schuster, 1956.

Wilensky, Harold L. "The Professionalization of Everyone?" The American Journal of Sociology, LXX, No 2 (September 1964), pp. 137-158.

Williams, C. "Reaching Isolated Older People: II. An Evaluation of An Alternative Model of Day Services." Journal of Gerontological Social Work, 8, Nos 1-2 (1984), pp. 35-49.

Williams, Leon and Carmen Diaz. "Family: Multigenerational." Encyclopedia of Social Work, Vol 1, 18th edition. Silver Spring, MD: National Association of Social Workers, 1987, pp. 529-540.

Wilson, Albert J. Social Services for Older Persons. Boston, MA: Little, Brown and Company, 1984.

Wood, J. B. "The Emergence of Adult Day Care Centers as Post-Acute Care Agencies." Journal of Aging and Health, 1, No 4 (1989), pp. 521-539.

Wood, Stephen. "Growing Opportunities." Mortgage Banking, 46, No 3 (1985), pp. 26-32.

Wood, Suzanne and William P. Harris. "Adult Day Care, A New Modality." The Journal of Long Term Care Administration, IV (Spring, 1976), p. 19.

Woodward, G. E. Kahana, et al. "Alternative Predictors of Formal and Informal Supports in Meeting Needs of Urban Elders. Presentation at 40th Annual Scientific Meeting of the Gerontological Society of America, Washington, DC, Nov. 19, 1987.

Yeatts, Dale, John Capitman, and Bruce Steinhardt. "Evaluation of Connecticut's Medicaid Community Care Waiver Program." The Gerontologist, 27, No 5 (1987), pp. 652-659.

Yee, Donna L. "On Lok Senior Health Services: Community-Based Long Term Care." Aging, Nos 319-320 (1981), pp. 26-30.

Zaki, Gamal and Sylvia Zaki. Day Care as a Long-Term Care Service. Brown University: Rhode Island College Gerontology Center, February 15, 1982.

Zarit, Steven H., et al. "Relatives of the Impaired Elderly: Correlates of Feelings of Burden." The Gerontologist, 20, No 6 (1980), p. 649.

Zimmerman, Shirley L. Adult Day Care: Its Effects on Families of Elderly Disabled Members. Unpublished paper, Family Social Science, University of Minnesota, St. Paul, Minnesota 55108, March 1984.

Zones, Jane, et al. "Gender, Public Policy and the Oldest Old." Aging and Society. 7 (1987), pp. 275-302.